PENNSYLVANIA

FODOR'S TRAVEL GUIDES

are compiled, researched, and edited by an international team of travel writers, field correspondents, and editors. The series, which now almost covers the globe, was founded by Eugene Fodor in 1936.

OFFICES
New York and London

FODOR'S PENNSYLVANIA:

Area Editor: Lenny Bughman, Gloria Hayes Kremer
Editor: Gerardyne Madigan
Editorial Associate: Paul Busby
Drawings: Ted Burwell, Sandra Lang (p. 1)
Cartography: Dyno Lowenstein

FODOR'S

PENNSYLVANIA

New
and
Revised

FODOR'S TRAVEL GUIDES
New York

Third Edition

All the following Guides are current (most of them also in
the Hodder and Stoughton British edition.)

CURRENT FODOR'S COUNTRY AND AREA TITLES:

AUSTRALIA, NEW ZEALAND
  AND SOUTH PACIFIC
AUSTRIA
BELGIUM AND
  LUXEMBOURG
BERMUDA
BRAZIL
CANADA
CARIBBEAN AND BAHAMAS
CENTRAL AMERICA
EASTERN EUROPE
EGYPT
EUROPE
FRANCE
GERMANY
GREAT BRITAIN
GREECE
HOLLAND
INDIA
IRELAND

ISRAEL
ITALY
JAPAN
JORDAN AND HOLY LAND
KENYA
KOREA
MEXICO
NORTH AFRICA
PEOPLE'S REPUBLIC
  OF CHINA
PORTUGAL
SCANDINAVIA
SCOTLAND
SOUTH AMERICA
SOUTHEAST ASIA
SOVIET UNION
SPAIN
SWITZERLAND
TURKEY

CITY GUIDES:

BEIJING, GUANGZHOU, SHANGHAI
CHICAGO
LONDON
LOS ANGELES
MADRID
MEXICO CITY AND ACAPULCO
NEW YORK CITY
PARIS

ROME
SAN DIEGO
SAN FRANCISCO
STOCKHOLM, COPENHAGEN,
  OSLO, HELSINKI, AND
  REYKJAVIK
TOKYO
WASHINGTON, D.C.

FODOR'S BUDGET SERIES:

BUDGET BRITAIN
BUDGET CANADA
BUDGET CARIBBEAN
BUDGET EUROPE
BUDGET FRANCE
BUDGET GERMANY
BUDGET HAWAII

BUDGET ITALY
BUDGET JAPAN
BUDGET MEXICO
BUDGET SCANDINAVIA
BUDGET SPAIN
BUDGET TRAVEL IN AMERICA

USA GUIDES:

ALASKA
CAPE COD
COLORADO
FAR WEST
FLORIDA
GRAND CANYON

HAWAII
NEW ENGLAND
PENNSYLVANIA
SOUTH
TEXAS
USA (in one volume)

MANUFACTURED IN THE UNITED STATES OF AMERICA
10 9 8 7 6 5 4 3 2 1

CONTENTS

PENNSYLVANIA

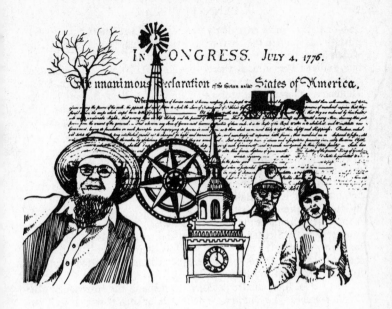

PENNSYLVANIA

The History Maker

by
GLORIA HAYES KREMER

Pennsylvania's 12 million residents are delighted with the slogan recently adopted to promote their state. "You've got a friend in Pennsylvania" genuinely reflects the warmth and hospitality of people eager to display the virtues of William Penn's "Greene Land." The Keystone State, nicknamed in early Colonial days due to the importance of the young state, boasts lush, wooded hills, dynamic cities and farmlands, green and fertile, where third and fourth-generation farm families, including the Amish, live and plow the land.

During 1982, Pennsylvania is celebrating its 300th birthday with year-long activities as part of the "Century IV" anniversary festival. It was on October 24, 1682, that Penn's ship, the *Welcome*, safely arrived at the Delaware River. Between that grand river and the broad Schuylkill River William Penn's brave band of Quakers established Philadelphia, the new home guaranteeing them their long-sought religious freedom.

Pennsylvania's ethnic diversity has added to its interest as a state that offers "something for everyone." In 1861, when William Penn, at age

1

36—one of the most engaging yet annoying of the English nonconformists—was granted the charter for Pennsylvania, he was given a land which never had a homogeneous population and would never acquire one. Indians were already there—possibly 20,000 of them—a handful of black people, Dutchmen, Welshmen, Africans, Englishmen, Scots, Huguenots, Germans (church and Plain), Swiss, Slavs, Italians, Scotch-Irish, Czechs, and others. This mixture of people who struggled together produced a dynamic combination of competitive, yet cooperative, individuals. Benjamin Franklin, innovative and daring, flourished in the atmosphere of the Philadelphia scene.

Although it is commonly believed that William Penn founded Pennsylvania, the Dutch and the Swedes were actually the first European settlers who arrived in the present Delaware Valley region. In August 1609, the Dutch East India Company's Henry Hudson made his way up the Delaware River in his tiny ship, the *Half Moon.* Thirty years later, Peter Minuit began the first permanent settlement in the Delaware region, for Sweden. New Sweden and especially New Netherland both grew during the next thirty years as their mother countries sent more expeditions. In 1664, the English government decided to enforce its claim to the entire Atlantic seaboard. The English King, Charles II, sent a fleet of four hundred soldiers to demand the surrender of the Dutch colonies. The Dutch were no match for such power, and Governor Peter Stuyvesant surrendered New Amsterdam (now New York City) and all other Dutch possessions in North America.

Charles II owed the estate of Admiral Penn (William's father) a large sum of money, which he was unable to repay. Thus when William Penn told the king his desire to establish a Quaker Society in the New World as repayment, Charles was delighted. He granted Penn all the land that lay between the thirty-ninth and forty-second degrees of north latitude, extending from the Delaware River westward five degrees longitude. The colony became known as "Pennsilvania," or "Penn's Woods." In 1681, William Penn thus became the largest landholder in the British Empire, save the king himself.

Of course, long before the advent of the white man, the Indians had lived here for at least ten thousand years. The Indians—some fifteen thousand of them—from the tribes of Delawares, Shawnees, Picts, Wyandotes and Mingoes, lived in peace under the powerful and benign Iroquois Federation.

Penn, unlike most early settlers in the New World, kept the peace with the Indians, inaugurating relations with them that were almost unique. Peace reigned between white settlers and the Indians in the Pennsylvania Colony for almost seventy years, time enough to give a good head start to what has since been called "Penn's holy experiment."

Under the progressive and idealistic leadership of Penn, the new colony developed a workable government under a charter called the "Great Law of Pennsylvania." It gave the vote to any male citizen who believed in God and met modest property requirements. It provided for public education so that children would learn to read, write and master a trade. No man could be denied "life, liberty, or estate" without trial by a jury of his peers. These were radical ideas three centuries ago in

Pennsylvania, or anywhere else in the world for that matter. In addition, settlers to the new colony were guaranteed religious freedom. Tolerance for all races and creeds was the law of the land.

It was a remarkable beginning for the young colony. Its political, religious, economic and historic impact is still felt today in the state, as well as in the nation whose first roots grew deep and thrived here. The guarantees of religious and political freedom drew early colonists by the droves. Most other colonies had restrictive laws concerning settlers. When Penn set foot on his new territories, only five hundred people lived here. Three years later, the population had mounted to seven thousand. By the time of the Revolution, less than a century later, Pennsylvania was the third largest colony of the original thirteen, having a population of 275,000. The early settlers were largely English, Swedish and German. They were followed by French Huguenots. Scotch-Irish immigrated by the thousands and, as time went by, were joined by a sprinkling of people from all the lands of Europe. In those early days, no colony ever had as many races and religions represented among its people as Pennsylvania.

Religious Diversity—The Keynote

The state's heritage of religious freedom and tolerance for all races and creeds, set almost three hundred years ago, still prevails in twentieth-century Pennsylvania. It is not surprising to find that the state today boasts the widest possible variety of religious and ethnic groups.

The Pennsylvania Dutch, the colorful and picturesque "plain people," still cling to their centuries-old ways and costumes. Travelers to the annual Kutztown Fair in July are amazed to find whole communities of people who shun automobiles, electricity and the whole world of American gadgetry. Visitors might be stepping back one hundred years in time.

Residents of the Keystone State have generally tolerated each other's religions with good grace. Besides William Penn's "Friends" (for such are the Quakers called), who laid a solid foundation of religious thought and custom, there were also the Presbyterians and other Protestant sects, who made great contributions to the thinking of the people. The Pennsylvania Dutch—actually a mixture of German and Swiss—settled here in search of religious freedom and practiced a very special code of daily life. The state also gave haven to a good many other special groups, such as the Harmony Society, with its belief in the imminent second coming of Christ and a simple, religiously inspired, but communal form of life.

The Central Colony

Pennsylvania was centrally located among the original colonies, rich in agricultural lands and abundant in resources, particularly coal, iron and timber. The temperate climate and the rivers which traverse the state afforded easy movement for people and produce. So located, the people of Pennsylvania played an important role in all of the continent's wars.

Long before the idea of revolution occurred to the patriots, Pennsylvania was the setting for "the dress rehearsal of the Revolutionary War." Many of the major tactical moves of the French and Indian War took place here.

In the middle of the 18th century, Virginia's Governor Dinwiddie sent a twenty-one-year-old militia officer named George Washington up to Fort Le Boeuf on Lake Erie to persuade the French to withdraw. They refused, and shortly afterward moved south and occupied the site of Pittsburgh, held by a small force of Virginia militia. Washington, coming up from Virginia with four hundred men to reinforce this post, clashed with the French in the mountains, withdrew to a stockade that he called Fort Necessity and was defeated there. The following year he accompanied General Edward Braddock on the latter's disastrous expedition against French Fort Duquesne. He was with General John Forbes when, in 1758, the strategic point at the junction of the Allegheny and Monongahela rivers finally was taken.

During the Revolution, Pennsylvania again played a central role. The colonial protests against "taxation without representation" finally led to the calling of the First Continental Congress, in September 1774. Philadelphia was selected as the meeting place of the Congress because it was the leading city of the thirteen colonies. Its central location among the colonies also made it a convenient place for the delegates to gather. Since Pennsylvania's General Assembly was in session in the State House, the delegates held their meeting in nearby Carpenter Hall. Many delegates still felt that a reconciliation could be reached with England. The situation had become extremely grave when the Second Continental Congress met in the State House in Philadelphia on May 10, 1775. On July 2, 1776, the great debate in the Continental Congress reached its climax. Thomas Jefferson, with the aid of Benjamin Franklin and three others, had been chosen to draft a Declaration of Independence. On July 4, 1776, the Declaration was approved. While other colonies, notably Massachusetts and Virginia, may be said to have sparked the Revolution, Pennsylvania was also in the forefront. John Dickinson's *Letters from a Farmer in Pennsylvania* and Thomas Paine's pamphlet *Common Sense* appeared in Philadelphia and were hungrily read by the literate colonists, helping to stoke the fire of revolt.

York, Pennsylvania, served as headquarters for the Congress for nearly a year while it drafted the Articles of Confederation. The United States Constitution was adopted in Philadelphia, which for ten significant years, from 1790 to 1800, served as the young nation's capital.

Here, in Pennsylvania, the battles of Brandywine, Paoli, Fort Mifflin and Germantown were fought. In 1777–1778, George Washington spent the horrible winter at Valley Forge, twenty-four miles from Philadelphia, with his ragged and poorly supplied army.

In addition to these roles, Pennsylvania provided vital supplies. From its iron forges came the guns, the cannons, the muskets and the pikes to arm the Continental Army. From its farms, the patriots sent vast supplies of food, such as sheep, hogs and grain, as well as horses for army transport. When the Continental Army went bankrupt and Washington lacked funds to pay his men, ninety wealthy Philadelphians raised a million and a half dollars—no small sum in those days—to pay the soldiers' salaries.

In the War of 1812, Pennsylvania again played a large role. Commodore Oliver Hazard Perry sailed out onto Lake Erie with his pitifully small fleet to meet the British. He lost his flagship but switched to another ship, the *Niagara*, and boldly flew his famed pennant, "Don't give up the ship," sewn for him by Pennsylvania women. Perry won this crucial naval battle, which helped to break the British hold on the colonies forever. In a message to General William Henry Harrison, later president of the United States, he boasted: "We have met the enemy and they are ours—two ships, two brigs, one schooner, and one sloop." Today, tourists can see Perry's ship, the *Niagara*, at a pier in Erie, Pennsylvania.

The Civil War and Its Aftermath

Almost half a century later, when the Civil War tore the states asunder, Pennsylvania was again the pivotal hinge in a decisive conflict. Not only was it a chief source of guns and military supplies for the North, with its three major cities of Philadelphia, Pittsburgh and Harrisburg, but Pennsylvania was also a strategically important target for the South. Harrisburg, the state's capital, was a rail, canal and highway center. Through it passed many of the supplies needed by the Union Army. The Confederacy hoped to break the back of the Union in Pennsylvania by seizing one or more of these centers.

From a military standpoint, Lee gambled for victory by trying to draw the military might of the North away from Washington. It was a big risk and the South went for broke. Lee had to stake his all in the battle for Pennsylvania, the richest prize in the war. From July 1st to 3rd, 1863, Robert E. Lee played the deadly game across the board. Backed by some of his most brilliant generals, "Jeb" Stuart, C. Fitzhugh Lee and G.E. Pickett, he met the Union forces at a little town called Gettysburg. This was the turning point of the Civil War, one of the most important battles in American—and world—history.

On the green sloping hills around Gettysburg, one-third of the Union Army, many of them from Pennsylvania, commanded by General George Meade, himself a Pennsylvanian, clashed with the Army of the South. Pickett made his memorable charge in the face of certain death. When the smoke cleared, 22,000 men of the Union Forces were killed, wounded or missing. The Grays lost 28,000 men "on this hallowed ground," and the war itself. Thus Pennsylvania was not only where our country began, but also where it was preserved.

In World Wars I and II, also, the Pennsylvania contribution was gigantic, in terms of men, munitions and intangible might. Pennsylvania's steel mills, in Pittsburgh, Bethlehem and other cities, spewed out the molten metal needed for the machines of war. Pittsburgh's Dravo boatworks along the banks of the Ohio River produced the LSTs (Landing Ship Tanks) and LSIs (Landing Ships Infantry) that stormed across invasion beaches from Guadalcanal to Normandy. Pennsylvania's sons manned the country's defense lines around the world in these conflicts. Today, many of the state's highways are marked in memory of Pennsylvania's famous 28th Division.

The Geographic and Economic Structure

In less than three centuries, Pennsylvania's population has grown from five hundred souls to more than twelve million. It is the nation's fourth largest state in population and a vital political force in national politics, even though it has given the country only one of its presidents, James Buchanan, in 1856. Traditionally the governor, like his counterparts in New York or New Jersey, is a logical contender for the presidential nominations of both major parties and usually gets a first-ballot vote as a "favorite son."

As for geographical size, the state's 45,330 square miles cannot hope to compare with Texas, Alaska or other giants. It is thirty-third in size among the fifty states, but it was generously endowed by nature: thousands of miles of comparatively level lands in the east and south-central parts are ideal for the growth of fruits, vegetables, cereals and grasses; it produces virtually all of the anthracite (or hard) coal mined in the United States; it stands second in the production of all kinds of coal; it boasts almost seventy thousand oil wells, including the nation's first (at Titusville), and good sources of natural gas. Eons before humans settled on these lands, geologic forces were at work to enrich it with sand and limestone, granite, basalt and iron ore.

Three great rivers, the Delaware, the Susquehanna and the Ohio (formed at Pittsburgh where the Monongahela and Allegheny come together), and the seven smoothed-off ridges of the Appalachian Mountains—South Mountain, Kittatinny, Tuscarora, Sideling, Allegheny, Laurel and Chestnut—all have played a part in shaping the destiny of the Keystone State.

Two hundred years ago the state's pioneers helped set the stage for America's technological growth. Pennsylvania's contribution to the Industrial Revolution, which reached its peak in the 19th century, was sparked in its earliest stages by the important iron industry which flourished around Pottsville and Reading in the 18th century. The nation's first oil well, drilled by Colonel Drake at Titusville only a hundred and fifteen years ago, gave rise to the world-wide petroleum industry.

This same business growth is still apparent in twentieth-century Pennsylvania. Today, the state produces one-third of America's steel and leads in the manufacture of items as varied as electrical parts and chocolate.

Today, Pennsylvania is the nation's fourth largest industrial production state. Pennsylvania's mineral wealth is almost limitless. Its varied manufactured products, raw materials, and agricultural bounty move rapidly, efficiently and cheaply over a fine network of highways, railways, waterways and through three of the country's biggest ports, Philadelphia, Pittsburgh and Erie, to the rest of the world.

The ability of versatile Pennsylvania to adjust its business complexion to changing times is best seen in the way the state snapped back after the coal industry was largely played out in the eastern-central part of Pennsylvania a generation ago. Cities like Scranton and Wilkes-Barre, which had depended for economic survival on coal mining, were becoming industrial ghost towns until new industries were developed to replace the failing one. The state has taken many steps to attract new industries, and tourism is now one of the Keystone State's large money earners.

Many Pennsylvanians are unaware of the beauty of the state's scenic wonders—its handsome forests and rolling hills. Its hardworking citizens are viewed as part of a "big northeastern industrial state." Although it is a big-town state, 31 of its 67 counties remain more than 30.7 percent rural. It has 30 cities and 112 boroughs with populations between 7,000 and 25,000. It is an important state, politically, in the national scene.

Pennsylvania's proximity to New York City and Washington, D.C. has caused some visitors to give the Keystone State a cursory glance. But in the last few years, tourism has increased throughout the state, particularly in Philadelphia, the City of Brotherly Love, where a restaurant resurgence has made it a gourmet's cornucopia. Now, throughout the state, one finds adventure, year-round sports and festivals, world-renowned cultural institutions, historical sites richly preserved from a 300-year history, and scenery to rival any place in the country. A genuinely warm and hospitable citizenry confirms the state's new slogan: "You've got a friend in Pennsylvania."

In the rich tapestry of American history, Penn's "holy experiment," begun nearly three hundred years ago, has paid off handsomely in an economic, cultural and social renaissance that has been fulfilled in Penn's "good and fruitful land." The creed the Quakers evolved in Philadelphia, "The City of Brotherly Love"—"Virtue, Liberty and Independence"—still remains valid in Pennsylvania, the cradle of America.

PENNSYLVANIA

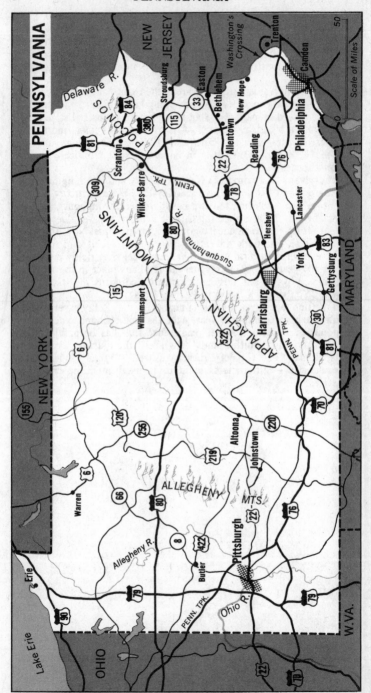

PRACTICAL INFORMATION

 FACTS AND FIGURES. In both area and population, Pennsylvania is the largest of the mid-Atlantic states with a land area of 44,832 miles and a population of over 12,000,000. It is a particularly compact state, well-organized, convenient to travel through, and filled with interesting things to do and see. Ethnically, culturally and economically, it is extremely diverse. It offers a rich combination of scenic, historical and human interest, as well as cultural and recreational attractions. It also has as an excellent tourist infrastructure of hotels, restaurants, resorts, roads, sources of information, and experience in receiving visitors.

Pennsylvania is not a natural region, but was created by royal charter in 1681. Its boundaries, for the most part, are artificial. The Delaware River on the east and some forty miles of Lake Erie shore at the northwest corner are its only natural boundaries. Elsewhere, the boundaries are regular, making the state almost a rectangle. For this reason, Pennsylvania cannot be said to have had a separate existence before 1681, and its history merges with that of the surrounding mid-Atlantic region before that time. A dissected plateau covers the northern and western section, ranging from about 2,000 feet above sea level in the northern tier of counties to about 1,200 feet south of Pittsburgh. A broad belt of wide valleys, alternating with narrow mountains, stretches across the state from the south-central boundary to the northeast corner. Next, to the east, is the Grant Valley; its southern, central, and eastern sections are known as the Cumberland, Lebanon, and Lehigh valleys respectively. This area is bordered on the east by discontinuous mountains, by lowlands of irregular form, and by a deeply dissected plateau of moderate height that gradually slopes to the Delaware River. There is another lowland along the shore of Lake Erie.

Woodlands of stately oaks, maples, pines and hemlocks are firmly rooted in more than half the state. There are rushing rivers, waterfalls, lakes, and streams, filled with fish, throughout the highlands and lovely rolling hills in the Pocono Mountains region—one of the East's most popular honeymoon resort areas. There are three important river systems: the Delaware, the Susquehanna, and the Ohio. Minor systems draining a part of the state are the Potomac and the Genesee; a small system drains into Lake Erie. The major rivers have important tributaries, one of the most important being the Schuylkill River in Philadelphia. Pennsylvania's streams provide transportation, water supply, power and fishing.

Since colonial days, Pennsylvania has been an important agricultural area. Today, it is also one of America's major industrial centers. When the state was first named after the father of its founder, William Penn, it became known as The Quaker State. Pennsylvania, which means Penn's Woods, quickly became the cultural and geographical center of the English colonies in America. Before long, it was the pivotal meeting place between the New England states and those as far south as Georgia, thus forming an "arch" that held together the factions of the north and south. Pennsylvania was appropriately nicknamed the "Keystone State."

The diverse state also gained the reputation of being "the workshop of the world" because its reserves of coal and oil attracted giant industries. Today, gigantic mills in cities such as Bethlehem, Harrisburg, Johnstown, Lewistown,

Pittsburgh and Washington produce about one-fourth of the nation's steel. Important chemical and synthetic textile firms operate in Easton, Lewistown, Scranton and Williamsport. Many of the nation's most important products are produced in the state, among them: clothing and shoes, paper and wood products, glass, coke, cigars, beverages, electric machinery and appliances and transportation equipment.

For you, the tourist, however, the principal attractions of this multi-faceted state will be human rather than natural or industrial, deriving from the arts and activities in a pleasant and temperate area. The pleasures of this region are frequently urban and urbane. Its landscapes are muted, orderly and moderate, with none of the vastness or ruggedness that begins west of the Mississippi. There are marvelous festivals all year long, with exciting events that will interest the most sophisticated traveler. There are exquisitely manicured farms, particularly in the Pennsylvania Dutch region. One can stay with a farming family for a unique vacation experience, sharing farm chores and enjoying home-cooked, family-style meals after a full day of unusual pleasures.

Sports for activists range from horse-pulling contests, whitewater rafting, mountain climbing, skiing, boating, golfing and tennis, to square dancing. One can also ride horseback, hang glide, rock climb, fish, hunt, swim, skate, or visit any one of hundreds of beautiful state parks and campgrounds. Or one can root for one's favorite team, for there are many big league winning teams to cheer for—the Phillies, Pirates, Eagles, Flyers, 76ers, and more. For just relaxing, the lovely state can be used as your own private retreat, in which to think, write, read, or paint—an exquisite, tranquil locale for unwinding.

As a cultural center, Pennsylvania abounds in delights for the mind as well as the body. A marvelous ethnic and cultural mix offers an assortment of people, rich in heritage and proud of their contribution to this country. Throughout the state there are sites like Valley Forge National Park, Hershey (with its marvelous Chocolate World), quaint covered bridges, breathtaking caverns (ten in all) and more operating caves than in any other state. And everywhere, one finds warm, hospitable people—happy to share the best of Pennsylvania pride and hospitality.

 WHEN TO GO. With prevailing winds from the west, Pennsylvania has a continental climate. However, the weather can take sudden turns. A humid, summer day may turn chilly if a squall sweeps in from the sea or a blustery January day may be followed by an unexpected warm spell. Temperatures range from an average low of 23 degrees to a high of 38 in December to an average high of 86 and low of 65 in July. A drop of 40 degrees within 24 hours is not unusual, so it is advisable to bring clothing that covers all exigencies. Philadelphia can have pleasant, breezy summer days or a heat spell that chases people to the mountains or the seashore. Spring and fall are particularly lovely, when temperatures are usually pleasant and the foliage exquisite. Winters are often mild, but snow storms do appear to the delight of skiiers who have an abundance of areas in which to indulge their pastime. Numerically speaking, summer welcomes the largest number of visitors to the state. Festivals (folk, craft, art and music) explode throughout Pennsylvania as do sports and seasonal events. There are state and local fairs from early spring through fall. Historical commemorations, particularly in 1981 and 1982, are likely to occur at any time of the year, due to Pennsylvania's unique position marking William Penn's receiving a charter for Pennsylvania from Charles II on March 14, 1681 and on October 24, 1682—the date of Penn's arrival in Philadelphia.

PLANNING YOUR TRIP. In the *Practical Information* sections you will find detailed sources for information on general tourism, national and state parks, tours, gardens, festivals, sports, museums, historic sites and monuments, and much more. If you don't want to bother with reservations on your own, a travel agent won't cost you a cent, except for specific charges like telegrams. He gets his fee from the hotel or carrier he books for you. A travel agent can also be of help for those who prefer to take their vacations on a "package tour"—thus keeping your own planning to a minimum. If you prefer the convenience of standardized accommodations, remember that the hotel and motel chains publish free directories that enable you to plan your overnights very precisely and to reserve everything ahead of time. If you don't belong to an auto club, now is the time to join one. They can be very helpful about routings and emergency service on the road. If you plan the route yourself, make certain the map you get is dated for the current year (highways and thruways are appearing and being extended at an astonishingly rapid rate). A few of the major oil companies will still send maps and mark preferred routes on them, if you tell them what you have in mind. Try: *Exxon Touring Service*, 1251 Avenue of the Americas, New York, N.Y. 10020, or 450 Decoma, Houston, TX 77001; *Arco Travel Service*, P.O. Box 93, Versailles, KY 40383; *Texaco Travel Service*, P.O. Box 1459, Houston, TX 77001; or *Mobil Oil Corp. Travel Service*, P.O. Box 25, Versailles, KY 40383. In addition, most states have their own maps, which pinpoint attractions, list historical sites, parks, etc. City chambers of commerce are also good sources of information. Specific addresses are given under *Tourist Information* in the individual city chapters.

PACKING. What to take, what to wear. Make a packing list for each member of the family. Then check off items as you pack them. It will save time, reduce confusion. Time-savers to carry along include extra photo film (plenty), suntan lotion, insect repellent, sufficient toothpaste, soap, etc. Always carry an extra pair of glasses, including sunglasses, particularly if they're prescription ones. A travel iron is always a good tote-along, as are some transparent plastic bags (small and large) for wet suits, socks, etc. They are also excellent, of course, for packing shoes, spillable cosmetics, and other easily-damaged items. If you fly, remember that despite signs to the contrary airport security X-rays do in fact damage your films in about 17% of the cases. Have them inspected separately or pack them in special protective bags. Useful extras to carry include binoculars, a compass, and a magnifying glass—for fine print maps.

All members of the family should have sturdy shoes with non-slip soles. Keep them handy in the back of the car. Carry rain gear in a separate bag in the back of the car (so no one will have to get out and hunt for it in a downpour en route).

Women should stick to one or two basic colors for their wardrobes, so that they can manage with one set of accessories. If possible, include one dress or a pants suit. Wrinkle-free fabrics are, of course, the easiest to pack and wear. For dress-up evenings, take along dresses or pants you can vary with a simple change of accessories. That way you can dress up or down to suit the occasion.

If you go in spring or summer, plan to dress as lightly as possible, but have along a light sweater for overcast days, cool evenings, and air-conditioned interiors. Women should have sleeveless dresses of cotton, linen, or synthetic fabrics that breathe. For men, tropical-weight suits of synthetic blends that breathe easily and are wrinkle-resistant are best. Cotton shirts are more absorbent than synthetics. A lightweight raincoat that can double as an overcoat in cooler weather, or as a windbreaker over warmer clothes in winter, will be handy. November through March be prepared for cooler weather, especially as you go inland and into higher ground.

Turtlenecks are now accepted almost everywhere and are a comfortable accessory. Don't forget extra socks.

Planning a lot of sun time? Don't forget something to wear en route to the pool, beach, or lakefront, and for those first few days when you're getting reacquainted with sun on tender skin.

A common-sense list of handy things to have along in the car might include: 1) a First-Aid kit, with plenty of Band-Aids; 2) a supply of tissues, a roll of paper towels, and a roll of toilet paper; 3) a moist washcloth in a plastic bag; 4) insect repellant; 5) a bottle opener and a can opener; 6) a whisk broom; 7) a jacknife.

WHAT WILL IT COST? This is a crucial question, and one of the most difficult. The American Automobile Association estimates that during 1982 expenses for a couple driving across the country would average around $40 per day for meals, $40 for lodging, and $7 for each 100 miles for gasoline (at 20 miles to the gallon—subject to change). We hope you can do it for less, and we have included a number of concrete and practical suggestions for cutting costs wherever you can. We think two people can travel comfortably in this part of U.S. for about $79 a day (not counting gasoline or other transportation costs), as you can see in the table below.

In some areas you can cut expenses by traveling off season, when hotel rates are usually lower. The budget-minded traveler can also find bargain accommodations at tourist homes or family-style YMCA's and YWCA's. Some state and federal parks also provide inexpensive lodging. And in this six-state area 26 colleges and universities offer dormitory accommodations to tourists during the summer vacations at single-room rates of $2–$10 per night, with meals from $0.60–$3.50. A directory of some 200 such opportunities all over the U.S. is *Mort's Guide to Low-Cost Vacations and Lodgings on College Campuses, USA–Canada.*

Another way to cut down on the cost of your trip is to look for out-of-the-way resorts. Travelers are frequently rewarded by discovering very attractive areas which haven't as yet begun to draw quantities of people.

Typical Expenses for Two People

Room at **moderate** hotel or motel	$38.00	plus tax
Breakfast, including tip	5.50	
Lunch at **inexpensive** restaurant, including tip	8.00	
Dinner at **moderate** restaurant, including tip	16.00	
Sightseeing bus tour for two	6.00	
An evening drink for two	3.00	
Admission to museum or historic site for two	2.50	
	$79.00	

If you are budgeting your trip, don't forget to set aside a realistic amount for the possible rental of sports equipment (perhaps including a boat or canoe), entrance fees to amusement and historical sites, etc. Allow for tolls for bridges and super-highways (this can be a major item), extra film for cameras, and souvenirs.

After lodging, your next biggest expense will be food, and here you can make very substantial economies if you are willing to get along with only one meal a day (or less) in a restaurant. Plan to eat simply, and to picnic. It will save you time and money, and it will help you to enjoy your trip more. That beautiful scenery does not *have* to whiz by at 55 miles per hour. Many states have set aside picnic and rest areas, often well-equipped and in scenic spots, even on highways and thruways, so finding a pleasant place to stop usually is not difficult. Before you leave home put together a picnic kit.

Sturdy plastic plates and cups will be cheaper in the long run than throw-away paper ones; and the same goes for permanent metal flatware rather than the throw-away plastic kind. Pack a small electric pot and two thermoses, one for water and one for milk, tea, or coffee. In other words, one hot, and one cold. Also, at least one sharp knife, a bottle opener, a can opener, and some paper towels. If you go by car, take along a small cooler. Bread, milk, cold cereal, jam, tea or instant coffee, fruit, fresh vegetables that need no cooking (such as lettuce, cucumbers, carrots, tomatoes and mushrooms), cold cuts, cheese, nuts, raisins, eggs (hard boil them in the electric pot in your room the night before)—with only things like this you can eat conveniently, cheaply, and well.

If you like a drink before dinner or bed, bring your own bottle. Most hotels and motels will supply ice free or for very little, but the markup on alcoholic beverages in restaurants, bars, lounges and dining rooms is enormous, and in some states peculiar laws apply anyway.

 INSURANCE. In planning your trip, think about three kinds of insurance: property, medical, and automobile. The best person to consult about insuring your household furnishings and personal property is your insurance agent. For Americans, he is also the person to ask about whatever special adjustments might be advisable in medical coverage while traveling. Foreigners visiting the United States should bear in mind that medical expenses in this country can be astronomical compared to those elsewhere, and that the kind of protection that some countries (Britain, for example) extend not only to their own nationals but to visiting foreigners as well simply does not exist here.

Every state has some sort of Financial Responsibility law establishing minimum and maximum amounts for which you can be held liable in auto accidents. Most states require insurance to be offered, and 17 states require you to have it in order to register a car or get a license within their jurisdictions. In any case, it is almost essential to have third-party coverage, or "liability insurance," as claims can run very high for both car repairs and, particularly, medical treatment. Insurance premiums vary according to place and person; they are generally highest for males under 25 and for drivers who live in large urban areas.

One possibility is the *American Automobile Association* (AAA), which offers both group personal accident insurance (from $2,500 to $3,750) and bail bond protection up to $5,000 as part of its annual membership (fee $35). The AAA can also arrange the validation of foreign driving permits for use in the United States. Foreigners should consider getting their insurance before leaving their own countries since short-term tourists will find it difficult and expensive to buy here. For the AAA, write to AAA, 28 East 78th St., New York, NY 10021.

If you are over 50, write to the American Association of Retired Persons/ AIM, P.O. Box 2400, Long Beach, Calif. 90801 for information about its auto insurance recommendations and other travel services.

14   PENNSYLVANIA

HOW TO GET THERE. By car: There is easy access to Pennsylvania by Interstate Highway. From New York on the east, I–95 runs to Philadelphia, in the northeast I–81 passes through Binghamton, N.Y., to Scranton and down the state to Harrisburg, the state capital. I–80 bisects the state on an east-west axis. I–79 has its northern terminal in Erie, Pa., passing through Pittsburgh and leaving the state near Morgantown, West Virginia. The Pennsylvania Turnpike, the granddaddy of all turnpikes, snakes across the breath of the state, linking New Jersey in the east with Ohio in the west. The turnpike, which has a northeastern extension, carves through Pennsylvania's hills near Philadelphia, Harrisburg, and Pittsburgh. Breezewood, a town of motels (service stations and restaurants) is on the turnpike, east of Pittsburgh, where Interstate 70 curves up from the south.

By train: *Amtrak* has service to Philadelphia, Harrisburg, and Lancaster on interstate routes.

By bus: *Greyhound* and *Trailways* are the major carriers to Pennsylvania. *Continental* also has service to the major cities.

By air: Philadelphia and Pittsburgh have the major airports. Major airlines serving these airports include *USAir, Eastern, American, Northwest, TWA,* and *United.*

HOW TO GET AROUND. By car: The Pennsylvania Turnpike winds its way west from the New Jersey line near Philadelphia, past Harrisburg, just north of Pittsburgh to the Ohio line. Some tunnels in the mountains have been eliminated and mostly newly paved surfaces are a big help.

By train: *Amtrak* has good service in the southern half of the state between Philadelphia and Pittsburgh. There is also commuter service in the Philadelphia suburbs. Contact your travel agent or Amtrak office for rates and schedules.

By bus: *Trailways, Greyhound* and *Continental* provide fairly complete coverage within the state.

By air: *USAir* is the major interstate carrier. Besides Philadelphia and Pittsburgh, USAir's *Allegheny Commuters* fly to: Erie, Bradford, Williamsport, Scranton and Wilkes-Barre, Hazelton, Allentown, Reading, Lancaster, Harrisburg, Johnstown, Altoona, Clearfield, Dubois and Franklin.

TOURIST INFORMATION. *The Travel Development Bureau,* Pennsylvania Department of Commerce, 416 Forum Building, Harrisburg, Pa. 17120, is ready to answer any questions you might have. A list of county tourist-bureaus is available from the same source, 717–787–5453.

HINTS TO THE MOTORIST. Pennsylvania is well supplied with interstates, freeways, turnpikes and other systems that enable you to whiz through an area swiftly and smoothly and see absolutely nothing, but it would be self-defeating to plan your visit in those terms. Distances in the region are not long, and many of the major points of interest are remarkably close to each other. The Pennsylvania Turnpike is a well-designed highway, when you need it.

Driving through Pennsylvania can be a delightful experience, especially along the state's paved secondary roads. Its rolling countryside, handsome farms, and quiet towns are lovely, and the magnificent mountain scenery in the east and the west should not be missed. Along the back roads in the Pennsylvania Dutch region are enchanting sights. Horse and buggy riders clip-clop through the Amish countryside. See our cover if you have any doubts!

You will find 23 service plazas on the *Pennsylvania Turnpike,* each with a restaurant and gas station offering normal automotive services. You will also find 38 interchanges equipped with patron facilities. Over 600 vehicles, in constant touch with each other and with the *Turnpike's Communications Center,* patrol the highway for the ultimate in user service. The Pennsylvania Turnpike adheres to the national speed limit of 55 miles per hour. There are no motels or independent restaurants along the Turnpike, but they can be found near many interchanges, such as Breezewood, Harrisburg, Philadelphia or Pittsburgh.

The first precaution you should take is to have your car thoroughly checked by your regular dealer or service station to make sure it is in good shape. You may also find it advisable to join an auto club that can provide you with trip planning information, insurance coverage and emergency and repair service along the way.

If you are a member of the NRTA/AARP, that organization has a motoring plan in cooperation with the *Amoco Motor Club* offering a number of emergency and repair services. Write to *NRTA/AARP Motoring Plan,* P. O. Box 390, Long Beach, Calif. 90801. The *National Institute for Automotive Service Excellence,* which tests and certifies the competence of auto mechanics, publishes a directory of about 10,000 repair shops all over the U. S. which employ certified mechanics. It is available from NIASE, Suite 515, 1825 K Street N.W., Washington, D. C. 20005.

SEASONAL EVENTS. January: In Philadelphia, the traditional *Mummers Parade* is staged annually on New Year's Day. It features elaborate and spectacular floats, and thousands of paraders clad in colorful costumes, going through the mid-city for hours. In Harrisburg, the *State Farm Show,* held in the second week of January, features the biggest agricultural exhibit to be seen anywhere, and it's free. In Pottsville, the *Greater Pottsville Winter Carnival* is one of the state's largest winter festivals. In Philadelphia, the *U.S. Professional Indoor Tennis Championships* are held at the Spectrum at the end of the month.

February: Philadelphia celebrates the *Chinese New Year* in Chinatown.

March: Special spring flower shows are held in Pittsburgh at the Phipps Conservatory—also in Philadelphia. Philadelphia hosts its annual *St. Patrick's Day Parade.*

April: Somerset County schedules a 3-day *Maple Festival,* crowning a Maple Queen, plus a crafts show. In Philadelphia, the nation's top track and field events, the *Penn Relays,* are held at Franklin Field on the University of Pennsylvania's campus, last weekend of the month.

May: Annual *Apple Blossom Festival* is staged at South Mountain Fairgrounds in Adams County. Folklore, folk dances and celebrations are available at Pittsburgh's *Folk Festival.* In nearby Devon, there is equestrian competition

and a gala outdoor fair. *Northern Appalachian Festival* features "The Great Bed
Race," in Bedford. In Allentown, the unique *Historic Covered Bridge Festival*
features four famous sites. *Bach Music Festival,* Packer Memorial Chapel, Lehigh University in Bethlehem, presents four days of concerts.

June: Pittsburgh schedules its *Three Rivers Arts Festival* in Gateway Center,
displaying works and crafts of local artists, plus band concerts and entertainment, June 10–26. In Philadelphia concerts are offered free in Robin Hood Dell
in Fairmount Park. Also in Philadelphia, first Saturday in the month, *Elfreth's
Alley* people hold their annual Fete in colonial costumes. The *Ringling Brothers
Barnum and Bailey Circus* returns for its annual visit to the Spectrum. The state
flower, the mountain laurel, is featured in laurel festivals in the Poconos, Brook-
ville and elsewhere. The *Pennsylvania State Laurel Festival* in Wellsboro combines a craft fair, art exhibits, amusements, a beauty pageant, and more.

July: The *Kutztown Folk Festival* is a most unique gathering. The heritage
of the Pennsylvania Dutch is reflected through the festival's crafts and folkways,
its food and pageantry, its quilts and demonstrations. At Ephrata Cloister,
during July and August, the *Vorspiel* is a spectacular event, where music two
centuries old is performed. The *Bavarian Summer Festival,* in Barnesville, is
America's original and greatest "Oktoberfest in July." The annual *Pocono 500*
is held at the Pocono International Raceway in Mt. Pocono in July. Philadelphia
continues to celebrate *Freedom Week* as well as Independence Day ceremonies.
The end of July features the *IVB-Philadelphia Golf Classic;* more low-cost
outdoor summertime music is performed at the Robin Hood Dell. The *Central
Pennsylvania Festival of Arts* is held in State College. A 3-day *Sommerfest* in
Somerset is a little bit of Bavaria in the Laurel Highlands area of the Southern
Alleghenies.

August: Last weeks of August, the *Little League World Series* is played at
Little League Stadium, Williamsport. August is a time for county and local fairs.
Check the local newspapers for details. The *Old Fiddlers Picnic* is held in
Chester County.The *Philadelphia Folk Festival,* in nearby Schwenksville, offers
day and night concerts, workshops, dance sessions, fireside singing, and craft
exhibitions. The biggest *Woodsmen's Show* in the country is held at Cherry
Springs State Park, 8 miles south of *Galeton.* The *Siberian Husky Dog Exhibit*
is held on Woodward Cave's campground in *Woodward.*
    Great Allentown Fair presents top-name performers, agricultural demonstra-
tions and a midway. On the Fairgrounds, Allentown.

September: A custom more than two centuries old is revived at West Grove's
Star Rose Gardens, where the *annual rent of one red rose* is presented to the
descendants of the family of William Penn, following the tradition in force since
1731. In Uniontown, near Pittsburgh, the annual *Fall Foliage Festival* in the
Laurel Highlands attracts many people. The first week of September, the *Ukrainian Festival* boasts bands and dance groups from the United States and
Canada in Nanticoke. *Grand Irish Jubilee* highlights traditional Irish dancing,
arts, crafts and delicacies. Lakewood Park, Barnesville. *Ligonier Highland
Games* is a gathering of the Scottish clans. *Rolling Rock Races,* in Ligonier, is
America's biggest steeplechase event. *Autumn Leaf Festival* highlights the foli-
age season. Clarion.

October: At the Pennsylvania Farm Museum, located on US 222 near Lancaster, *Harvest Festival Days* are scheduled Oct. 1–9 for a fine display of two-centuries-old farm customs and antiques. In Harrisburg, the *Pennsylvania National Horse Show,* a famous event, is held in the Farm Show Arena. In West Chester, for *Chester County Day,* the old, gracious colonial homes are opened up for visitors.

November: Philadelphia stages its annual, colorful *Thanksgiving Day Parade.* The annual *Army-Navy Football Classic* is held in Philadelphia's John F. Kennedy Stadium that same day. The *Philadelphia Craft Show* is held at Memorial Hall in Fairmont Park. In Pittsburgh, the *Fall Flower Show* is scheduled in Phipps Conservatory. At Gettysburg, Lincoln's famous *Gettysburg Address* is commemorated.

December: Christmas season is best to spend in *Bethlehem* for special services, displays and holy music sung by the Moravian Choir Group. Special events are staged by the *Valley Forge Historical Society* at Valley Forge to honor Washington's encampment there during the Revolutionary War. Also, a *Christmas Ceremony* is held at Washington Crossing State Park, to mark Washington's famous crossing of the Delaware.

 NATIONAL PARKS. **Gettysburg National Military Park** surrounds the town of Gettysburg at the junction of US 30 and 15 and 140 about 7 miles north of the Maryland border. It comprises the battlefield on which, on July 1, 2 and 3 of 1863, was fought one of the bloodiest and most decisive battles of the Civil War. Here, too, is the spot on which President Abraham Lincoln delivered his most famous speech, the *Gettysburg Address,* on November 18, 1863. The park covers 25 square miles and has almost 30 miles of roads through the fighting areas, with monuments, markers, and tablets of granite and bronze; and 400 cannon in battle positions are located on the field. Battlefield guides, licensed by the National Park Service, conduct two-hour tours to all the points of interest, describing the troop movements and highlights of the battle. Tours are also available in air-conditioned sightseeing buses that supply the sounds of the battle and a dramatized description in stereophonic sound. Tours are also available at the Wax Museum. A *Park Visitors Center,* located on US 15 and State 134, features many instructive exhibits and dioramas in a large museum, as well as a 356-foot cyclorama painting of *Pickett's Charge.* The center is open 8 to 5 P.M. daily and is free, but adults pay 50¢ admission to the cyclorama. *Eisenhower's Farm* is another famous place to visit. For a complete description of the park, see *Gettysburg: A Living Battlefield.*

Valley Forge National Historical Park, 2,073 acres on State 363 adjacent to town of Valley Forge, marks the site where Washington's half-clothed, half-starved army wintered in 1777–78. Restorations of cabins and remains of entrenchments as well as many national and state monuments may be seen, including Washington's headquarters; the Bake House, an 18th-century bakery, and the headquarters of Generals von Steuben and Varnum. Observation tower on Mt. Joy affords fine view of countryside. There is a small museum of battlefield relics. Washington Memorial Chapel and Carillon on State 363 contains relics; its windows tell our early history in stained glass. Museum adjoining chapel contains Washington's tent and flag. The Potts House, Washington's headquarters on Valley Creek Road, has Washington mementos, and is the site of an annual Spring Dogwood Festival.

The **Allegheny National Forest,** established by proclamation of President Calvin Coolidge in 1923, lies in the Allegheny Plateau country. The forest extends from the New York-Pennsylvania boundary 45 miles into the state, in the general vicinity of the communities of Warren, Bradford and Kane. The forest, covering more than 471 thousand acres, has been a center for forestry research since 1927, and is important as well as a recreation area serving more than 47 million people who live within a 300-mile radius. There are 260 miles of trout streams, and bass may be found in the Allegheny and Clarion rivers and in 32 acres of lakes. Hunting turkey, deer and bear is popular in season. Facilities for camping, picnicking, boating, and swimming are provided in numerous areas throughout the forest. Recreation is administered with the least possible restriction, in keeping with the safety of the public and the protection of the forest. At all times, unless the camping and picnicking are at one of the specially improved areas, a campfire permit is necessary. The permits are issued without cost at the Forest Supervisor's Office in Warren, or by district rangers at Sheffield, Marienville, Bradford and Ridgeway.

Hopewell Village National Historic Site is a restored iron-making village 6 miles south of Birdsboro, near Reading.

STATE PARKS. The State of Pennsylvania urges native residents and visiting tourists alike to "Come to Penn's Woods" . . . enjoy the outdoors in a vast forest area covering half of the state's 30 million acres . . . where you'll find beautiful mountain, plateau, and valley country . . . where there are parks virtually everywhere to provide health and recreation benefits. There is boating on lakes and streams, camping in patrolled forests, fishing in placid lakes and swift streams, hiking in woods and rolling hills, picnicking in pleasant groves and swimming in guard-protected lakes and pools. For you to enjoy the great outdoors, Pennsylvania has provided 113 state parks, 105 picnic areas, 21 state forests, and natural forest areas, some open throughout the year, but all open from at least Memorial Day to Labor Day. The state parks and forests are well distributed throughout the state so that no matter where you may find yourself, you are not too far removed from outdoor recreation facilities. In addition to the activities mentioned above, a number of the areas provide rustic or primitive vacation cabins which may be reserved for up to two weeks by writing the Pennsylvania Department of Environmental Resources, Harrisburg, Pa., or by applying directly to the local state park ranger in the park where you wish to stop. In the mountainous parts of the state, recreation areas are provided with facilities for winter sports: ski slopes and tows, toboggan runs, ice rinks, lodges and other types of accommodations.

The following state parks are among the most outstanding in Pennsylvania:

Big Pocono State Park, 1,305 acres, 6 mi. northwest of Tannersville in Monroe Co., off State 611—no camping but picnicking at a scenic 2,000 ft. above sea level.

Hickory Run State Park, 15,500 acres, northeast of Hazelton via State 940 and 534 in Carbon Co. on border of Poconos; stream fishing, swimming. *Boulder Field*—within the park is a geological wonder from the last glacial period.

Presque Isle State Park at Erie, 3,100 acres, 5 mi. from Erie on State 832. Park includes the beautiful peninsula and bay of Presque Isle and the landlocked harbor of the city of Erie. A monument in the park commemorates Admiral Perry's historic victory over the British at the Battle of Lake Erie in 1813. Presque Isle has a 7-mile guarded beach with facilities for swimming, fishing, boating, and winter sports; no camping. A 110-acre lake connected with harbor offers inland water sports. Wildlife refuge and conservation area also located here. Commercial ferry service is available.

Pymatuning State Park, 20,075 acres, on southwest end of Pymatuning Lake, on US 6 and State 332, in Crawford Co.; wildlife refuge, boating, fishing, swimming, camping.

Ricketts Glen State Park, 13,000 acres, 17 mi. west of Wilkes-Barre on State 118 and 487, cutting into Columbia, Luzerne, and Sullivan counties; camping, swimming, hiking, picnicking, fishing, 28 spectacular waterfalls—some 100 ft. high.

Shawnee State Park, 3,840 acres, with a 450-acre lake, 10 mi. west of Bedford between US 30 and Penna. Tpke., in Bedford Co.; boating, fishing, swimming, picnicking, camping.

Washington Crossing State Park (478 acres on Delaware River 7 miles south of New Hope on State 32, in Bucks Co.) is the site of Washington's historic crossing of the Delaware River to surprise the Hessians at Trenton. The park is connected to Washington Crossing State Park, N.J., by a bridge. It has a wildflower preserve, picnicking.

For a complete list of all the state parks in Pennsylvania, write the Bureau of State Parks, Dept. of Environmental Resources, P.O. Box 1467, Harrisburg, Pa. 17120.

 CAMPING OUT. There are private campgrounds throughout the state; most have facilities for both tents and travel trailers. Campgrounds range from merely an open space to pitch a tent to elaborate facilities including movies, churches, organized social activities, in fact, all the amenities of a resort. The Travel Development Bureau publishes a *Pennsylvania Campground Guide* that lists over 100 private campgrounds. Write: The Travel Development Bureau, Department of Commerce, 416 Forum Building, Harrisburg, Pa. 17120. Also see listings in the chapters on Sports, Gettysburg, and the Poconos.

 TRAILER TIPS. The increasing popularity of trailer travel in recent years is evidenced in Pennsylvania by an ever-growing number of accommodations and facilities for this pleasantly informal mode of travel and vacation. All of the state parks that provide camping facilities accommodate the smaller and moderate-size travel trailers at the same rates as for tent camping. However, no electricity or hookups are provided. In addition, there are many private, well-equipped trailer and mobile home parks throughout the state. **Melody Lakes Mobile Park** is in Quakertown in beautiful Bucks County. Another working farm that features a campground is **Twin Bridge Meadow Valley Campground,** R.D. 4, Chambersburg, Pa.

FARM VACATIONS AND GUEST RANCHES. Pennsylvania has many working farms that take in guests. At most of the farms you are welcome to help with the chores if you wish, or you can just laze about and enjoy the countryside. *Beaver Creek Farm Cabins,* State 1, Strasburg, is in Amish country not far from Gettysburg. This working chicken farm has plenty of room for the guests to roam. There are accommodations for sixty in eight heated cabins. Harold and Miriam Brubaker are your hosts.

The Bassak family runs the *Dyberry Glen* dairy farm in Honesdale. Adults and children alike enjoy helping the Bassaks work their many cows. There are excellent walking trails in the area.

Hillstone Farms, Mrs. Jerry Webster, R.D. #6 in Wellsboro, is in the Pennsylvania Grand Canyon country. This is a 600-acre working dairy farm with milk cows, pigs, and saddle horses. Main attraction is horseback riding through canyon country.

Tom and Jean Trone own and operate *Quality First Acres.* This picturesque, modern 197-acre farm, located in the heart of southcentral Pennsylvania, has over 50,000 laying hens. Rife Road, R.D. 2, East Berlin, Pa. 17316.

For more information on farms in Pennsylvania write Pennsylvania Dutch Tourist Bureau, 1800 Hempstead Rd., Lancaster 17601.

  MUSEUMS AND GALLERIES. The town of Gettysburg has many museums under privated management where admissions are usually around $1 for adults, and about half that for children. **Gettysburg National Museum,** on US 15, has the largest collection of Civil War relics plus an electrical map which lights up in a vivid display of the famous three-day battle. The **Hall of Presidents,** at the main gate of the **National Cemetery** on US 140, has life-size figures in wax of all the Presidents. At the intersection of US 15 and 30, you will find the **Wills House,** or the **Lincoln Room Museum,** and see the room where he put the finishing touches to his famous address. You may also hear a stereophonic rendition of the speech. **Horse'n' Buggy Museum,** one mile north on US 15, contains about two hundred old buggies, carriages, and wagons. The Visitor's Center in the **Gettysburg Park** itself is free, and it too has exhibits of the Civil War and the Battle of Gettysburg. The **Gettysburg Battle Theatre** features a half-hour film, a complete "Battlerama" of handpainted miniatures, exhibits, statistics, and plenty more.

At Chadds Ford, in Chester County, some twenty-five to thirty miles from Philadelphia, is the **Brandywine River Museum.** It houses works by the famous Wyeth family. There are slide lectures daily except Christmas season, and movies on N.C. Wyeth.

The town of Bethlehem boasts the first museum in America. The **Annie S. Kemerer Museum,** which is open in the afternoon, re-creates the spirit and appearance of Victorian times with its rare carpets, gas chandeliers, hand-blocked wallpapers, Grunewald paintings and lithographs.

At **Reading Public Museum and Art Gallery,** at 500 Museum Road, in Museum Park, you will find exhibitions of art, science, and commerce set in a park of beautiful gardens. The stress here in on Dutch folk art.

York, one-time capital of the United States, has one of the largest collections of original Currier and Ives lithographs extant. Three hundred prints are on display at the **Currier and Ives and Antique Gallery** at 43 King St.

A glimpse into the life of Christopher Columbus after he made his famous voyage may be had in central Pennsylvania at Boalsburg. At the **Boal Estate,** along US 322, now a memorial park run by the state, you may see the Columbus family chapel, which has original furnishings, the family's ornate carved wood escutcheon, letters and other relics. The Boal mansion, part of it dating from the eighteenth century, is rich in paintings, glass, china and other beautiful furnishings. In a separate building on the estate is the museum replete with a varied and rich collection of items, including memorabilia of Pennsylvania's famed 28th Division. This site is open daily from May 1 to Oct. 31.

In Strasburg, near Lancaster, the state has opened a **Railroad Museum** which tells the history of railroading and has a fine collection of historic locomotives and passenger cars. It attracts nearly double the number of visitors of any other state museum. Nearby is the **Strasburg Railroad,** a standard-gauge, steam-driven train which is the oldest short-line train in the nation.

In the **Pennsylvania Farm Museum** in Landis Valley, north of Lancaster on US 222, you'll find one of the largest collections of rural Americana in the country and also have the opportunity to see how our forefathers made soap, churned butter, made brooms and rolled tobacco leaves into cigars.

The **Mercer Museum of Early American Tools and Implements** at Doylestown in Bucks County has re-creations of an 18th-century blacksmith shop, clockmaker's shop and wood-worker's shop plus many other tools and a large library to supplement the collection.

Also in Doylestown is the **Moravian Pottery and Tile Works Museum,** part of the Bucks County Park System. Open Wed. to Sat. Take a guided tour of this tile factory built in 1910. Closed Jan. and Feb.

The **Colonial Pennsylvania Plantation** in Ridley Creek State Park, in Media, is a 200-year-old restored farm re-creating the life of a typical farm family of the late 1700s. Visitors encouraged to participate in the activities. Also in Media is the **Franklin Mint and Museum of Medallic Art.** Featured are the coining process and works by James Wyeth and Norman Rockwell.

The **Allentown Art Museum** houses a permanent collection of 15th-18th-century European paintings, and 18th-20th-century American works.

In Easton is the **Canal Museum** in Hugh Moore Park. Displayed are exhibits on canals and certain featured waterways, such as the Lehigh and the Delaware.

The **William Penn Memorial Museum,** in Harrisburg, is a six-story circular building housing an authentic early country store, period rooms, Indian life exhibits, a planetarium, natural history exhibits, and more. Across the street from the capital. Inquire for times.

The **Forbes Road Gun Museum,** in Ligonier, features a collection of firearms from 1450, including Revolutionary and Civil War rifles and muskets.

The **Pocono Indian Museum,** in Bushkill, is dedicated to the history of the Delaware Indians. There are thousands of Indian artifacts and a chronological story of the Indian from 10,000 B.C.

The **Hershey Museum of American Life** features exhibits of artifacts, grouped into themes which explore the cultures of the American Indian, Eskimo, and Pennsylvania Dutch.

The **Westmoreland County Museum of Art** in Greensburg focuses on American Art and area artists. There is also a permanent collection of European paintings. It's a remarkable museum for a city the size of Greensburg.

 HISTORIC SITES. Pennsbury Manor in Morrisville is a re-creation of William Penn's house of 1699–1701. Pennsbury has beautifully furnished rooms with 17th-century antiques (the largest collection in Pennsylvania) and has handsome grounds.

In Ambler, **Fort Washington State Park** commemorates the winter of 1777. Hope Lodge, one mile south of Fort Washington, was General Nathanael

Greene's headquarters after the battle of Germantown. The house dates from 1750.

Washington Crossing State Park, near Buckingham, was Washington's embarkation point for the battles of Trenton and Princeton. There are two preserved houses that Washington and his officers used before crossing the Delaware on Christmas of 1777 to fight at Trenton and again on Jan. 3, 1778, to fight at Princeton. A museum of Revolutionary War artifacts was built in 1959 housing, among other things, Emanuel Leutze's famous painting *Washington Crossing the Delaware.* A 110-ft. lookout tower on Bowman Hill commands an excellent view of the Park and surrounding countryside. The Park and buildings are open daily.

In Fallisington are three hundred years of American architectural history. There are preservations of **Quaker houses** from the early 1700s, two dozen later **18th-century houses,** and elaborate **Victorian buildings** from the 19th century. Open Wed. to Sun., 1 P.M. to 5 P.M. Closed Jan. and Feb.

New Hope has the **Parry House** dating from the late 18th century. Open Fri. to Mon., May to Sept. The **New Hope-Delaware Canal Locks** and the **Barge Landing** (1790) are just south of town. The **New Hope town hall** dates from 1790.

The **Parsons-Taylor House** (1757) in Easton was owned by George Taylor, a signer of the Declaration of Independence.

Bethlehem, now known for its steel mills, has many 18th-century Moravian buildings. The **Central Moravian Church** at Main and West Sts. is regarded as the predominant church for this old Protestant sect. The **Bretheren's Church** (1748) was used as an army hospital during the Revolutionary War. The **Moravian Cemetery** (1742) at Hackewelder Pl. and the **Bell House** (1746) are also of interest.

A monument in Public Square in Wilkes-Barre marks the site of **Fort Wilkes-Barre.** In Wyoming, 7 mi. W on US 115, are the **Swetland Homestead** and the **Wyoming Massacre Site.** The Homestead shows the progress of a family in the first half of the 19th century. Open June 15 to Labor Day, except Mondays. The Massacre Site Monument memorializes an Iroquois attack on settlers in 1778.

Erie was an important town in early American history and has many sites and monuments to preserve its heritage. On US 19 16 mi. S of the city is **Fort Le Boeuf,** which was controlled by the French in 1759, the English in 1760, Indians in 1763 and finally the Americans in 1790. Oliver Hazard Perry's famous ship the **U.S.S. Niagara** and the **Perry Memorial House** on French St. are open to the public. The **Wayne Blockhouse** is a reconstruction of the building in which "Mad Anthony" Wayne succumbed to illness in 1793. 56 3rd St. The **Old Custom House** at 407 State St. is a preservation from the 19th century.

Titusville has the **Drake Well Memorial Park** with a working replica of the first oil well and related exhibits. Open Mon. to Sat. 9 to 5; Sun. 12 to 5.

Old Economy Village in Ambridge is a restoration of the Harmony Society buildings. The Harmonists, a communal society, enjoyed much success in the 19th century but celibacy and dwindling profits finally dissolved the community in 1905. Nearby is **Logan Cemetery,** a Revolutionary cemetery at the site of Logstown Indian Village, which was a major Indian stronghold important in the French and Indian Wars. General "Mad Anthony" Wayne encamped nearby in his winter quarters before the battle of Fallen Timbers broke the Indian power and made this part of the West safe for expansion.

On Route 30 in Ligonier is **Fort Ligonier,** originally constructed in 1758 to provide the settlers with refuge from the Indians. Beside the Fort itself, there are interesting museum exhibits plus reconstruction of 18th-century rooms.

The **Campass Inn Museum,** in nearby Laugulintown, is a restoration of an early 18th-century roadside inn. It has been carefully restored by the Ligonier Valley Historical Society.

Friendship Hill, 1 mi. S of New Geneva on State 166, was the home of Albert Gallatin, a noted diplomat serving Presidents Jefferson and Madison. This extraordinary house gives an insight into an 18th-century renaissance man. This National Historic Landmark is open daily Apr. to Oct.

The French and Indian War in America and the Seven Years War in Europe is said to have begun at the lonely outpost of **Fort Necessity** in 1754. Colonel George Washington led the Virginians and Indians against the French here. Two months later the French returned with an overpowering force of seven hundred soldiers and Indians and forced Washington to surrender. The conditions of the surrender were mild; the Colonials were allowed to withdraw, leaving their cannons behind, and the French burned the fort. General Edward Braddock was then sent to remove the French from Fort Duquesne but died during the retreat from the Battle of Monongahela. A monument at Fort Necessity memorialized Braddock and his defeat by the French.

The **Espy House** at 123 Pitt St., Bedford, was Washington's headquarters in 1794 during that series of anti-taxation riots known as the "Whiskey Rebellion."

Gettysburg National Military Park is, of course, the site of the most famous and decisive battle of the Civil War. Confederate and Union forces totaling 160,000 men fought here on the first days of July in 1863. General George Meade prevailed over Robert E. Lee, but casualties amounted to over 50,000 men. This beautiful park commemorates a very dark day in the history of America. There are numerous museums, tours, monuments and points of interest. Information is obtainable from the Gettysburg Travel Council, 35 Carlisle St., Gettysburg 17325.

The **York County Colonial Court House,** on Market St. and Pershing Ave., is the restored meeting place where the Continental Congress met from September 30, 1777 through June 27, 1778. Here, the Articles of Confederation and the new nation's first Constitution were adopted, thereby creating the United States of America and designating York as the nation's first capital. The Historical Society of York County maintains the **Golden Plough Tavern** and **General Gates' House,** both dating from the middle of the 18th century. Here, Lafayette made his famous "Toast That Saved a Nation" after an attempt to oust Washington as Commander in Chief. The **Bonham House** and **Log House** are 19th-century restorations at the same location.

In Harrisburg visit the **John Harris Mansion** (1776) at 219 S. Front St. It was the home of the city's founder. Open Mon. to Sat. The **State Capital Building,** between N. and Walnut Streets, is a beautiful statehouse designed after St. Peter's in Rome.

The **James Buchanan Birthplace,** in Mercersburg, features the cabin where the only President of the U.S. from Pennsylvania was born.

The **Daniel Boone Homestead,** on Rt. 422 E. of Reading, is the birthplace of America's great frontiersmen.

 TOURS. A great many bus tours are run from New York and other eastern cities, including some cities in Pennsylvania itself, to the Pennsylvania Dutch country, Philadelphia, Gettysburg and other points. Some are operated by *Greyhound, Gray Line* and *Trailways. Talmage Tours,* out of Philadelphia, slates tours to the same areas. *Casser Tours,* 201 W. 41st St., New York, has a good variety of Pennsylvania tours. *Parker Tours,* 125 W. 43rd St., New York, offers package weekend trips to and around the Dutch country at around $43 per person. *Conestoga Tours,* 825 E. Chestnut St., Lancaster, Pa., offers tours around that city and county, heart of the Dutch country.

 GARDENS. Longwood Gardens, which is near the town of Kennett Square, in the eastern part of the state, draws about a half million enthusiastic visitors a year.

Pierre Samuel du Pont made a gift of these extraordinary gardens, filled with both rare and everyday flowers, special seasonal displays, fountains to challenge Versailles, conservatories, an arboretum and an open-air theater. The central fountain shoots 1,000 gallons of water a minute in a dazzling 140-foot spray. Special displays, using color, music, and lights to enhance the fountains are open to the public without charge during the summer. Here you may see the world's largest analemmatic sundial, 40 feet in diameter, which tells time to the minute along principles laid down by the ancient Egyptians. Hershey has **Hershey Gardens** (Park Dr.). Over 40,000 plants; 800 varieties spread over 23 acres near Hotel Hershey—also tulip gardens (30,000 blooms) and arboretum. Open April 15 to late fall.

The **Phipps Conservatory** in Schenley Park, Pittsburgh, is the second largest conservatory of its kind in the country. Of special interest are the spring (March –April) and fall (November) flower shows. Outstanding orchid collection. Admission.

 MUSIC. Some large cities in the state offer symphony orchestras. There are many local and specialized music festivals here, including the **Vorspiel,** a spectacular of religious music staged annually in summer months at Ephrata in the ancient cloister. In the Pennsylvania Dutch country, the **Dutch Folk Festival** at Kutztown offers folk music, crafts, food, etc., for the over-100,000 visitors who come annually for the affair in early July.

There are many seasonal music and folk festivals around the state. Check local papers for details and dates.

DRINKING LAWS. The legal drinking age in Pennsylvania is twenty-one. Bottled liquor is sold only in state stores.

 SUMMER SPORTS. Summer sports are many and varied, and Pennsylvania affords nearly all in one location or another. The state is supplied with many excellent **golf** courses, both public and private. Among the courses are *Hershey, Shawnee-on-the-Delaware, Pocono Manor, Oakmont* and *Laurel Valley* in Ligonier. **Baseball** events, in addition to the big-league games, include the *World Series of Little League Baseball,* played each summer at Williamsport. The realm of fine **horses** may be enjoyed at the following tracks: *Keystone* (flats) and *Liberty Bell,* Philadelphia (flats and harness racing); *Pocono Downs,* between Scranton and Wilkes-Barre (harness); the *Meadows,* at Meadowlands (harness); *Commodore Downs,* Erie (flats); and *Penn National,* thirteen miles east of Hershey (flats). In addition, each September the *Rolling Rock Races,* a steeplechase for charity, is held in Ligonier. For the nature enthusiast, Pennsylvania provides excellent **hunting, fishing,** and **hiking.** Lakes and streams throughout the state provide a wide variety of fresh-water fish, from catfish to trout, from sunfish to muskelunge. And for the hunter the woods and forests abound in deer, bear, small game and game birds. The fields and hills and mountains of the state are a hiker's paradise, for they are criss-crossed by hundreds of miles of delightful hiking trails. For the rugged individual who enjoys the more strenuous paths, the *Appalachian Trail,* a footpath which runs from Maine to Florida, enters the state near Stroudsburg and runs in a south-westerly direction, to pass on into Maryland near Waynesboro. It is joined above Harrisburg by the *Horse Shoe Trail,* which continues east to Valley Forge. For the water enthusiast, the many many lakes and rivers throughout the state afford ample opportunity for **sailing, boating, canoeing, white-water rafting, water skiing, swimming,** and **diving,** as well as **scuba** and **skin diving.** Sand beaches can be found at Lake Erie and in many of the state parks, and public and private pools are to be found everywhere. For a more complete description of summer sports, consult the following chapter, *Sports in Pennsylvania.*

WINTER SPORTS. In the area of sports no part of the state is far removed from facilities to suit every taste. Among the winter sports, **skiing,** which has leaped in popularity in recent years, leads the rest, with a concentration of facilities in the Pocono Mountains in the northeast and in the Allegheny Mountains in the southwest. However, no part of the state really lacks facilities for this popular winter pastime. In the Pocono Mountain area, *Big Boulder, Camelback, Buck Hill, Pocono Manor, Jack Frost, Elk Mountain, Shawnee Mountain, Mt. Airy* and *Pocono Manor* are the major ski centers. Many other Pocono resorts have maintained limited ski facilities for years. In addition to skiing, a number of resorts that stay open all winter offer **sleighing, ice skating, tobogganing, sledding,** and **ice fishing.** Some of the Pocono lakes, most notably *Lake Wallenpaupack,* provide **ice boating** and even **sports-car racing on ice.** In the Allegheny Mountains area, *Seven Springs, Laurel Mountain, Hidden Valley,* and *Blue Knob* are the more popular and accessible ski facilities. Here too, the associated pastimes of tobogganing, sleighing and skating are provided for those who seek a variety of snowy activity. *Ski Liberty,* in Fairfield, is a fine ski area close to Gettysburg. Elsewhere in the state wintersports provisions are located at *Harley's Ski Roundtop,* southwest of Harrisburg; *Tussey Mountain,* east of University Park; *Happy Hill,* at Eagles Mere; *Denton Hill,* near Coudersport; *Cook Forest,* at Cooksburg; *Mt. Pleasant,* north of Cambridge Springs; and *Boyce Park,* Pittsburgh. Hockey is popular in Hershey, Pittsburgh and Philadelphia. The sports arenas of the principal cities also feature **boxing** and **wrestling** matches, while college **football** and **basketball** may be seen on the many campuses throughout the state. For a more complete description of summer sports, see the following chapter, *Sports in Pennsylvania.*

SHOPPING. Pennsylvania, one of the most beautiful states of the Union, has a multitude of unique shopping opportunities. In its cities you will find the large, typical American department stores that offer everything from safety pins to Aubusson rugs. Easy to find, they are often nationally known— *John Wanamaker, Gimbel's* or *Strawbridge and Clothier* in Philadelphia as well as super shopping complexes like New Market and the Gallery. You will often spot their suburban branches in shopping centers as you approach a city.

For **Pennsylvania Dutch articles,** there is *The Distelfink,* housed in a miniature red barn, at 31st and Tilghman Sts., in Allentown, which carries a wide assortment of **hand-crafted objects** and a special collection of **candles, Christ-**

mas decorations and stocking stuffers. Hand-blown glass is a specialty at *The Country Cousin,* on State 72 and US 222 about three miles south of Lancaster. Other articles in this gift shop include ironstone dinnerware and copies of Early American decorative items in copper, pewter and wood. *Walnut Grove Farm,* on US 30, some seven miles west of Coatesville, makes its specialty just as the old folks used to make it, with butter and cream, and stirred by hand. The *Amish Homestead,* three miles east of Lancaster on US 30, is a scenic seventy-one-acre farm dating back to 1744. It is in full operation and has a gift shop with Pennsylvania Dutch wares. There also is *Dutch Haven Barn,* on State 340 at Intercourse. In the same quaint village you can get jams, jellies, preserves and other distinctive foods at *Kitchen Kettle Village.*

Shops abound in the Berks County area, of which Reading is the principal city. In Montgomery County, the *Court* at King of Prussia is being hailed the largest mall in the country. Among its handsome stores are Bloomingdale's, Abraham and Straus, Wanamaker's, and hundreds of fine specialty stores.At Shartlesville, along US 22, you will come upon *Roadside America,* which calls itself the "World's greatest indoor miniature village," and the *Pennsylvania Dutch Gift Haus.* Throughout the area you'll find patchwork quilts made with Pennsylvania Dutch motifs; you'll eye collections of old Amish wagons, traps and bobsleds; you'll watch potters at work and then buy their handsomely shaped vases and bowls. And don't forget pretzels—this could be called the pretzel capital of the world. Hearth-baked pretzels are the specialty of *Tom Sturgis'* shop at 235 Lancester Pike W., in Shillington, near Reading.

Up in the Pocono region, at Mt. Pocono, you'll find a multitude of shopping spots. Among them are *Memorytown, U.S.A.,* which houses a number of stores, a motor lodge and the *Pennsylvania Dutch Farm,* which offers foods and a doll shop. *Holley Ross Pottery,* at La Anna, gives free demonstrations Monday through Friday. Others in the area are *Sciota Craft Shop,* at Sciota, which has crystal, pewter, baskets, unusual jewelry and pottery.

Many of these are open only seasonally, and the Pocono Mountains Vacation Bureau, 1004 Main St., Stroudsburg 18360, can fill you in.

Located in the northeast part of the state are many of the mills and factories that mass-produce clothing. Those of you with an eye for a bargain should look out for the factory outlets that sell merchandise for just a fraction of its usual retail price. In Reading alone you'll find such shops run by *David Crystal, Vanity Fair* and *Talbott's.* Also in the northeastern part of the state you can purchase slate—especially if you can load it in your car and carry it home, thus avoiding shipping costs, which are high because of the weight involved. This split-faced slate may be used to make a beautiful and easily-cared-for coffee table. It may be brought at one of the many quarries in the area.

 WHAT TO DO WITH THE CHILDREN. On a trip most children prefer action and adventure to playing the passive role of observers. Well distributed throughout the state of Pennsylvania are countless attractions especially designed for youngsters, and grown-ups as well. The majority of the attractions are not only entertaining but also informative and instructive.

A number of parks in the state feature fairy tales and characters from children's literature. Here the youngster may meet Red Riding Hood, Bambi, Jack-the-Giantkiller, and Santa Claus and his elves. They may visit the Gingerbread House, Ali Baba's Cave with its riches, a medieval castle, a riverboat, the North Pole, or a Lollipop Garden. At these parks they may ride a hay slide, a donkey cart, a fire engine, or even a 1910 Buick on a "magic" turnpike. The parks where all this takes place are **Storybook Forest,** on US 30 at Ligonier; **Dutch Wonderland,** on Rte. 30 east of Lancaster; **Storybookland,** on US 209 at Bushkill in the Poconos area; **Fairyland Forest,** at Conneaut Lake Park; and the **Poconos' Magic Valley** and **Winona Five Falls,** in Bushkill.

Just outside Philadelphia, on Rt. 1, in Langhorne, Bucks County, is **Sesame Place,** a 15-acre theme park that stresses intelligent, fun-filled entertainment.

For the more adventuresome child a trip of exploration through one of Pennsylvania's many underground caves and caverns to see the unusual rock formations and sparkling lighting displays may prove appealing. In southwestern Pennsylvania the largest caves are **Indian Caverns,** on State 45 at Spruce Creek. **Coral Caverns** are at Bedford, on State 31; **Laurel Caverns** on US 40 east of Uniontown, **Penn's Cave,** at Centre Hall in the center of the state, treats the visitor to a mile-long boat ride under ground. In the eastern part of the state lovely **Crystal Cave** and **Onyx Cave** are both just off US 222 near Kutztown; and the children will marvel at the **Lost River Caverns** on State 412 at Hellertown. **Indian Echo** is another cave at Hummelstown, near Hershey. **Woodward Cave** is the largest dry cavern in Pennsylvania. This 400-million-year-old cave features 14-foot-high stalagmites. Located in Woodward, Pa., midway between State College and Lewisburg. Lincoln Caverns, a "mysterious world of color," is on US Route 22, just west of Huntingdon.

Two coal mines in the state are open to visitors. In the westcentral part of the state is the **Seldom Seen Valley Mine,** on State 36 near St. Boniface; the **Pioneer Tunnel** at Ashland is in the heart of America's only anthracite region, north of Reading.

Rides are fun. The cable cars at Johnstown and Pittsburgh will give the kids a never-to-be-forgotten thrill. The **East Broad Top Railroad** at Rockhill Furnace and the **Strasburg Railroad** at Strasburg are two old-fashioned lines that still operate over lines as old as 130 years.

There are some other, rather unusual attractions, too. The sight of rattlesnakes being milked of their venom attracts thousands to the **Pocono Snake Country,** in Marshalls Creek. An exciting trip through the 150-year-old man-of-war, **Niagara,** Perry's flagship, which won decisive victories in the War of 1812, is available at Erie.

Good zoos, including children's zoos, may be visited in Philadelphia, Erie, and Pittsburgh. In the latter city they'll enjoy the **Aviary-Conservatory,** where tropical birds fly free in a jungle. Pennsylvania also features a variety of different animal parks. **Clyde Peeling's Reptiland** is on US Rt. 15 in Allenwood. This specialized zoo offers guided tours of the fascinating world of reptiles. **Animaland** is in Wellsboro, Pennsylvania's Grand Country region. The **Forest Zoo,** 3 mi. W. of Horseshoe curve in Gallitzin, exhibits hundreds of live, wild animals in their natural surrounding.

Children can ride a mule-drawn canal boat at New Hope.

HOTELS AND MOTELS in Pennsylvania range from deluxe resorts, mostly in the southeast quarter, to the plain highway accommodations that blend with the less glamorous life-style of the northern half of the state west of the Poconos. Price categories are, for double occupancy, *Super Deluxe* over $70, *Deluxe* $60 average, *Expensive* $50 average, *Moderate* $35 average and *Inexpensive* under $30. A 6% state tax will be added to your bill.

General Hints. Don't be one of those who take potluck for lodgings. You'll waste a lot of time hunting for a place, and often won't be happy with the accommodations you finally find. If you are without reservations, by all means begin looking early in the afternoon. If you have reservations, but expect to arrive later than five or six P.M., advise the hotel or motel in advance. Some places will not, unless advised, hold reservations after six P.M. And if you hope to get a room at that hotel's *minimum* rate be sure to reserve ahead or arrive very early.

If you are planning to stay in a popular resort region, at the height of the season, reserve well in advance. Include a deposit for all places except motels (and for motels if they request one). Many chain or associated motels and hotels will make advance reservations for you at affiliated hostelries along your route.

A number of hotels and motels have one-day laundry and dry cleaning services, and many motels have coin laundries. Most motels, but not all, have telephones in the rooms. If you want to be sure of room service, however, better stay at a hotel. Many motels have swimming pools, and even beachfront hotels frequently have a pool. Even some motels in the heart of large cities have pools. An advantage at motels is the free parking. There's seldom a charge for parking at country and resort hotels.

Hotels and motel chains. In addition to the hundreds of excellent independent motels and hotels throughout the country, there are also many that belong to national or regional chains. A major advantage of the chains, to many travelers, is the ease of making reservations en route, or at one fell swoop in advance. If you are a guest at a member hotel or motel, the management will be delighted to secure you a sure booking at one of its affiliated hotels at no cost to you. Chains also usually have toll free WATS (800) lines to assist you in making reservations on your own. This, of course, saves you time, worry and money. In addition, the chains publish directories giving complete and detailed information on all their members so that you can, if you prefer this style of travel, plan your entire trip ahead with much precision, albeit less flexibility. Request a free copy either from your nearest member or by the chain's toll-free (800) line. The insistence on uniform standards of comfort, cleanliness and amenities is more common in motel than in hotel chains. (Easy to understand when you realize that most hotel chains are formed by buying up older, established hotels, while most motel chains have control of their units from start to finish.) This is not meant to denigrate the hotel chains; after all, individuality can be one of the great charms of a hotel. Some travelers prefer independent motels and hotels because they are more likely to reflect the genuine character of the surrounding area. There are several aids to planning available in this sphere. *The Hotel and Motel Redbook,* published annually by the American Hotel and Motel Association, 888 Seventh Avenue, New York City, N.Y. 10019, covers the entire world and sells for around $16.00. *Hotel and Travel Index,* published quarterly by Ziff-Davis, sells for about $20. These are probably best consulted at your travel agent's office. On a more modest scale, the AAA supplies, *to its members only,* regional *Tour Books* that list those establishments recommended by the Association.

HOTEL AND MOTEL CATEGORIES. Hotels and motels in all the Fodor guidebooks to the U.S.A. are divided into five categories, arranged primarily by price, but also taking into consideration the degree of comfort, the amount of service, and the atmosphere which will surround you in the establishment of your choice. Occasionally, an establishment with deluxe prices will only offer *expensive* service or atmosphere, and so we will list it as *expensive*. On the other hand, a hotel which charges only *moderate* prices may offer superior comfort and service, so we will list it as *expensive*. Our ratings are flexible and subject to change. We should also point out that many fine hotels and motels had to be omitted for lack of space.

Although the names of the various hotel and motel categories are standard throughout this series, the prices listed under each category may vary from area to area. This variance is meant to reflect local price standards, and take into account the fact that what might be considered a *moderate* price in a large urban area might be quite expensive in a rural region. In every case, however, the dollar ranges for each category are clearly stated before each listing of establishments.

Since the biggest single expense of your whole trip will be lodging, you may well be discouraged by the prices of many hotel and motel rooms, particularly when you know that you are paying for things that you may neither need nor want, such as a heated swimming pool, two huge double beds for only two people, a cocktail lounge, meeting rooms, and a putting green. Nationwide, motel prices for two people now average around $29–$37 a night; and hotel prices run from $35–$68 with the average around $40–$50. This explains the recent rapid rise of a number of budget chains where rates, nationwide, average $12.50 a night for a single and $15 for a double, an obvious advantage. The budget chains publish their own directories, too, free of charge. So far, most of the budget chains are only regional rather than nationwide; here, therefore, are the ones which operate in the Pennsylvania area: *Red Roof Inns,* 500 South Fourth Street, P.O. Box 283, Columbus, Ohio 43216; *Days Inns of America, Inc.,* 2751 Buford Highway, NE, Atlanta, Georgia 30324; *Econo-Travel Motor Hotel Corp.,* 3 Koger Executive Center, Norfolk, Virginia 23502.

Super deluxe: this category is reserved for only a few hotels. In addition to giving the visitor all the amenities discussed under the deluxe category (below), the super deluxe hotel has a special atmosphere of glamor, good taste, and dignity. Its history will inevitably be full of many historical anecdotes, and it will probably be a favored meeting spot of local society. In short, super deluxe means the tops.

Deluxe: the minimum facilities must include bath and shower in all rooms, valet and laundry service, suites available, a well-appointed restaurant and a bar (where local law permits), room service, TV and telephone in room, air conditioning and heat (unless locale makes one or the other unnecessary), pleasing decor, and an atmosphere of luxury, calm and elegance. There should be ample and personalized service. In a deluxe *motel,* there may be less service rendered by employees and more by machine or automation (such as refrigerators and ice-making machines in your room), but there should be a minimum of do-it-yourself in a truly deluxe establishment.

Expensive: all rooms must have bath or shower, valet and laundry service, restaurant and bar (local law permitting), limited room service, TV and telephone in room, heat and air conditioning (locale not precluding), and pleasing decor. Although the decor may be as good as that in deluxe establishments, hotels and motels in this category are frequently designed for commercial travelers or for families in a hurry and are somewhat impersonal in terms of service.

As for *motels* in this category, valet and laundry service will probably be lacking; the units will be outstanding primarily for their convenient location and functional character, not for their attractive or comfortable qualities.

(Note: We often list top-notch ultra-modern hotels in this category, in spite of the fact that they have rates as high as deluxe hotels and motels. We do this because certain elements are missing in these hotels—usually, the missing element is service. In spite of automated devices such as ice-cube-making machines and message-signalling-buzzers, service in these hotels is not up to the standard by which we judge deluxe establishments. Room service is incredibly slow in some of these places and the entire atmosphere is often one of expediency over comfort, economy of manpower and overhead taking precedence over attention to the desire of guests.)

Moderate: each room should have an attached bath or shower, TV available, telephone in room, heat and air conditioning (locale not precluding), relatively convenient location, clean and comfortable rooms and public rooms. *Motels* in this category may not have attached bath or shower, may not have a restaurant or coffee shop (though one is usually nearby), and of course, may have no public rooms to speak of.

Inexpensive: bath or shower, telephone available, clean rooms are the minimum.

Free parking is assumed at all motels and motor hotels; you must pay for parking at most city hotels, though certain establishments have free parking, frequently for occupants of higher-than-minimum-rate rooms. *Baby sitter* lists are always available in good hotels and motels, and *cribs* for the children are always on hand—sometimes at no cost, but more frequently at a cost of $1 or $2. The cost of a *cot* in your room, to supplement the beds, will be around $3 per night, but moving an *extra single bed* into a room will cost around $7 in better hotels and motels.

Senior Citizens may in some cases receive special discounts on lodgings. The *Days Inn* chain offers various discounts to anyone 55 or older. *Holiday Inns* give a 10% discount year-round to members of the NRTA (write to National Retired Teachers Association, Membership Division, 701 North Montgomery St., Ojai, California 93023) and the AARP (write to American Association of Retired Persons, Membership Division, 215 Long Beach Blvd., Long Beach, California 90802). *Howard Johnson's Motor Lodges* give 10% off to NRTA and AARP members (call 800–654–2000); and the *ITT Sheraton* chain gives 25% off (call 800–325–3535) to members of the AARP, the NRTA, the National Association of Retired Persons, the Catholic Golden Age of United Societies of the U.S.A., and the Old Age Security Pensioners of Canada.

The closest thing America has to Europe's bed-and-breakfast is the private houses that go by the various names of Tourist Home, Guest Home or Guest House. These are often large, still fairly elegant old homes in quiet residential or semi-residential parts of larger towns or along secondary roads and the main streets of small towns and resorts. Styles and standards vary widely, of course, and the main generalizations that one can make are that private baths will be less common and rates will be pleasingly low. In many small towns such Guest Houses are excellent examples of the best a region has to offer of its own special atmosphere. Each one will be different, so that their advantage is precisely the opposite of that "no surprise" uniformity which motel chains pride themselves on. Few, if any, Guest Houses will have heated pools, wall-to-wall carpeting, or exposed styrofoam-wooden beams in the bar. Few if any will have bars. What you do get, in addition to economy, is the personal flavor of a family atmosphere in a private home. In popular tourist areas, state or local tourist information offices or chambers of commerce usually have lists of homes that let out spare rooms to paying guests, and such a listing usually means that the places on it have been inspected and meet some reliable standard of cleanliness, comfort, and reasonable pricing. A nationwide *Guide to Guest Houses and Tourist Homes U.S.A.* is available from Tourist House Associates of America, Inc., P.O. Box 335-A, Greentown, Pennsylvania 18426.

In larger towns and cities a good bet for clean, plain, reliable lodging is a YMCA or YWCA. These buildings are usually centrally located, and their rates tend to run to less than half of those of hotels. Non-members are welcome, but may pay slightly more than members. A few very large Y's may have rooms for couples but usually the sexes are segregated. Decor is spartan and the cafeteria fare plain and wholesome, but a definite advantage is the use of the building's pool, gym, reading room, information services and other facilities. For a directory, write to: *National Council of the YMCA,* 291 Broadway, New York, N.Y. 10007; and the *National Board of the YWCA,* 600 Lexington Avenue, New York, N.Y. 10022. In Pennsylvania, YMCA's and YWCA's offering transient lodgings number 15.

Colleges and universities often open their dormitories and cafeterias to budget travelers during school vacations. There are 14 schools in Pennsylvania in this category. For a directory, see under *What Will It Cost?* **Note:** For a complete list of hotels and motels in Pennsylvania, see the following chapters: *Sports in Pennsylvania, Philadelphia, Bucks County, The Poconos, Lancaster County, Gettysburg, Pittsburgh, Other Pennsylvania Highlights.*

In the listings below, price categories are, for double occupancy, *Super Deluxe* over $45, *Deluxe* $28–45, *Expensive* $22–27, *Moderate* $17–21 and *Inexpensive* under $17. A 6% state tax will be added to your bill.

ALLENTOWN

Sheraton Inn—Allentown. *Expensive.* 400 Hamilton St. High-rise building with family rates. Entertainment and dancing in the lounge, room service.

Holiday Inn. *Moderate.* US 22 at State 309. On spacious grounds, 5 mi. W of town, this typical chain member adds a heated pool to the expected features.

Americus. *Inexpensive.* 6th St. at Hamilton. They have suites available and, they claim, an all-night café. There are also a barber shop and beauty salon in this midtown hotel; free parking, too.

ALTOONA

Sheraton Altoona. *Expensive.* Rt. 220 S. 228 rooms. Restaurant, Coffee shop; nightly entertainment.

The Fountain. *Moderate.* 2906 Pleasant Valley Blvd. The grounds are attractively landscaped—with a fountain—but children stay free only up to the age of 7.

BLOOMSBURG

Quality Inn. *Moderate.* I–80 at State 41. It has 60 nicely furnished rooms.

Magee Hotel. *Inexpensive.* 20 W. Main St. (US 11). A well-maintained downtown establishment with 63 rooms. Under 14 free, crib free, cot $2. Free parking, restaurant and bar.

BREEZEWOOD

Holiday Inn. *Moderate.* US 30 at Turnpike exit 12. Two- and three-story motor inn with 122 rooms. Under 12 free, pool, entertainment in summer, restaurant, cocktails and lounge.

Holiday Inn. *Moderate.* 2915 Pleasant Valley Blvd. Swimming pool, dancing and entertainment and, of course, lounge and restaurant.

Howard Johnson's. *Moderate.* US 30 at I-70. Has 81 rooms, open from May 1 to Oct. 1. Pool, putting green, restaurant, café and bar.

Penn Alto. *Moderate.* 13th Ave. at 12th St. Located in the downtown area, but don't worry, parking is free. Dining room, coffee shop and lounge.

Quality Inn—Breeze Manor. *Moderate.* US 30, E of Turnpike exit 12. Has 50 rooms. Open from Memorial Day to Sept. 15. Lovely grounds, large attractive rooms, heated pool, playground, restaurant a block away.

Town House. *Moderate* 1114 11th St. at Green Ave. Entertainment and dancing in the lounge; restaurant. You can enjoy a sauna bath here.

CARLISLE

Allenberry Inn. *Expensive.* State 174 S of town in Boiling Springs. It has 65 rooms in lodges. Colonial atmosphere from the restored buildings to the 100-year-old gardens and old, majestic trees. Under 12 free, heated pool, playground. Restaurant, bars, entertainment. Summer theater.

Howard Johnson's. *Expensive.* I-81 at US 11. Has 98 rooms, heated pool, recreation room, restaurant.

Quality Inn—Embers. *Moderate.* US 11 5 mi N of town. Has 122 rooms, pool, gift shop, golf privileges, putting green. Restaurant and bar.

Starlite. *Moderate.* 4 mi. N on US 11. Pool, restaurant and bar. Some rooms have refrigerators. Entertainment Fri. and Sat.

CHAMBERSBURG

Holiday Inn. *Moderate.* Junction I-81 and State 316, exit 5. Has 139 rooms, heated pool. Under 12 free. Dining room and coffee shop, cocktails and lounge, dancing and entertainment.

Howard Johnson's. *Moderate.* I-81 at US 30. Has 82 rooms, heated indoor pool, sauna. Rec room has pool table. Under 12 free. Restaurant, cocktails and lounge.

TraveLodge. *Inexpensive.* 565 Lincoln Way E. (US 30). It has 50 rooms, a restaurant and cocktail lounge.

CHAMPION

Seven Springs Mountain Resort. *Super Deluxe.* Ten mi. E of Pennsylvania Turnpike exit 9. Has 107 rooms in a lodge, guest houses, chalets and cottages. Heated indoor and outdoor pool, plus tennis courts, golf course, and Alpine slide.

CLARION

Holiday Inn. *Moderate.* State 68 at I-80, exit 9. Has 158 rooms with some expensive suites. Under 12 free. Restaurant and coffee shop, cocktail lounge, dancing and entertainment. Heated pool, 2 units for handicapped.

CLEARFIELD

Ramada Inn. *Expensive.* RD2 just NE of I–80, exit 19. Has 123 rooms, indoor heated pool, entertainment and dancing nightly, except Sunday.

Holiday Inn. *Moderate.* I–80 exit 19 at State 879. Has 121 rooms with some expensive suites. Heated pool, playground. Dining room, cocktail lounge, entertainment.

DENVER

Holiday Inn. *Expensive.* US 222 at Turnpike exit 21. Has 110 attractively furnished rooms. Pool, restaurant and cocktail lounge.

Colonial Motor Lodge. *Moderate.* On US 222 at Turnpike exit 21. Twenty minutes from Reading by car. Has 106 nicely furnished rooms, pool, spacious grounds.

Howard Johnson's. *Moderate.* US 222 at Turnpike exit 21. Has 50 rooms, with extra charge for waterbeds in two rooms. Swimming pool, restaurant.

DOWNINGTON

Downington Ramada Inn. *Deluxe.* US 30, 1 mi. east of town. 550 rooms, two pools, 18-hole golf course, indoor/outdoor tennis, indoor ice rink. Entertainment, dancing, theater.

Tabas Hotel. *Deluxe.* US 30. New hotel; gourmet dining. Dinner theater. Farmer's market just up the street. Indoor/outdoor pools. Tours of historic sites.

Sheraton Inn-Greensburg. *Deluxe.* US 30 East. 10 mi. N of Pa. Turnpike. 146 rooms, suites, meeting rooms. Restaurant, lounge, indoor pool, saunas, 9-hole golf course, racquet ball. Heliport on premises.

HARRISBURG

Host Inn Harrisburg. *Deluxe.* Rts. 283 and 441. Complete resort and convention center includes: a dinner theater, indoor and outdoor pool, a Roman bath near the outdoor pool, tennis, volleyball, two restaurants, whirlpools in some rooms, pitch-and-putt, and winter ice skating.

Holiday Inn Harrisburg–Mechanicsburg. *Expensive.* 5401 Carlisle Pike (US 11). 211 rooms, some suites. Under 12 free. Heated pool. Restaurant, bar, entertainment and dancing. Six mi. SW of the city.

Holiday Inn Town. *Expensive.* 2nd and Chestnut Sts. Nicely furnished rooms. Dining room, cocktail lounge.

Howard Johnson's. *Expensive.* I–83 at State 322, five mi. E of city. Under 12 free. Pool, playground. Restaurant, cocktail lounge.

Nationwide Inn. *Expensive.* 525 S. Front St. (State 322). 125-room, downtown motor hotel with complete services and family plan. Heated pool. Restaurant, cocktail lounge.

Penn Harris Motor Inn. *Expensive.* North on Taylor St. bypass, US 11 and 15. 200 rooms, some suites. Under 12 free. Pool, sauna. Restaurant, bar, entertainment and dancing.

Sheraton Inn East. *Expensive.* I–83 at Turnpike exit 18A. 200 rooms, 32 with steam baths; some suites. Under 17 free. Heated pool, sauna, putting green, recreation room. Restaurant, bar, entertainment and dancing.

Congress Inn. *Moderate.* At 1350 Eisenhower Blvd. Under 12 free. Has 62 rooms. Pleasant accommodations, pool. Restaurant and bar.

HAZLETON

Holiday Inn. *Moderate.* State 309, 1½ mi. N of town. 108 rooms. Under 12 free. Heated pool, restaurant, bar, dancing Tues., Wed., Fri. and Sat. Coin laundry, 2 wheelchair units.

Mount Laurel. *Inexpensive.* State 309. 18 rooms. Free for children up to only six years old. At-door parking, with restaurant opposite. One mile S of town.

IRWIN

Conley's. *Moderate.* US 30, 1 mi. E of town. 44 rooms including 2 kitchen units available monthly. Heated indoor pool, sauna, whirlpool, rec room, putting green. Restaurant, cocktail lounge.

Quality Inn. *Moderate.* 1½ mi. E. on 30, just east of Pa. Turnpike exit 7. Children under 12 stay for free. There is a heated pool with a lifeguard.

Jacktown. *Inexpensive.* US 30, near Turnpike exit 7. Children under 11 stay free. Restaurant a quarter-mile away, bar.

JOHNSTOWN

Downtowner. *Moderate.* 212 Main St. (State 53, 56). 44 rooms. Free continental breakfast. Restaurant, cocktail lounge, coin laundry nearby.

Holiday Inn. *Moderate.* 1540 Scalp Ave. (State 56 at US 219). 112 rooms. There's shopping center across the road. Heated pool, wading pool, playground. Restaurant, cocktail lounge, entertainment, dancing.

Towne Manor. *Inexpensive.* 155 Johns St. Under 12 free. Continental breakfast on the house. Restaurant nearby.

KING OF PRUSSIA

Stouffer's Valley Forge Inn. *Deluxe.* 480 N. Gulph Rd. (exit 24 from Turnpike). Brand new with 300 rooms on 3 levels. Outdoor pool and sun deck in enclosed garden court, health club and sauna. Gift shop. Handsome Brandywine restaurant, coffee shop and Grog shop for fun and entertainment.

Valley Forge Hilton. *Deluxe.* 251 W. DeKalb Pike (US 202 at Turnpike, exit 24). Family rates available. Heated pool, ice skating in winter. Restaurants and coffee shop, bars, entertainment and dancing except Mon.

Holiday Inn. *Expensive.* 260 Goodard Blvd. (US 202 at Turnpike exit 24). Heated pool, wading pool, saunas. Restaurant, cocktail lounge, dancing and entertainment except Sun.

Howard Johnson's. *Expensive.* N of turnpike exit 24, US 202. Service by the pool, rec room, a restaurant is opposite.

Sheraton-Valley Forge. *Expensive.* State 363N, near Valley Forge Park. Newly opened with 247 rooms. In a plaza that includes shopping mall and twin theaters. Under 18 free. Heated pool, health club, tennis, etc. Sunflower coffee shop. Chumley's restaurant, closed Sun, requires reservations.

George Washington Motor Lodge. *Moderate.* Turnpike exit 24 on US 202. 405 rooms. Indoor heated pool, outdoor pool. Restaurant, coffee shop, cocktail lounge, entertainment.

LEBANON

Lebanon Treadway Inn. *Moderate.* Quentin Rd. at Poplar St. (State 72). 130 rooms. Under 12 free. Pool, wading pool. Restaurant; bar has dancing Sat. Barber and beauty shops.

LEWISTOWN

Holiday Inn. *Moderate.* On US 322 Burnham exit. Enjoy snacks and drinks by the heated pool, playground. Restaurant, bar, dancing, entertainment except Sun.

LIGONIER

Lord Ligonier Inn. *Moderate.* Dining room. Swimming pool.

MEADVILLE

Best Western David Mead Inn. *Moderate.* 455 Chestnut St. Children under 14 stay free. Heated pool with service. Restaurant, bar. Ask about inn's history and community ownership.

Holiday Inn. *Moderate.* 240 Conneaut Lake Rd., US 6, 19, 322. Typical chain operation. Under 12 free. Heated pool. Restaurant, bar, entertainment, dancing.

MORGANTOWN

Morgantown Motor Inn. *Inexpensive.* On State 10 near Turnpike exit 22. 42 rooms, a pool. Restaurant is closed Mon.

NEW STANTON

Inn America. *Expensive.* Half-mile S of Turnpike exit 8, just off I–70 and US 119. Free to children only up to 8 years old. A dining room, cocktail lounge, organist, dancing.

Holiday Inn. *Moderate.* At junction of I–70 and Turnpike exit 8. 160 rooms, under 12 free. Pool, restaurant, cocktail lounge.

READING

Holiday Inn-Downtown. *Expensive.* South 2 and Penn Sts. Good central location. Facilities include indoor heated pool, a kennel, entertainment, and dancing, except Sunday.

Abraham Lincoln Motor Lodge. *Moderate.* Fifth and Washington Sts. There are 300 rooms in this large, conveniently located and family-oriented inn. Dining room and coffee shop, cocktail lounge.

Reading Motor Inn. *Moderate.* Just off US 222 on Warren St. bypass. Free depot bus. Heated pool, playground. Restaurant, bar, dancing, entertainment Tues, through Sat.

ST. DAVID'S

St. David's Inn. *Expensive.* US 30 at Radnor-Chester Rd. Located on extensive grounds. Spacious rooms. Pool. Restaurant and coffee shop, cocktail lounge, entertainment. Golf nearby.

SCRANTON

Howard Johnson's. *Expensive.* US 13 at I–81, near Turnpike exit 37. 120 rooms, 40 of them just added. Heated pool, wading pool. Restaurant and bar with live music for listening and dancing.

Holiday Inn-Downtown. *Moderate.* Mulberry and Franklin Sts. Waterbeds are available. There's a pool, health club, sauna and barber shop. Restaurant, cocktail lounge with dancing Fri. and Sat. evenings.

SHARON

Shenango Inn. *Inexpensive.* 1330 Kimberly Rd. Has 90 rooms where children under 12 stay free. Restaurant and bar.

STATE COLLEGE

Toftrees Country Club. *Deluxe.* A soft country environment surrounds this 124-room complex. 18-hole golf course (greens fee $9), heated pool, tennis, platform tennis, lawn games, entertainment, and some balconies. 1 Country Club Lane, 2 mi. off 322. Book reservations for football weekends well in advance.

WILKES-BARRE

Sheraton Crossgates. *Expensive,* near I-81. Across from city park where performing arts program is delightful. Indoor pool; restaurant, Wanda's on the Park, seats 176 people.

 DINING OUT. With fertile land, plenty of water and a temperate climate, Pennsylvania could hardly fail to be fruitful, nor its culinary traditions delightsome. Specific hotels and restaurants and their specialties are listed under the various cities and regions, but here is a quick overview of some of the pleasures to look for as you travel through this diverse state.

Overwhelming in its number and quality of fine eating establishments is Philadelphia. There has literally been a restaurant renaissance in the last seven years, with over 200 new dining places opening throughout the city. Intimate restaurants as well as gourmet establishments have inspired gastronomic critics to call Philadelphia cooking "the new cuisine." In addition to the new restaurant culture, there has been a rebirth of purely ethnic eateries. Philadelphia, in addition to excellent steak and seafood houses, now offers an international array of cuisines from Morocco, Thailand, Cuba, India, Mexico, Hungary, Vietnam, Greece, Germany and Spain. A colorful and expansive Chinatown as well as heavily Italian South Philadelphia offer endless varieties in both these popular ethnic cuisines. Local dishes, such as scrapple (a kind of ground sausage), ice cream, soft pretzels and a soup called pepper pot are still favorites with visitors, as well as residents of the Brotherly Love city. *Western Pennsylvania* offers eating in the traditions of the various Eastern European ethnic groups that came to work in the steel mills of Pittsburgh. The eastern part of the state is famous as the home of the "Pennsylvania Dutch" (actually *Deutsch,* religious refugees from the Palatinate of Germany in the late 1600s). For this, a good place to start is *Lancaster,* 65 miles west of Philadelphia, where the Central Market is open on Tuesdays and Fridays, and the Southern Market on Saturdays. Nearby *Adams County* (north of Gettysburg) is one of the leading fruit-growing areas in the U. S. (apples, cherries, peaches). Chicken-corn soup is a local specialty, along with smoked hams, dumplings, apple and egg dishes, all kinds of home-made breads, puddings and cakes, the famous shoofly pie, and a wide variety of relishes, pickles, sausages, cheeses, salads and pies.

For evening dining, the best advice is to make reservations whenever possible. Most resort hotels and farm vacation places have set dining hours. For motelstayers, life is simpler if the motel has a restaurant. If it hasn't, try to stay at one that is near a restaurant.

Some restaurants are fussy about customers' dress, particularly in the evening. For women, pants and pants suits are now almost universally acceptable. For men, the tie and jacket remain the standard, but turtleneck sweaters are becoming more and more common. Shorts are almost always frowned on for both men and women. Standards of dress are becoming more relaxed, so a neatly dressed customer will usually experience no problem. If in doubt about accepted dress at a particular establishment, call ahead. Roadside stands, turnpike restaurants and cafeterias have no fixed standards of dress. If you're traveling with children, ask if a restaurant has a children's menu and commensurate prices (many do). When figuring the tip on your check, base it on the total charges for the meal, not on the grand total, if that total includes a sales tax. Don't tip on tax.

The restaurants mentioned in this volume which are located in large metropolitan areas are categorized by type of cuisine: French, Chinese, American, etc., with restaurants of a general nature listed as American-International. Restaurants in less populous areas are divided into price categories as follows: *Super deluxe, deluxe, expensive, moderate,* and *inexpensive.* As a general rule, expect restaurants in metropolitan areas to be higher in price, but many restaurants that feature foreign cuisine are surprisingly inexpensive. We should also point out that limitations of space make it impossible to include every establishment. We have, therefore, listed those which we recommend as the best within each price range.

RESTAURANT CATEGORIES. Although the names of the various restaurant categories are standard throughout this series, the prices listed under each category may vary from area to area. This variation is meant to reflect local price standards, and take into account the fact that what might be considered a *moderate* price in a large urban area might be quite *expensive* in a rural region. In every case, however, the dollar ranges for each category are clearly stated before each listing of establishments.

Super deluxe: this category will probably be pertinent to only one or two metropolitan areas. This indicates an outstanding restaurant which is lavishly decorated, some which may delight in the fear it inspires among the humble. It will charge the customer at least $12 for soup, entree, and dessert. The average price for the same is apt to be closer to $16, although some will run much higher than this. As in all our other categories, this price range does not include cocktails, wines, cover or table charges, tip, or extravagant house specialties. The price range here indicates a typical roast beef (prime ribs) dinner. The restaurant in this category must have a superb wine list, excellent service, immaculate kitchens, and a large, well-trained staff. Regrettably, these establishments are occasionally over-priced and over-rated.

Deluxe: many a fine restaurant around the country falls into this category. It will have its own well-deserved reputation for excellence, perhaps a house specialty or two for which it is famous, and an atmosphere of elegance of unique decor. It will have a good wine list where the law permits, and will be considered one of the best in town by the inhabitants. It will have a clean kitchen and attentive staff.

Expensive: in addition to the expected dishes, it will offer one or two house specialties, wine list, and cocktails (where law permits), air conditioning (unless locale makes it unnecessary), a general reputation for very good food and adequate staff, an elegant decor and appropriately dressed clientele.

Moderate: cocktails and/or beer where the law permits, air conditioning (when needed), clean kitchen, adequate staff, better-than-average service. General reputation for good, wholesome food.

Inexpensive: the bargain place in town, it is clean, even if plain. It will have air conditioning (when necessary), tables (not a counter), clean kitchen and attempt to provide adequate service.

Chains. There are now several chains of restaurants that offer reliable eating at good budget prices. Look for them as you travel, and check local telephone directories in cities where you stop. Some of the ones which operate in the region are: *Arthur Treacher's Fish and Chips* (low prices, limited menu, Tuesday night special). *Holiday Inns* (some offer all-you-can-eat buffets, check locally). *Red Barn Restaurants* (all-you-can-eat salad bars). Also *McDonald's* and *Gino's.*

For restaurants in other areas, see chapters on Philadelphia, Bucks County, The Poconos, Lancaster County, Gettysburg, Pittsburgh, and other Pennsylvania highlights. In the listings below, categories apply to mid-priced dinners on each menu. *Deluxe* $12–20, *Expensive* $9–12, *Moderate* $5–9, and *Inexpensive* under $5.

ALLENTOWN

Schoenersville Inn. *Expensive.* Airport and Schoenersville Rds. Located ½ mile north of the Allentown-Bethlehem-Easton Airport, this restaurant combines the charm of an old inn with early aircraft memorabilia. Specialties include broiled shrimp and scallops, surf and turf, and prime ribs.

Charles Inn. *Moderate.* 19th St. at Hamilton. Continental-American cuisine and home-baked pastries. Lunch and dinner. Children's prices lower. Located in shopping center.

Walps. *Inexpensive.* 911 Union Blvd. Family-style, with several pleasant dining rooms. Pennsylvania Dutch menu includes home-baked bread. Special children's platters. Open 7 A.M. to 11 P.M. Closed July 4, Dec. 25.

ALTOONA

Erculiani's. *Deluxe.* State 53, 4 mi. N of the city. Famed country-style family restaurant featuring Italian and American dishes. Fantastic antipasto served in many varieties. Good wine list. Specialties: lobster, veal parmigiana. Open 4 to 9 P.M., Sun., noon to 7 P.M. Closed Mon., also December-February.

BEAVER

Wooden Angel. *Expensive.* W. Bridgewater St. A modern restaurant with a fine wine cellar serving, among other things, prime ribs, lobster in sauce and homemade paté.

BIRD IN HAND

Plain and Fancy Restaurant. *Inexpensive.* State 340, E of the village. Pennsylvania Dutch foods served family style, no menu necessary. Children's prices. Own bakery, food shop. Carriage rides and tours available. Hours, 11:30 A.M. to 8 P.M. Closed Sun. and Christmas.

BLUE BELL

Blue Bell Inn. *Expensive.* State 73. This old historic inn, established in 1743, is a pleasant spot for good food and drinks. Children's menu. Open noon to 3 P.M. and 5 to 10 P.M., Saturday to 10:30. Closed Sun., Mon. and Christmas.

BUTLER

Morgan's Garden Gate Restaurant. *Inexpensive.* US 422, 8 mi. W of town. Popular family-style dining. Noted for evening buffets (Sun. from noon.) Children's portions. Open 7 A.M. to 8 P.M. Closed Dec. 25–26.

DENVER

Zinn's Diner. *Moderate.* Rt. 222, ¼ mile N of Turnpike exit 21. Open 24 hours. Pennsylvania Dutch menu includes specialties such as chicken and waffle, wiener schnitzel, pork and sauerkraut. They make their own pastries.

DONORA

Redwood. *Deluxe.* 87 Castner Ave. The owner, who is in personal charge, grows all his own herbs and vegetables, and also makes his own wine. The steaks and lobsters are the best on a very good menu. Reservations are a must.

DOYLESTOWN

Conti's Cross Keys Inn. *Expensive.* State 611 at State 313. Jackets required for men. This restaurant offers a bountiful combination of Italian dishes and good fellowship. Bar to midnight. Children's platters half price. Open 11:30 A.M. to 11 P.M. Closed Sun., major holidays and second week in August.

GREENSBURG

Mountain View Inn. *Moderate.* US 30, 4 mi. E of town. Perched high on Huckleberry Hill, this dining spot is open 7:30 A.M. to 10 P.M., Sun. 8:30 A.M. to 8 P.M. Cocktails.

HARRISBURG

Inn 22. *Expensive.* 5 mi. E of US 22, Steak, prime ribs, baked stuffed shrimp served in pleasant Early American establishment, with fireplaces and background music. Open to 10 P.M., Sat. to 11. Closed Sun.

Lombardo's at Locust Court. *Expensive.* 212 Locust St. Haute cuisine. Fresh lobsters served daily. Across the street from the capital, and a favorite for the politicians. Reservations suggested. Valet parking.

La Truffe D'Argent. *Expensive.* 3901 N. Front St. Housed in old Georgian mansion. Fine French cuisine in elegant atmosphere.

Aujour Le Jour. *Moderate.* 540 Race Street. Continental cuisine. Intimate, rustic setting.

Castiglia's. *Inexpensive.* 706 N. 3rd St. This restaurant features an assortment of pasta with Italian embellishments. Also American dishes. Children's platters. Bar and background music. Open to midnight, 10 P.M. Sun.

IRWIN

Ben Gross. *Expensive.* 822 Lincoln Highway W. Fine dining in a restaurant noted for over 35 years for gourmet specialties. Japanese dinners are served in the Sukoshi Room. Children's plates $1 less. Entertainment Wed. through Sat. Closed Sun. and holidays. Reservations advisable.

KIMBERTON

Kimberton Country House. *Moderate.* Six miles W of Valley Forge. Early American building now tastefully converted into a restaurant for sophisticated tastes. Open for dinner only. On weekends, it's a good idea to reserve a table.

KING OF PRUSSIA

The Sting. *Expensive.* Rt. 363. Specialties include Coquille St. Jacques and Steak Marianna.

KUTZTOWN

Glockenspiel. *Moderate.* US 222, 2 mi. W of town. An inviting Pennsylvania Dutch establishment blending local and British decor. Waitresses garbed in Colonial costume. Lunch, dinner to 8 P.M., Sat. to 9. Bring your own wine. Reservations advised weekends. Closed Jan. 1–15.

The Willows. *Inexpensive.* 2425 Lincoln Highway E. (US 30). Pennsylvania Dutch cooking, good for families. They bake their own pastries and serve children's specials. Open 7:30 A.M. to 7:45 P.M. Closed Dec 25–27.

LEBANON

The Fernwick Tavern and Restaurant. *Moderate.* 2200 W. Cumberland St. Special features include fresh broiled flounder, fresh broiled haddock, crab imperial, steaks, and a variety of seafood. Daily after 5 P.M.

LIGONIER

M's. *Expensive.* 201 East Main St. This new, tastefully elegant restaurant features French cuisine. Piano-bar-lounge upstairs. Open for dinner 5:00 to 10:00 P.M.

MEADVILLE

Cottage Restaurant. *Inexpensive.* 1039 Park Ave., half a mile W of town (US 6). Leisurely dining in agreeable surroundings. Open for lunch; dinner to 8 P.M. The management and staff are very friendly. Closed Sun.

MEDIA

Towne House. *Expensive.* 117 South Ave., at Baltimore Pike. This establishment attracts a large local following with its Italian fare, seafood and prime ribs. Children's plates. Piano bar. Open until midnight, Fri. and Sat. to 1 A.M. Closed Sun. and July 1–15.

Newtown Squire. *Moderate.* State 252, 5 mi. N of town. Another one the local folks go for. Prime ribs, lobster (from the tank), steak. Own baking. Piano bar. Open 11:30 A.M. to 2 P.M., 5 to 10 P.M. Closed Sun. and holidays.

NEW WILMINGTON

The Tavern. *Moderate.* 108 N. Market St. Agreeable spot where fine food is nicely served. Children's plates. Specialties include creamed chicken, stuffed pork chops. Closed Tues. and Christmas.

PENNSYLVANIA

NORRISTOWN

Tiffany Saloon. *Moderate.* US 202 at Center Square. An 1890s restaurant with Victorian furnishings. Good food, Tiffany lampshades, lounges with soft velvet love seats. Try their Steak Teriaki. There's a help-yourself salad bar.

PHOENIXVILLE

Columbia Hotel. *Moderate.* 148 Bridge St. Specialties every nite. Varied menu in pleasant surroundings. Closed Sundays in summer. Hours are 4:30–10:00. Children's menu. Reservations are suggested.

POTTERS MILL

The Eutaw House. *Expensive.* 12 mi. E. of Rt. 80 at Bellefonte exit. 13 mi. E. of State College on 322. Antique atmosphere, built in 1823. Old country house remodeled into a charming, country restaurant. Varied menu.

POTTSTOWN

Coventry Forge Inn. *Deluxe.* State 23, 6 mi. SW of town. Famed for its French cooking. Original Queen Anne pine paneling and old fireplaces, antiques on display. Menu offers such favorites as quiche Lorraine, steak au poivre, duck à l'orange. Open for dinner only. Bar, wine cellar. Reservations are strongly recommended. Closed Sun., holidays, week before Labor Day, Dec. 15–Jan. 15 and Mon. from late Oct.-late Apr.

READING

Joe's. *Expensive.* 450 S. 7th St. Not to be missed. Mushrooms are what this place is all about, and they are treated with tender, loving care. Try the Wild Mushroom Soup and the Filet Mignon Entrecôte with Duxelles of Wild Mushroom. A good wine list. Closed Mon., Tues. and September. Reservations a must.

Stokesay Castle. *Moderate.* Hill Rd. and Spook Lane. A copy of a Shropshire castle nestled in the foothills of the Blue Mountains. Dine on Canvas-covered patio or indoors. French, American cuisine, buffet in summer. Service charge 15 percent. Wine list. Children's menus half price.

Ye Olde Ironmaster. *Moderate.* 1319 Lancaster Ave. (US 222). Wine and dine in friendly surroundings. Specialties: steak, seafood. Children's menu. Closed Christmas, Aug. 1–10. You should make reservations during weekends.

SCRANTON

Preno's. *Moderate.* 602 Lackawanna Ave. Pleasant place with a Continental-American cuisine. Specialties: tournedos of beef chasseur, filet of sole meunière. Children's dinners are half price. Closed holidays.

Castle. *Inexpensive.* 1826 N. Main St. Well-known spot with American menu, their own baking and a wine list. Children's menu. Open until midnight, closed Christmas, July 9–14.

SHARTLESVILLE

Haag's Hotel. *Inexpensive.* US 22 downtown. Pennsylvania Dutch delights served in an authentic atmosphere. Family-style lunch and dinner, using locally grown products and their own baked goods. Open 11 A.M. to 7 P.M., closed Christmas.

SOMERSET

Oakhurst Tea Room. *Moderate.* State 31, 6 mi. W of downtown. Regional specialties served in pleasant surroundings. Open noon to 11 P.M. Near Seven Springs resort.

STATE COLLEGE

L' Chaumier. *Expensive.* On College Avenue. French dining in a country atmosphere. French onion soup is their specialty. Good wine list. Outside patio in spring and summer.

Nittany Lion. *Moderate.* 1274 N. Atherton St. Spacious dining room in a handsome old inn. Specialties: Lobster Newburg, duck, ribs of beef. Children's portions. Closed Mon.

Tavern. *Moderate.* 220 E. College Ave. A friendly place with Colonial decor and a collection of Pennsylvania prints on the walls. International cuisine, but you can also get pizza. Bar open until midnight, closed Sun., holidays.

VALLEY FORGE

Bull Tavern. *Expensive.* 1221 Valley Forge Rd. The specialty is beef. Family dining in a pleasant atmosphere. Children eat for half-price. Piano bar Tues. to Sat., dancing Fri. and Sat. Closed Christmas, New Year's.

WASHINGTON

Century Inn. *Moderate.* US 40, 12 mi. E. in Scenery Hill. Historic establishment dating back to 1794. There's Colonial decor and a mountain view. Cocktail lounge, fireplaces. Children's platters. Closed July 4, Dec. 20-mid-April.

WILKES-BARRE

Aldino's Manor. *Moderate.* East End Blvd. Italian-American menu in a pleasant atmosphere. Specialties include sliced beef tenderloin a la pizzaiola, boneless chicken breast a la marsala, and rum cake.

WILLIAMSPORT

Double U Steak House. *Inexpensive.* 912 Arch St. (US 220). Charcoal-broiled steaks are featured here. Cocktails. Open 5 to 10 P.M.

Obstfeld's. *Inexpensive.* 452 Market St. This simple, unpretentious Jewish bakery and delicatessen serves simple but good food. The cheesecake is a triumph.

YORK

Lincoln Woods Inn. *Expensive.* 2510 E. Market St. (State 462). The theme is Merrie England. The specialties are steak and seafood. There's a cocktail lounge, entertainment and dancing. Children at reduced prices. Closed Sun. and Christmas.

Seven Cousins. *Expensive.* 2400 E. Market St. (State 462). Very pleasant establishment with Italian and American menus, featuring Maine lobster on weekends and prime ribs. There's a bar and background music. Closed major holidays.

BUSINESS HOURS AND LOCAL TIME. As a result of recent Federal legislation, Pennsylvania is on Eastern Daylight Time.

Most businesses keep about the same hours as do those in your own community. In areas which cater to tourists, however, you will find some stores stay open later than the usual five, five-thirty or six o'clock closing.

Hours during which you may purchase liquor (as well as who may purchase it and where) vary greatly in this region. Check locally.

ROUGHING IT. More, and improved, camping facilities are springing up each year across the country, in national parks, national forests, state parks, in private camping areas, and trailer parks, which by now have become national institutions.

Farm vacations continue to gain adherents, especially among families with children. Some are quite deluxe, some extremely simple. Here and there a farm has a swimming pool, while others have facilities for trailers and camping. For a directory of farms which take vacations (including details of rates, accommodations, dates, etc.) write to *Adventure Guides, Inc.,* 36 East 57 Street, New York, N.Y. 10022 for their 224-page book *Country Vacations U.S.A.* Their other directory, *Adventure Travel U.S.A.,* gives details on guided wilderness trips, backpacking, canoeing, rock climbing, covered wagon treks, scuba diving and more.

Because of the great size of the United States and the distances involved, Youth Hostels have not developed in this country the way they have in Europe and Japan. In the entire 3½ million square miles of the U.S. there are upwards of 200 Youth Hostels, and because they are, in any case, designed primarily for people who are traveling under their own power, usually hiking or bicycling, rather than by car or commercial transportation, they tend to be away from towns and cities and in rural areas, near scenic spots. Although their membership is mainly younger people, there is no age limit. In the U.S. they are most frequent and practical in compact areas like New England. You must be a member to use Youth Hostels, write to *American Youth Hostel Association, Inc.,* National Campus, Delaplane, Virginia 22025. A copy of the Hostel Guide and Handbook will be included in your membership. Accommodations are simple, dormitories are segregated for men and women, common rooms and kitchen are shared, and everyone helps with the cleanup. Lights out 11 P.M. to 7 A.M., no alcohol or drugs allowed. Membership fees: under 18–$5; 18 and over—$11; family—$12. Hostel rates vary; $1.75 to $2.50 per person per night is average. In season it is wise to reserve ahead; write or phone directly to the particular hostel you plan to stay in. In the Mid-Atlantic region Youth Hostels number 2 in New Jersey, 12 in Pennsylvania, 3 in Maryland and 1 each in Washington and West Virginia.

Useful addresses: *National Parks Service,* U.S. Dept. of the Interior, Washington, D.C. 20025; *National Forest Service,* U.S. Dept. of Agriculture, Washington, D.C. 20025. For information on state parks, see the addresses given in the *Practical Information* sections for the individual states you are interested in.

The National Campers & Hikers Assoc., Box 451, Orange, New Jersey 07051. Commercial camping organizations include: *American Camping Assoc., Inc.* Bradford Woods, Martinsville, Indiana 46151, and *Camping Council,* 17 East

48 Street, New York, N.Y., 10017. Also *Kampgrounds of America, Inc.,* P.O. Box 30558, Billings, Montana 59114. Headquarters of the *Appalachian Mountain Club* is 5 Joy Street, Boston, Massachusetts 02108.

Canoe trips are extremely popular in some areas, while, here and there, travelers are making long vacation trips aboard their own power cruisers and sailboats. The coast of the Mid-Atlantic region is deeply indented and contains much excellent boating territory in addition to an important segment of the Inland Waterway, the sheltered boating route that runs from New York to Miami.

 TIPPING. Tipping is supposed to be a personal thing, your way of expressing your appreciation of someone who has taken pleasure and pride in giving you attentive, efficient, and personal service. Because standards of personal service in the United States are highly uneven, you should, when you get genuinely good service, feel secure in rewarding it, and when you feel that the service you got was slovenly, indifferent or surly, don't hesitate to show this by the size, or non-size, of your tip. Remember that in many places the help are paid very little and depend on tips for the better part of their income. This is *supposed* to give them incentive to serve you well.

These days, the going rate for tipping on *restaurant* service is 15% on the amount *before* taxes. Tipping at counters is not universal, but many people leave $0.25 on anything up to $1, and 10% on anything over that. For *bellboys,* 25¢ per bag is usual. However, if you load him down with all manner of bags, hatboxes, cameras, coats, etc., you might consider giving an extra quarter or two. For one-night stays in most *hotels* and *motels* you leave nothing. If you stay longer, at the end of your stay leave the maid $1–$1.25 per day, or $5 per person per week for multiple occupancy. If you are staying at an *American Plan* hostelry (meals included), $1.50 per day per person for the waiter or waitress is considered sufficient and is left at the end of your stay. If you have been surrounded by an army of servants (one bringing relishes, another rolls, etc.) add an extra few dollars and give the lump sum to the captain or *maitre d'hotel* when you leave, asking him to allocate it.

For the many other services that you may encounter in a big hotel or resort, figure roughly as follows: doorman—25¢ for taxi handling, 50¢ for help with baggage; bellhop—25¢ per bag, more if you load him down with extras; parking attendant—50¢; bartender—15%; room service—10–15% of that bill; laundry or valet service—15%; pool attendant—50¢ per day; snackbar waiter at pool, beach or golf club—50¢ per person for food and 15% of the beverage check; locker attendant—50¢ per person per day, or $2.50 per week; masseurs and masseuses—15%–20%; golf caddies $1–$2 per bag, or 15% of the greens fee for an 18-hole course, or $3 on a free course; barbers—50¢; shoeshine attendants —25¢; hairdressers—$1; manicurists—50¢.

Transportation: Give 25¢ for any taxi fare under $1 and 15% for any above. Limousine service—20%. Car rental agencies—nothing. Bus porters are tipped 25¢ per bag, drivers nothing. On charters and package tours, conductors and drivers usually get $5–$10 per day from the group as a whole, but be sure to ask whether this has already been figured into the package cost. On short local sightseeing runs, the driver-guide may get 25¢ per person, more if you think he has been especially helpful or personable. Airport bus drivers—nothing. Redcaps, in resort areas—35¢ per suitcase, elsewhere, 25¢. Tipping at curbside checkin is unofficial, but same as above. On the plane, no tipping.

Railroads suggest you leave 10–15% per meal for dining car waiters, but the steward who seats you is not tipped. Sleeping-car porters get about $1 per person per night. The 25¢ or 35¢ you pay a railway station baggage porter is not a tip but the set fee that he must hand in at the end of the day along with the ticket stubs he has used. Therefore his tip is anything you give him above that, 25–50¢ per bag, depending on how heavy your luggage has been.

 HINTS TO HANDICAPPED TRAVELERS. One of the newest, and largest, groups to enter the travel scene is the handicapped, literally millions of people who are in fact physically able to travel and who do so enthusiastically when they know that they can move about in safety and comfort. Generally their tours parallel those of the non-handicapped traveler, but at a more leisurely pace, and with all the logistics carefully checked out in advance. Three important sources of information in this field are: 1) the book, *Access to the World: A Travel Guide for the Handicapped,* by Louise Weiss, published by Chatham Square Press, Inc., 401 Broadway, New York, N.Y. 10013. This book covers travel by air, ship, train, bus, car and recreational vehicle; hotels and motels; travel agents and tour operators; destinations; access guides; health and medical problems; and travel organizations. 2) The *Travel Information Center,* Moss Rehabilitation Hospital, 12th Street and Tabor Road, Philadelphia, Penn. 19141. 3) *Easter Seal Society for Crippled Children and Adults,* Director of Education and Information Service, 2023 West Ogden Avenue, Chicago, Illinois 60612. *The President's Committee on Employment of the Handicapped,* Washington, D.C. 20210, has issued a list of guidebooks for handicapped travelers that tells where to write for information on nearly 100 U.S. cities. The Committee also has a guide to Highway Rest Area Facilities that have been designed to be accessible to the handicapped. And for a list of tour operators who arrange travel for the handicapped, write to: *Society for the Advancement of Travel for the Handicapped,* 26 Court St., Brooklyn, N.Y. 11242.

Two publications which give valuable information about motels, hotels, and restaurants (rating them, telling about steps, table heights, door widths, etc.) are *Where Turning Wheels Stop,* published by Paralyzed Veterans of America, 3616 16th St., N.W., Washington, D.C., 20010 and *The Wheelchair Traveler,* by Douglass R. Annand, Ball Hill Road, Milford, N.H. 03055. A new guide for the handicapped, *Washington: The City for Everybody,* can be obtained by writing Handicap, Washington Area Convention and Visitors Bureau, 1129 20th St., N.W., Washington, D.C. 20036. Many of the nation's national parks have special facilities for the handicapped. These are described in *National Park Guide for the Handicapped,* available from the U.S. Government Printing Office, Washington, D.C. 20402. *TWA* publishes a free 12-page pamphlet entitled *Consumer Information About Air Travel for the Handicapped* to explain all the various arrangements that can be made, and how to get them. For rail travel, see *Access Amtrak,* a 16-page booklet published by the National Railway Passenger Corporation.

SPORTS IN PENNSYLVANIA

A State for All Seasons

Pennsylvania ranks number one in the nation in hunting and number four among the states in fishing. In terms of the volume of visitors to state parks each year, Pennsylvania is ranked number 5.

With its four distinct seasons, its rolling hills, inland waters, mountains, valleys, forests and sandy beaches, no part of the state is far removed from a wide range of sports facilities. Almost every sport is available in one location or another.

Although Pennsylvania is not a coastal state, sandy beaches can be found along the shores of Lake Erie and in many of the state parks. For the water enthusiast, lakes and rivers throughout Pennsylvania are perfect for swimming, sailing, boating, canoeing, water skiing and white water sports. The Olympic white water canoe team trains on the Loyalsock Creek in north central Pennsylvania. Other water sports available include diving, snorkeling and scuba diving. Public and private pools are found everywhere.

The hiking and backpacking enthusiast will appreciate the Applachian Trail, a footpath that extends from Maine to Florida. It enters Pennsylvania, near Stroudsburg, and runs in a southwesterly direction to Maryland. It is joined above Harrisburg by the Horseshoe Trail, which continues East to Valley Forge. The entire state is a hiker's paradise because the fields, hills, forests and mountains are criss-crossed by hundreds of miles of scenic trails.

Horseback riding and bicycling are particularly enjoyable in beautiful Pennsylvania. Nature enthusiasts and photographers will find an abundance of wild flowers in the spring and some of the world's most spectacular foliage in the autumn.

Hunting and fishing are excellent throughout the state. The woods and forests abound in deer, bear, small game, and game birds. Lakes and streams provide a wide variety of freshwater fish.

Tennis players will find courts at most resorts, and a large number of private clubs welcome visitors. Public courts can be found in many parks, and most schools have tennis and paddle tennis courts that often can be used by the public.

Many excellent golf courses are located throughout Pennsylvania; some of them can be enjoyed all year. Several of the more well-known courses are Hershey, Oakmont, Mt. Airy Lodge, Buck Hill, Shawnee-on-the-Delaware, Merion, Saucon Valley, Lancaster, Laurel Valley, Sky Top and Moselem Springs. In addition, many of the resorts have their own golf courses for guests. Public courses can be found in most areas. Private clubs often require that guests be acquainted with a club member; some will extend guest privileges to golfers who are members of clubs in other locations. It is advisable to bring a letter of recommendation from your golf pro.

During the winter months, some golf courses offer snow-mobiling to the public. Other winter sports found in Pennsylvania are sledding, ice skating—both indoor and outdoor, tobogganing, sleigh-riding and ice fishing. Some of the Pocono lakes, most notably Lake Wallenpaupack, provide ice boating and even sports-car racing on ice. Of course, downhill skiing is still Pennsylvania's leading winter sport, but cross country skiing, which has gained in popularity in recent years, is offered at most ski areas and in the state parks and forests.

Sports buffs will find accommodations in the area where they are participating in their favorite sport, or close by. In addition, several campgrounds are now open all year.

Skiing

Downhill skiing enthusiasts will find the largest concentration of ski areas in the Pocono Mountains in the northeast and the Allegheny Mountains in the southwest. However, no part of the state lacks facilities for this popular winter sport.

More than half of the downhill ski areas also offer cross country skiing. For enthusiasts of this sport there are picturesque trails leading through forests, past waterfalls, laurel thickets, lakes, creeks and streams. In addition, the state parks and forests have exceptional trails with breathtaking scenery.

Most of the ski areas are located near resorts that offer attractions to keep non-skiing members of the family happily occupied with **snow-mobiling, ice skating, sledding, tobogganing, ice fishing, indoor tennis** and **swimming** and more. A popular vacation time is the last week in February and first week in March, when the *Pocono Winter Carnival* is held. Besides the usual winter sports, there are races, contests, parties and free skiing and skating clinics. Because this is such a well attended event, reservations should be made well in advance.

Downhill Skiing—Pocono Area. *Big Boulder,* Lake Harmony, 5 miles from Blakeslee (Exit 43, I–80 via 115 and 903). *Buck Hill,* Buck Hill Falls (6 miles from Mt. Pocono, 16 miles from Stroudsburg off exit 52 of I–80). *Camelback,* NW of Stroudsburg (off I–80 exit 45). *Elk Mountain,* Union Dale (9 miles east of I–81). *Fernwood,* Bushkill (Route 209, 8 miles north of I–80, exit 52). *Hanley's Happy Hill,* Laporte Ave., Eagles Mere (Rt. 42 northeast of Williamsport). *Jack Frost,* White Haven (3 miles west of Blakeslee off Rt. 940). *Lodge at Split Rock,* Lake Harmony (Exit 42, off I–80 on Rt. 940). *Masthope Mountain,* Lackawaxen (near Hawley). *Mt. Airy Lodge,* Mt. Pocono (off Rt. 611, 3 miles south of Mt. Pocono). *Mount Tone,* Lake Como (2 miles from Rt. 247). *North Mountain* (2 miles north of Muncy Valley on Rt. 220). *Oregon Hill,* Morris (off Rt. 287, 45 minutes NW of Williamsport). *Pocono Manor* (15 miles NW of Stroudsburg off Rt. 611). *Saw Creek,* Bushkill (off Rt. 209). *Shawnee Mountain,* Shawnee-on-Delaware (near Stroudsburg). *Tamiment,* Tamiment (off U.S. 209).

Allegheny Mountain Area—*Blue Knob,* Claysburg (21 miles north of Pa. Turnpike; Exit 11 at Bedford, Rt. 220 to 869, left at Osterburg). *Boyce Park* (675 Old Frankstown Rd., Pittsburg). *Buckaloons* (Youngville, Rt. 6 along Brokenstraw Creek, 7 miles west of Warren). *Denton Hill* (U.S. Rt. 6 east of Coudersport). *Hidden Valley* (Rt. 31, 12 miles west of Somerset). *Mount Pleasant,* Cambridge Springs (7 miles southeast of Edinboro on Washington Valley Road). *Seven Springs,* Champion (12 miles off Pa. Turnpike, exit 9). *Laurel Mountain* (8 miles east of Ligonier Rt. 30).

Other Ski Areas—*Chadds Peak,* Chadds Ford (U.S. Rt. 1, 4 miles west of Rt. 202). *Doe Mountain,* Macungie (15 miles southwest of Allentown off Rt. 29 and 100). *Hahn Mountain,* Kempton (Rt. 22 at Lenhartsville). *Little Gap* (5 miles east of Palmerton, 30 minutes north of Allentown). *Mount Heidelberg* (half mile south of Bernville on Rt. 183). *Spring Mountain* (30 miles north of Philadelphia, off Rt. 29 and 73). *Ski Liberty* (Rt. 116, 8 miles southwest of Gettysburg).

For additional information contact: Commonwealth of Pennsylvania, Department of Commerce, Bureau of Travel Development, Harrisburg, Pa. 17120. Request charts of ski areas. In addition, most of the ski areas mentioned will send, upon request, a complete listing of nearby accommodations.

Cross Country Skiing

Cross Country Ski Areas—Poconos. *Fernwood,* Bushkill (Rt. 209, 8 miles north of I–80). *Hanley's Happy Hill* (Rt. 42 northeast of Williamsport at Eagles Mere). *Inn at Starlight Lake* (1 mile off Rt. 370, in Wayne County, 5 miles south of Hancock, N.Y.). *Masthope Mountain,* Lackawaxen (near Hawley). *Crystal Lake Camps* (7 miles off Rt. 220 at Tivoli). *Mt. Airy Lodge,* Mt. Pocono (off Rt. 611, 3 miles south of

Mt. Pocono). *Oregon Hill* (off Rt. 287, 45 minutes northwest of Williamsport). *Panorama,* Forest City (8 miles off I–81, exit 63 on Rt. 247). *Pocono Manor* (15 miles northwest of Stroudsburg off Rt. 611). *Tamiment,* Tamiment (off U.S. 209). *Tanglewood,* Tafton (Rt. 390 at Lake Wallenpaupack).

Cross Country Ski Areas—Allegheny Mountains. *Denton Hill* (U.S. Rt. 6, east of Coudersport). *Hidden Valley* (12 miles west of Somerset on Rt. 31). *Seven Springs,* Champion (12 miles off Pa. Turnpike at exit 9). *Laurel Mountain* (8 miles east of Ligonier Rt. 30).

Cross country skiing is also available in 55 Pennsylvania state parks and forests. The trails range in length from three quarters of a mile to twenty miles. The following list identifies trails over ten miles long: *Ohiopyle,* 20 miles of scenic trails along and within the Youghiogheny River Gorge; *Black Moshannon,* Philipsburg, 12 miles of trails encircle Black Moshanon Lake; *Blue Knob,* Imler, 17 miles long, utilizing several old logging trails; *Caledonis,* Fayetteville, 10 miles of trails in beautiful wooded area; *Shawnee,* Schellsburg, 12 miles of trails in varied terrain; *Ridley Creek,* Media, 12 miles of trails in one of the few areas in Delaware County where cross country skiing is permitted; *Elk State Forest,* Emporium, 25 miles of trails in the Quehanna Wild Area—for well-equipped, experienced skiiers only; *Tiadaghton State Forest,* S. Williamsport, 15 miles of trails that follow abandoned logging railroad grades; *Forbes State Forest,* Ligonier, 14 miles of well-marked trails on Laurel Ridge.

For further information, contact the Bureau of Travel Development.

Snowmobiling

This thrilling, fast-moving sport has captured the fancy of many people who used to think winter was a time to sit by the fireplace. Many resorts offer snowmobiling as an additional enticement for their guests.

The ski resorts that offer snowmobiling are: *Buck Hill, Denton Hill, Fernwood, Hickory Ridge, Lodge* at Split Rock, *Mt. Airy Lodge, Oregon Hill, Pocono Manor, Tamiment* and *Vacation Village.* In addition, the *Pocono Snowmobile Center* in Mt. Pocono allows the public to use their 35-acre golf course for snowmobiling. *Robinwood Country Resort* in Saylorsburg has a 40-acre course for snowmobiling. *Pocono Hershey,* in Whitehaven, opens their golf course. *Otter Lake Camp Resort* in Marshalls Creek offers 160 acres of land surrounded by state forests. *White Beauty View Resort* in Greentown has snowmobiling along the 52-mile shoreline of Lake Wallenpaupack. *Alvins Log Cabins* in Henryville has trails through woodlands and fields.

Hunting

The woods and forests in Pennsylvania abound in deer, bears, small game and game birds. Hunting is strictly regulated as to hours and bag limits. Besides the thousands of acres open to public hunting in the state, many private land owners open their property to licensed hunters. Always ask for permission to hunt or trap on private property.

Due to the geology of the state, certain animals are found in more abundance in different areas. For convenience, it is best to divide the state into six sections, with a description of which species is in more abundance in each.

Northwest—The best waterfowl hunting in Pennsylvania is found in this area. It is also good for hunting deer, bears, grouse and woodcocks and for fur trapping.

Southwest—This area is best for hunting rabbits, squirrels and deer. Game birds, such as grouse and pheasants will also be found here.

North central—Best for hunting bears. This is also the leading turkey-hunting area. Hunters will also find an abundance of deer, grey squirrels and rabbits.

South central—This area leads the state in quail hunting and is also good for bears.

Northeast—A vast variety of wild animals will be found here. It is the leading area in the state for the snowshoe hare and woodcock.

Southeast—This corner of the state offers more small game hunting than any other division of Pennsylvania. The state's best pheasant hunting is found in this region in which many deer abound. Farm game and dove hunting is also good.

License information can be obtained from the Pennsylvania Game Commission, License Section, P.O. Box 1567, Harrisburg, Pa. 17120. A non-resident license costs $50.50. The Game Commission has several publications of interest to the hunter. A digest of hunting and trapping regulations will be sent upon request. This useful booklet has information on licenses, hunting and trapping regulations, seasons, hours and bag limits. The Game Commission also has detailed pamphlets on each of the six areas previously mentioned.

State Park hunting maps can be obtained from the Department of Environmental Resources, Office of Public Information, P.O. Box 2063, Harrisburg, Pa. 17120.

Fishing and Boating

It is almost impossible to find a five-square-mile area lacking facilities for fishing in Pennsylvania. The state has 5000 miles of stocked trout streams, 90 lakes stocked with trout and 30,000 miles of rivers and streams inhabited by muskellunge, small mouth bass, walleye and other game fish. The fishing seasons are: *trout*—mid April to mid-February; bass—mid June to mid-April, *northern pike, muskellunge, pickerel* and *walleye*—early May to March 14th.

The serious fisherman can find many kinds of accommodations. Most areas have overnight mooring, boat rentals and launching ramps. Campsites can also be found close to fishing areas.

Anyone 16 and over must have a fishing license. The non-resident fee is $20 for one year. A special 7-day tourist license is available for $15. Fishing licenses can be obtained at most sporting goods stores, the county treasurer's office and the regional headquarters offices of the Pennsylvania Fish Commission. The Pennsylvania Fish Commission will also send a license application. When requesting the application, ask for a copy of the Summary of Fishing Regulations and Laws. The address is: The Pennsylvania Fish Commission, Box 1673, Harrisburg, Pa. 17105-1673.

Boating

Many lakes and larger streams throughout the state offer boating opportunities to fisherman as well as pleasure boaters. Some have restrictions on horsepower ratings, some are limited to the use of electric motors. All power boats operating on Pennsylvania waters must display the current validation sticker for the state in which it is registered. In addition, all boats must carry a Coast Guard-approved flotation device for each person on board. For more information about boating, contact the *Bureau of Waterways* at the Pennsylvania Fish Commission.

Whitewater Rafting

This is America's newest participant sport for those who enjoy challenging nature. Four to ten people (per raft) paddle their way through dizzying whirlpools, around boulders and through foaming rapids. Minimum age limits vary from 10 to 16, depending upon the location. Beginners are welcome, although swimming ability is strongly recommended, and good physical condition is important.

Whitewater Rafting—Southeastern Pennsylvania. The 8-mile-long *Youghiogheny River,* with its 8 major rapids, was the first river rafted on a professional basis; it is one of the most popular river trips in the east. The season is from mid-April through October. The minimum age is 12. Rates vary from $16 per person per day, Tuesday, Wednesday and Thursday to $23 per person per day on Monday and Friday, and $28 per person per day on weekends and holidays. For further information, contact *Whitewater Adventurers,* Inc., P.O. Box 31, Ohiopyle, Pa. 15470; *Wilderness Voyageurs,* Inc., P.O. Box 97, Phiopyle, Pa. 15470; *Laurel Highlands River Tours,* P.O. Box 107, Ohiopyle, Pa. 15470.

Whitewater Rafting—Poconos Area. There is whitewater rafting through the *Lehigh River Gorge.* The highest water levels occur early in the spring. The minimum age here is 10. The Lehigh Gorge trip consists of 15 to 18 miles of almost continuous rapids. A new, upper *Lehigh Raft Trip* is exciting without being over-powering. The season is March 1 through June 30 and mid-September through mid-November. Trips are also held on the third Saturday in July and August, which are the scheduled water release dates. Fees range from $18 per person on weekdays to $28 per person on weekends.

For further information, contact: *Pocono Whitewater Rafting Center,* Rt. 903, P.O. Box 44, Jim Thorpe, Pa. 18229; *Whitewater Challengers, Inc.,* Star Route 6A 1, White Haven, Pa. 18661; *Pocono Mountain River Tours,* Inc., P.O. Box 45, Whitehaven, Pa. 18661.

Camping

Camping resorts in Pennsylvania aren't what they used to be. They are better! Some of the East's finest camping resorts, with complete facilities, are available for as little as $5.25 a night. More and more families are becoming camping enthusiasts, able to enjoy the same great skiing, snowmobiling, seasonal hunting and excellent fishing as resort guests, who pay a great deal more.

Families are finding that they enjoy camping in the winter months as well as the rest of the year, and at least 40 campsites throughout the state are open all year. Most have facilities for both tents and travel trailers. Campgrounds range from open spaces for pitching tents to those with elaborate facilities and all the amenities of a resort.

No longer is today's campground just a place to stop and rest overnight. Many are equipped with pools, playgrounds, miniature golf courses, laundromats and recreation halls. Special activities, such as sports tournaments, square dances, movies and covered dish suppers are planned.

Some camping resort operators are offering storage of campers during the week for visitors who want to come only on weekends. This service is most helpful for cutting fuel costs, as it eliminates the necessity of transporting the campers back and forth.

Because camping has become so popular, it is a good idea to make plans early. Some campgrounds require advance notices and reservations, especially for weekends and anticipated busy periods.

More than 600 campgrounds can be found in the state of Pennsylvania. The following lists some of the larger campgrounds with the longest seasons in each area of the state. This is not to say that bigger is better, since many campers prefer smaller campgrounds. See also the *Pennsylvania Campground Directory,* available from the Bureau of Travel Development.

Northwest. *Mercer Grove* (RD#6, Box 6794, Mercer, Pa. 16137). *Bear Run Campground* (RD#1, Portersville, Pa. 16051). *Red Oak Campground* (RD#1, Box 243, Russell, Pa. 16345). *White Haven Campground* (Hartstown Rd., Westford, Pa. 16134).

Southwest. *Cutty's Family Resort Campground* (Route 711, Champion, Pa. 15622). *Benner's Meadow Run Camping Grounds* (RD#2, Box 483, Farmington, Pa. 15437). *Pioneer Park Campground* (RD#4, 31 W, Somerset, Pa. 15501). *Woodland Campsites Inc.* (P.O. Box 493, Somerset, Pa. 15501).

Northcentral. *Higley Park* (Forksville, Pa. 18616). *Nittany Mountain Campground* (RD#1, Box 209, New Columbia, Pa. 17856). *Happy Acres Campground* (Waterville, Pa. 17776). *Stony Fork Creek Camping Grounds* (RD#5, Wellsboro, Pa. 16901).

Southcentral. *Park Away Parks* (RD#2, Box 2324, Etters, Pa. 17319). *Mountain Creek Campground* (Box 302, RD#2, Gardners, Pa. 17324). *Round Top Campground* (RD#9, Box 243, Gettysburg, Pa. 17325). *Hershey High Meadow Camp* (One Chocolate Ave., Hershey, Pa. 17033).

Northeast. *Timothy Lake Camp Resort* (RD#1, Box 317P, East Stroudsburg, Pa. 18301). *Otter Lake Camp Resort* (Box L, Marshalls Creek, Pa. 18335). *Lake Adventure Camp Resort* (Box 5000, Milford, Pa. 18337). *Keen Lake Camping Cottage Resort* (RD#1, Box 278, Waymart, Pa. 18472).

Southeast. *Appalachian Campsites* (P.O. Box 27, Shartlesville, Pa. 19554). *Mountain Springs Camping Resort* (P.O. Box 381, Shartlesville, Pa. 19554). *Oak Creek Camping and Trailer Reservation* (Box 128-C,

Bowmansville, Pa. 17507). *Birchview Farm Campground* (RD # 2, Coatsville, Pa. 19320). For further information, write to Pennsylvania Campground Owners Association,.P.O. Box 31, Coburn, Pa. 16832 or: *Pennsylvania Campground Owner's Association,* Box 306, Bowmansville, Pa. 17507; *Pennsylvania Bureau of Travel Development,* 432 South Office Building, Harrisburg, Pa. 17120.

PHILADELPHIA

City of Brotherly Love

"Let every house be pitched in the middle of its plot so that there may be ground on each side for gardens or orchards or fields, that it may be a greene countrie towne that will . . . always be wholesome."

So said William Penn of Philadelphia in 1681. And so it is. As you wander throughout this kaleidoscopic city that reflects the founding themes of this country, you will see a people proud of their 300 years of history, yet forged with a dynamic surge of vitality evident in restoration and renewal.

Pull a coin of the United States out of your pocket and look at the printing on it: *E Pluribus Unum* (One from many). Many cultures. Many religions. Many esthetics—all united in William Penn's "holy experiment," this heterogeneous city.

Whether it be in the restored **Independence National Historical Park**—the "most historic square mile in America"—the cobblestone streets of Society Hill, or the 8,400 acres of Fairmount Park, visitors to Philadelphia will find an incredible number of new things to see and do while visiting this historic city.

An ideal spot for beginning a walking tour is the National Historical Park. Independence Hall, a graceful red brick Georgian structure, topped by a white clock tower, was built between 1732 and 1741 as the colonial capital of Pennsylvania. It was designed by Andrew Hamilton, a lawyer best remembered for his defense of New York's anti-Tory newspaper editor John Peter Zenger in the first fight for freedom of the press in the American colonies. Nobody dreamed at the time that representatives of a defiant Continental Congress would gather here, that they would ratify the Articles of Confederation, commission George Washington commander-in-chief of the American armed forces, sign the Declaration of Independence and the Constitution of the United States, all in this historic hall.

Perhaps the most famous historical treasure in Independence Mall is the cracked Liberty Bell, one of the cherished symbols of American freedom. Made in England in 1751, the bell cracked while it was being tested in Philadelphia, probably because it contained too much copper. Recast, it rang when the Declaration of Independence was signed—thereby earning an immortal name. It rang also—but cracked again—when knelling for Chief Justice John Marshall. Cast on the bell is the legend "Proclaim Liberty Throughout the Land and Unto All the Inhabitants Thereof." The words come from the Old Testament book of Leviticus. Philadelphia has given this historic bell its own home in the *Liberty Bell Pavillion,* in Independence Mall.

On one side of Independence Hall is **Congress Hall,** where Congress met from 1790 to 1800 (legislative chambers authentically restored); on the other, the Old City Hall of Philadelphia. The **Supreme Court Building,** constructed in 1789–91, was slated to be the City Hall of Philadelphia, but housed the nation's Supreme Court from 1791 to 1800. Built in 1743 by Benjamin Franklin, **Philosophical Hall** has housed one of the nation's revered scholastic groups. Nearby is the **Second United States Bank,** built between 1819 and 1824, and known also as the Old Custom House. It was fashioned after the Parthenon and is one of the finest examples of Greek Revival architecture in the United States.

Carpenters' Hall, at 320 Chestnut Street, was originally the guild hall for Philadelphia's carpenters. In 1774, it served as the meeting place for the First Continental Congress. The chairs used by the patriots remain. **The First Bank of the United States** is at 116 S. 3rd Street. It was founded in 1795 by Alexander Hamilton, the first Secretary of the Treasury.

Church Built by a Lottery

On 2nd Street, between Market and Arch, stands the red brick **Georgian Christ Church.** Founded in 1695, it ranks as the oldest of the city's churches, although the present structure was built between 1727 and 1754. The church's two-hundred-foot steeple was financed by a lottery organized by Benjamin Franklin. Both Franklin and Washington had family pews at Christ Church, and at 5th and Arch Sts., in its burial ground, is Franklin's grave. His epitaph is self-composed, pious, witty and perhaps prophetic: "The body of B. Franklin, Printer, like the cover of an old book, its contents torn out, and stript of its lettering and gilding, lies here, food for worms. But the work shall not be lost; for it will, as he believ'd, appear once more in a new and more elegant edition, corrected and improved by the Author . . . " It would be well nigh impossible to list and assess all that Philadelphia owes to this adopted son, but among his many contributions—in addition to the Philosophical Society—were the *Saturday Evening Post,* the University of Pennsylvania and Pennsylvania Hospital.

Philadelphia is a city of "firsts," including the first American hospital, medical college, women's medical college, bank, art school, mint, stock exchange, steamboat, lending library, fire fighting company, daily newspaper, abolition society, and public school for black children (1750).

Just north of Arch Street, between Front and 2nd, is Elfreth's Alley, which Philadelphians claim is the oldest residential street in the North. Before the alley was laid out, some Quaker settlers lived in caves that they dug along the Delaware River. Later, Penn had the city laid out in blocks and it was one of the spaces left in between that in 1700 was cut into the cobblestone lane that became Elfreth's Alley. The alley is still flanked by narrow Colonial houses rising straight up from the sidewalk. In the early days, these were the homes of blacksmiths, cabinetmakers and river pilots. On the first weekend in June each year, Elfreth's Alley has a gala Fete Day.

Legend of Betsy Ross

At 239 Arch Street, only a short walk from Elfreth's Alley, is the doll-like structure believed to have been **Betsy Ross's house.** It is a two-and-a-half-story brick Restoration building, originally erected about 1700. The house remains a leading tourist attraction of the city and is filled with interesting memorabilia of Betsy Ross's era.

Among other houses of note in the city is the **Samuel Powel House** at 244 South 3rd Street, a superb example of an 18th-century town house. It is a commanding red brick structure, three stories high, with wrought-iron railings on its broad front steps. The Powel House was built about 1765 by the last Colonial and first post-Colonial mayor of Philadelphia, and a friend and frequent entertainer of Washington and Lafayette. In the **Edgar Allan Poe House** on 7th Street, the poet and author wrote "The Raven" and "The Gold Bug." The house was erected in 1800, and Poe lived in it for about two years in the 1840s. Architecturally, it is fairly characteristic of city dwelling of that era, though not outstanding, and does contain an interesting collection of Poe manuscripts and first editions.

Two burial grounds of historic importance in the city are at **Washington Square,** where the Tomb of the Unknown Soldier of the Revolutionary War stands, and the **Mikveh Israel Cemetery** near Pennsylvania Hospital. Buried here are Haym Solomon, the prominent financier who aided Washington during the Revolution, and Rebecca Gratz, who might have been the model for Rebecca in Sir Walter Scott's *Ivanhoe.*

In addition to Christ Church, the other churches of interest to tourists are **St. Mary's Church,** on South 4th Street, and the **Old Swedes Church,** or Gloria Dei, at Swanson Street and Delaware Avenue. In St. Mary's churchyard is the grave of John Barry, father of the American Navy. The Swedish church, built in 1700, replaced a log structure that had been erected in 1677. It is an attractive red brick building with a figurehead inside of two gilded angels above a Bible. The figurehead came from Sweden with settlers who arrived in 1643. It was not until 1681 that William Penn received his charter from King Charles to what is now most of Pennsylvania.

Penn landed his ship, the *Welcome,* on the left bank of the Delaware River in 1682. That spot, now known as **Penn's Landing,** has today become the largest freshwater port in the world. Penn's Landing offers an exciting and scenic array of majestic sailing vessels. The *Olympia,* Admiral George Dewey's flagship, is presently a public museum at the foot of Spruce St. on the Delaware River. The *Gazela Primeiro,* an 18th-century Portuguese sailing vessel, is open for tours during the summer months. Nearby is the *Becuna,* a WWII submarine. The *Moshulu,* a 1904 sailing square-rig ship, has been converted into a restaurant. Penn's Landing has unique restaurants, museums, landscaped gardens and more.

A short walk away, discover one of the most exciting, inviting, and delighting places in Philadelphia: **NewMarket** at Head House Square, in Society Hill. NewMarket is hundreds of historic nooks and contemporary crannies. A visitor has a chance to relax, dine, wander, and shop in one of America's most historic neighborhoods. Penn's Landing and NewMarket Square should not be missed.

The **Bourse,** one of the country's most architecturally interesting historic buildings, is a handsome mall housing dozens of eclectic shops and boutiques. It is located between Market and Chestnut Streets on Fifth Street.

The visitor who has finished his tour of old Philadelphia should not miss the attractions at the other end of town. The principal shopping streets of the city are Chestnut and Market Streets, with handsome, fashionable department stores. Recently opened is the new 125-store **Gallery Mall** at Market Street between 8th and 10th Streets, with dozens of international fast-food shops. A popular outdoor market is the Italian Market, located on 9th Street from Wharton to Christian Streets. Neighborhood merchants sell every variety of food imaginable. Open Tuesday through Saturday; a few stands open on Sunday.

Museums and Parks

Beyond City Hall and Penn Center, where the Tourist Center is located, Benjamin Franklin Parkway begins. On it is the oldest natural history museum in the United States, the **Academy of Natural Sciences.** The **Franklin Institute,** a museum of mechanics and applied science, is just a short distance farther on. Children love to climb into the cab of the huge locomotive on display. The **Free Library of Philadelphia** is close by.

Next along the highway comes the **Rodin Museum,** which houses, barring France, the largest collection of the 19th-century sculptor. In front of the museum, which is a branch of the Philadelphia Museum of Art, is a replica of *The Thinker.* In addition to many works in plaster, there are numerous drawings and watercolors.

The **Museum of Art** is at the junction of Benjamin Franklin Parkway and Spring Garden Street in Fairmount Park. It houses an ex-

tremely fine collection of American art, including works by Thomas
Eakins, Gilbert Stuart, John Singer Sargent, Charles Peale and Thomas
Sully.

There's lots more to see in Fairmount Park. *Belmont Mansion,* near
Belmont Ave., is where Washington, Madison and Franklin were once
entertained; *Carousel House,* Belmont and Parkside Ave., was built in
1900 as an indoor carousel. It is now a center with adjoining playground, for the handicapped. *Chamounix,* at the end of Chamounix
Dr., is a Federal-style mansion built in 1800 by a Quaker merchant.
Now it is the Philadelphia headquarters for American Youth Hostels.
Japanese House and Garden, Lansdowne Dr. and Belmont Ave., is a
reconstruction of a 17th-century Japanese scholar's house, tea house
and garden. *Memorial Hall,* near 42nd St. and Parkside Ave., is the
only remaining major building from the Centennial Exposition of 1876.
Scale model of Centennial grounds on display. Also indoor and outdoor recreational facilities. *Robin Hood Dell East,* near 33rd and Dauphin Sts., holds popular music, big bands, ethnic programs June
through August. *Mann Music Center* (formerly Robin Hood Dell
West), George's Hill near 52nd St. and Parkside Ave., is the summer
home of the Philadelphia Orchestra. Concerts in June and July. Tickets
free by submitting coupons in major daily newspapers or available at
the Tourist Center, 16th St. and JFK Blvd., on day of concert. *Smith
Memorial Playground,* Reservoir Dr. near 33rd St., has a sliding board
that is "10-children-wide," swimming pool, gardens. *Tom Moore Cottage,* West River Dr. north of Montgomery Dr., is claimed to have been
residence of the Irish poet for a brief time. *Waterworks,* East River Dr.,
has Greek Revival buildings. It was a former city aquarium. A year-
round café, with indoor dining, was added in 1977. During the 19th
century, water was pumped from the Schuylkill River to a nearby
reservoir from this facility. *Philadelphia Zoological Gardens,* 34th St.
and Girard Ave., opened in 1874. The country's first zoo covers 42
acres, houses 1,700 animals and a Children's Petting Zoo. In *Boathouse
Row,* East River Dr., just north of Art Museum, there are Victorian
boathouses occupied by local rowing clubs. Watch the scullers practice;
maybe you'll be lucky enough to be on hand for one of the competi-
tions. At night the roofs and turrets of the buildings are outlined with
strings of electric lights.

Historic Houses in the Park were once the homes of ten important
Philadelphians of the 18th century. All open to the public. However,
not all are open every day of the week. (Call MU 6–2176 or 568-6599.)
They include:

Lemon Hill, off Sedgely Dr. Robert Morris, signer of the Declaration
of Independence and financier of the Revolution, purchased this property for a farm and greenhouse in 1770. Later, when Morris was
sentenced to debtors' prison, the property's new owner developed it
into a beautiful garden spot where lemon trees grew in the greenhouse.
The house is a gem of late 18th-century architecture. Note oval draw-
ing rooms, Federal furnishings.

Mount Pleasant, off 33rd and Oxford Sts. When John Adams dined here in 1775 he described it as "the most elegant seat in Pennsylvania." An elaborate house, built in 1761, it was purchased by Benedict Arnold as a wedding present for his bride Peggy Shippen, but he was convicted of treason before they could occupy it. An example of Georgian symmetry; ornate woodwork, Chippendale-style furnishings.

Laurel Hill, off 33rd and Diamond Sts. In 1760 the center section of this mansion was built on the laurel-covered hill overlooking the Schuylkill River. A kitchen wing and an octagonal wing were added later. Note the decorative use of delft tiles, the Chinese export porcelains and the unusual corner fireplace in the kitchen.

Woodford, near 33rd and Dauphin Sts. General Howe was entertained here during the winter of 1777 while George Washington and his troops were encamped at Valley Forge. Before Woodford became a Tory home, Benjamin Franklin was a frequent visitor. This early Georgian-style house is now a museum of colonial furniture and household gadgets.

Strawberry Mansion, off Ridge Ave. near Robin Hood Dell East. The Marquis de Lafayette and Daniel Webster were entertained in this stately mansion that is furnished with a mixture of Federal, Regency and Empire styles. The library contains a collection of Tucker porcelain, one of the first true porcelains made in America. The attic is filled with antique toys. This is the largest mansion in the park.

Cedar Grove, off Block Rd. and West River Dr. A Quaker house built in 1748 as a summer cottage in the city's Northeast section. The house was doubled in size in the 1790s and a porch was added, giving it the appearance of a 19th-century Friends' Meetinghouse. In 1926 the house was dismantled and moved, stone by stone, to the park.

Sweetbriar, next door to Cedar Grove. Built in 1797 by a family who wanted to escape the yellow fever epidemic that killed 10,000 Philadelphians, this Federal-style house is an example of the Adam style in America with its floor-to-ceiling windows.

Hatfield House, near 33rd St. and Girard Ave. Built as a simple frame farmhouse in 1760, a Greek Revival portico was added in 1835. This is another house that was moved from its original location (in Philadelphia's Nicetown section).

Letitia Street House, southeast of Sweetbriar, off Girard Ave. In 1715 this house was built as a row home and stood near the Delaware River. Some claim that William Penn built it for his daughter Letitia. However, Letitia Penn never left England. The house has two rooms, a corner fireplace and a winding staircase, common in the 18th century.

Solitude, on the grounds of the Philadelphia Zoo. John Penn, grandson of William Penn, built this house in 1785. Note the detailed plaster ceilings, the handwrought railings and the intricately carved moldings.

Getting Around Fairmount Park: From late April to late October (Wed. through Sun.) the *Fairmount Park Trolley* leaves the Convention and Visitors Bureau, 1525 JFK Blvd., for the Museum of Art and the Park Houses, 9:30 A.M. to 4 P.M. June 15 to September 14, the *Cultural Loop Bus* leaves from 3rd and Chestnut Sts., stopping at the Convention and Visitors Bureau, before arriving at the Museum of Art. (Wed. through Saturday, 9:30 A.M. to 5:30 P.M.)

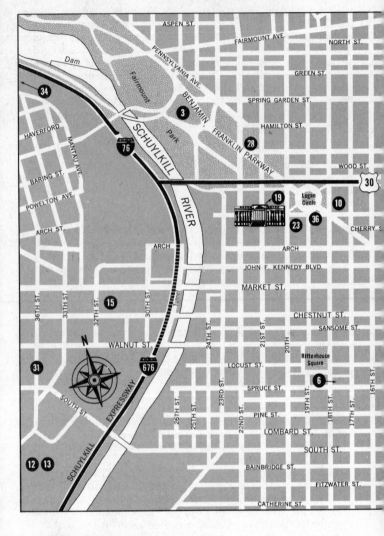

Points of Interest

1) Academy of Music
2) American Philosophical Society
3) Philadelphia Museum of Art
4) Antique Row
5) Arch Street Friends Meeting House
6) Art Alliance
7) Atwater Kent Museum
8) Betsy Ross House
9) Carpenter's Hall
10) Cathedral of St. Peter and St. Paul
11) City Hall
12) Civic Center
13) Convention Hall
14) Congress Hall
15) Drexel University
16) Elfreth's Alley
17) Forrest Theater
18) Franklin's Grave

19) Franklin Institute and Fels Planetarium
20) Independence Hall and Mall
21) Franklin Court
22) U.S. Mint
23) Moore College of Art
24) New Locust Theater
25) Old City Hall
26) Pennsylvania Academy of Fine Arts
27) Phila. College of Art
28) Rodin Museum
29) Shubert Theater
30) Theater of Living Arts
31) University of Pennsylvania
32) Visitors Bureau
33) The Gallery
34) Zoological Gardens
35) New Market
36) Academy of Natural Sciences

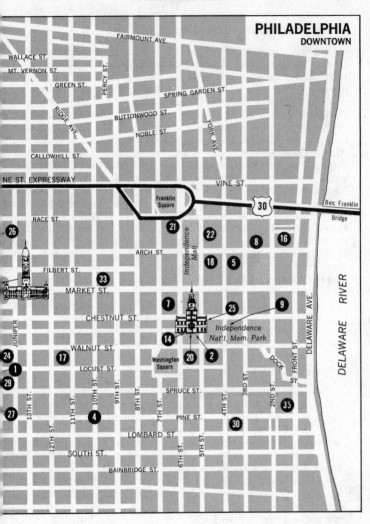

PHILADELPHIA
DOWNTOWN

FAIRMOUNT AVE.

WALLACE ST.
MT. VERNON ST.
GREEN ST.
PERCY ST.
SPRING GARDEN ST.
RIDGE AVE.
BUTTONWOOD ST.
NOBLE ST.
YORK AVE.
CALLOWHILL ST.

NE ST. EXPRESSWAY
VINE ST.
30
Ben. Franklin
Bridge

Franklin
Square

RACE ST.
26
21
22
8
16
18
5

ARCH ST.

Independence Mall

FILBERT ST.
33
MARKET ST.
7
CHESTNUT ST.
25
9

DELAWARE AVE.
DELAWARE RIVER

14
Independence
Nat'l. Mem. Park
JUNIPER
WALNUT ST.
24
17
LOCUST ST.
20
2
1
Washington
Square
29
DOCK ST.
FRONT ST.
27
SPRUCE ST.
4
PINE ST.
30
2ND ST.
3RD ST.
4TH ST.
35
13TH ST.
12TH ST.
11TH ST.
10TH ST.
9TH ST.
8TH ST.
7TH ST.
6TH ST.
5TH ST.
LOMBARD ST.
SOUTH ST.
BAINBRIDGE ST.

City of Schools and Colleges

On the University of Pennsylvania campus is the **University Museum,** with an excellent anthropological and archaeological collection. Incidentally, although Harvard was a college in 1636, it was not a university until 1780, whereas the University of Pennsylvania received that status in 1779. Other well-known schools in the city include the Curtis Institute of Music, Temple University, Community College of Philadelphia, Drexel Institute of Technology, St. Joseph's College, Chestnut Hill College, Hahnemann Medical College, Dropsie College, LaSalle College, Philadelphia College of Osteopathic Medicine, Philadelphia College of Pharmacy and Science, Medical College of Pennsylvania, Philadelphia College of Textiles and Science, Jefferson and Temple Medical Colleges.

A visit to Philadelphia would be incomplete without an exploration of its "Main Line" suburbs, so named after the **Main Line of the Penn-Central Railroad** that passes through it. Paoli marks the end of the Main Line towns, which include Ardmore, Radnor, Haverford, Bryn Mawr, Merion and Wynnewood, among others. In the early days, much of this land belonged to gentlemen farmers from Wales, hence the predominance of Welsh names. Today, these are wealthy residential communities, with rolling lawns, commanding houses, spectacular rose gardens and graceful pussywillow trees. This is also an area of Quaker-founded colleges—Haverford, Bryn Mawr and Swarthmore—and of outstanding preparatory schools. Villanova University, founded by the Augustinian Fathers in 1842, is also on the Main Line.

Growth and Changes

While John Adams' description of Philadelphia as "happy, peaceful, elegant and hospitable" is in some respects and in some areas still accurate, the usual urban blights have struck Philadelphia, like most major cities, in recent years. **Rittenhouse Square,** which has been completely restored, gives a true picture of Old Philadelphia, and is certainly worth a visit, but to expect a city of Old World or even 19th-century charm would be delusive.

Still the efforts of movers and shakers have given the city a "with it" look, and a kind of renaissance has occurred in the mid-city area, with high-rise office buildings, condominiums and cooperatives stretching their necks thirty or forty stories into the sky. The bicentennial gave Philadelphia a freshness and vitality that this city has not had in years. It is a very hospitable city and with the improved transportation links —including a Victorian trolley, bus "loops" and horse-drawn buggies —it is easy to get around to enjoy the amazing quantity of attractions. A visit to Philadelphia can be "a Great American Experience."

PRACTICAL INFORMATION FOR PHILADELPHIA

 HOW TO GET THERE. By car: I–95 and US 1 pass through Philadelphia on an east-west axis. The Pennsylvania Turnpike (I–76) runs east-west and intersects I–80 just north of the city.

By air: Numerous airlines serve Philadelphia International Airport including *Northwest, United* and *TWA. USAir* provides connections throughout the state.

By train: Philadelphia is on the *Amtrak* line. The station is at 30th and Market Sts. Call (215) 824-1600. The station in North Philadelphia is at Broad St. and Glenwood Ave. Their phone number is the same as the Market St. station.

By bus: The *Greyhound* terminal is at 17th and Market. Their number is LO 8-4800. *Trailways* is at 13th and Arch. Call LO 9-3100. *Martz, Merz,* and *The Gray Line* also provide service.

 HOW TO GET AROUND. By bus: The fare in the city is 70¢. Maps of the bus system are available from the Convention and Visitors Bureau at 1525 J. F. Kennedy Blvd., near the bus station, or at newsstands. 568-6599.

The Cultural Loop Bus covers historical and cultural attractions from Penn's Landing to the zoo, with special discounts at tourist attractions. The bus operates Wed.–Sat. in season 9:30 A.M. to 5:30 P.M. Information and schedules are available at the Visitors Center.

By taxi: *Yellow Cab's* number is WA 2-8400.

From the airport: A bus will take you to downtown hotels. *Yellow Cab* limousine will take you downtown.

By subway: The fare is 75¢ and exact change is required. Lateral transfers to other lines cost 15¢.

TOURIST INFORMATION. The *Convention and Visitors Bureau* is located at 1525 J. F. Kennedy Blvd., downtown. (215)568-6599. *Special Event Information* (also called the *Philly Fun Phone*) is (215)568-7255.

 CITY PARKS. The four thousand acres of *Fairmount Park*—the largest city-owned park in the world—not only houses the Zoo and Art Museum, but has a variety of activities such as biking, hiking, golf, tennis and sculling. It has more cherry blossoms than Washington, more than 2,000 azaleas, eight Colonial houses and, among other sights, a Japanese house.

 MUSEUMS AND GALLERIES. With its long history and deep cultural instincts, Philadelphia abounds in museums and art galleries catering to the diverse tastes and interests of its people. They range from fine arts to museums and include museums dedicated to photography, health, science, rare books, medical artifacts, history, furniture and fabrics. Among the most renowned are the following: The **Academy of Natural Sciences,** at 19th and Franklin Parkway, is the nation's oldest museum of its kind and is noted for its two-story-high dinosaur, fossils, special children's museum and live animal shows. The **Franklin Institute Science Museum,** 20th St. at Franklin Parkway, includes exhibits on space exploration, atomic energy, anatomy, physics, aviation, and communications. It has 6,000 science exhibits showing such things as how a locomotive moves, a plane flies, and a heart beats. The **Fels Planetarium,** part of the institute, presents astronomy shows and lectures. The **Pennsylvania Academy of Fine Arts,** Broad and Cherry Streets, is another American first of its kind—especially noted for its collection of fine American portraits from Revolutionary times to the present, but it also rates for its large collection of American paintings, sculpture and graphics. The **Philadelphia Museum of Art,** 26th and Franklin Parkway, has gathered under its lofty roofs several exceptional collections of art. Its fine displays of medieval, renaissance and modern art works make it one of the outstanding art museums of the world. Guided tours available. Its tea room and terrace restaurant are open daily. Free guided tours in eight languages: French, Spanish, Italian, German, Swedish, Polish, Russian and Turkish. The **Art Museum** has very recently added an American Wing, devoted to the contributions of Americans to the world of art, in addition to the new Arms and Armor Wing. The **Rodin Museum,** 22nd and Franklin Parkway, contains the largest collection outside of France of the famed sculptor's work. The **University Museum,** 33rd and Spruce Streets, has an extensive collection of ancient and primitive art from Europe and the Middle East, plus Chinese, Indian, African, Pacific, and other archeological and anthropological exhibits.

There are other good, though lesser known, museums, too. You may want to turn to the **American Swedish Historical Museum,** at 1900 Pattison, which traces the history of Swedes in America. The **Atwater Kent Museum,** 15 S. 7th Street, is a folk museum which tells the story of Philadelphia's 300-year history. **Civic Center Museum,** 34th Street and Civic Center Blvd., has an exhibit of raw materials; and its Philadelphia panoramas of the past and the future may appeal to you. It is advisable to write for an appointment or phone MO 7-0290 in order to view the world-famous collection at the **Barnes Foundation,** 300 N. Latch's Lane, in nearby Merion. The **Rosenbach Museum,** 2010 Delancey Place, houses the family collection of art objects, books and manuscripts. The **Norman Rockwell Museum,** 601 Walnut St., displays different forms of works covering sixty years of this artist's career. The **Brandywine River Museum,** in nearby Chadds Ford, is primarily devoted to the paintings of three generations of the Wyeth family.

The **Chinese Cultural and Community Center** is at 125 N. 10th St. The **Balch Institute,** at 18 S. Seventh St., is a truly unique educational center that spotlights the immigrant and ethnic experience in America. The **Mummers Museum,** Two St. and Washington Ave., is jammed with an array of colorful sounds and sights representing the pageantry and excitement of Philadelphia's New Year's Parade along Broad Street. Recently opened are the **Afro-American Historical and Cultural Museum** at 7th and Arch Sts., and the **Ile-Ife Museum of Afro-American Culture,** 2300 Germantown Ave.

Peale House, 1811 Chestnut St., is part of the Pennsylvania Academy of the Fine Arts and features changing exhibits. It will soon be moving to a newly renovated building across the street. The **Philadelphia Art Alliance,** 251 S. 18th St. at Rittenhouse Square, shows contemporary paintings, sculpture, crafts and prints. The **Institute of Contemporary Art** is at 34th and Walnut Sts. and the **Print Club** at 1614 Latimer St.

The **Philadelphia Maritime Museum,** 321 Chestnut St., tells the history of Philadelphia's port through exhibits and artifacts. The **Mutter Museum,** College of Physicians, 19 S. 22nd St., has anatomical and pathological collections and includes instruments used by Curie and Lister.

The **Athenaeum of Philadelphia,** 219 S. 6th St., features Victoriana and both art and furniture from the collections of Joseph and Napoleon Bonaparte. The **Buten Museum,** 246 N. Bowman Ave., contains over 10,000 pieces of Wedgwood. The **Historical Society of Pennsylvania,** 1300 Locust St., owns a collection of items associated with Penn, Washington, Jefferson and Lincoln.

The **Perelman Antique Toy Museum,** 270 S. 2nd St., exhibits over 4,000 old toys. The **Philadelphia Fire Museum,** or Firemen's Hall, 2nd and Quarry Sts., depicts the history of the Philadelphia Fire Department since its beginning in 1736: Rare old apparatus, equipment, uniforms and library.

 HISTORIC SITES. Philadelphia contains some of the nation's most important historic treasures—lovely old Georgian buildings, many of them grouped around Independence Square, bordered by Chestnut, Walnut, 5th and 6th Sts. The most famous, of course, is **Independence Hall,** at 6th and Chestnut Sts., open daily from 9 A.M. to 5 P.M.; July to Sept., 9 A.M. to 8 P.M. This is where the Declaration of Independence was adopted on July 4, 1776. The Liberty Bell is housed in its own pavilion on Independence Mall. **Congress Hall,** next door at 6th and Chestnut Sts., is where the Continental Congress met from 1790 to 1800. Also see **Carpenters' Hall,** on Chestnut below 4th St., where the first Continental Congress met in 1774. This guild hall was founded to teach architecture to carpenters and to help men in need.

The **Betsy Ross House** is located at 239 Arch St. Decorated in period furniture. Outside hangs a copy of the original 13-star flag that Ross is said to have designed. The **Edgar Allan Poe House** is at 530 N. 7th St. Poe lived here when he wrote "The Raven" and "The Gold Bug." The **Hill-Physick-Keith House** at 321 S. 4th St., was the home of the father of American surgery, Dr. Philip Syng Physick. Federal period furnishings and architecture.

Elfreth's Alley, between Arch and Race, Front and 2nd Sts., is one of the oldest continuously occupied streets in America, with 33 houses dating back to the early 1700s. Originally the homes of tradesmen, they are open to the public on the first weekend of June each year. Number 126 is **Elfreth's Alley Museum.**

The **Todd House,** a 200-year-old home once owned by Dolley Madison (née Todd), is at the northeast corner of 4th and Walnut Sts. The **Bishop White House,** at 309 Walnut St., was the home of the first Episcopal bishop in the U.S. Now restored and furnished with period pieces. The oldest Jewish cemetery in the U.S., the **Mikveh Israel Cemetery,** is located at 8th and Spruce Sts. Haym Solomon, who helped finance the Revolution, and Rebecca Gratz, thought by some scholars the model for the Rebecca in *Ivanhoe,* are buried here. Also at 8th and Spruce Sts. is the **Pennsylvania Hospital,** the oldest in the country (founded in 1751). The original building still stands and tours are available (free) upon request. Benjamin West's *Christ Healing the Sick* hangs in the lobby.

Two other homes worth visiting are the **Powel House,** at 244 S. 3rd St. and **Bartram's House and Garden,** at 54th and Elmwood Ave. The *Powel House* was the home of the mayor of Philadelphia during, before and after the Revolution. Washington and Lafayette were entertained here. *Bartram's House and Garden,* now in an industrial area, was once part of a 300-acre farm owned by America's first naturalist, John Bartram. The house is on 27 acres now and contains an unusual tree and plant collection. The **Graff House,** 701 Market St., is where Thomas Jefferson lived when he wrote the Declaration of Independence.

Franklin Court, on Market St. between 3rd and 4th Sts., contains frame and remnants of Benjamin Franklin's home. Also archeological discoveries, an underground museum filled with audio-visual exhibits (don't miss the film on Franklin's life!) and the **Ben Franklin Post Office**—the only one in the country where employees dress in colonial garb, open seven days a week. The **Thaddeus Kosciuszko House** at 3rd and Pine Sts. is a memorial to the Polish patriot. The **Man Full of Troubles Tavern,** 127 Spruce St. is a restored 18th-century tavern, now a museum. The **Tomb of the Unknown Soldier** of the Revolutionary War is located in Washington Square, just back of Independence Hall. This is also the burial place for hundreds of Revolutionary soldiers.

At Island Ave. and the Delaware River, near Philadelphia International Airport, is **Fort Mifflin,** used in 1777 to protect the Delaware River; in 1850 it served as a Civil War prison.

HISTORIC SITES IN THE GERMANTOWN AREA. (Each of the following is on or near Germantown Ave., Rt. 422, in the northwest section of the city.) *Cliveden,* 6401 Germantown Ave. An elegant 18th-century Georgian house. Site of the 1777 Battle of Germantown during the Revolution. Home of Benjamin Chew, Chief Justice of Colonial Pennsylvania. Chippendale and Federal furnishings. *Deshler-Morris House,* 5442 Germantown Ave. Built in 1759, occupied by George Washington during the summers of 1793 and 1794. Period furnishings. *Ebenezer Maxwell House,* Greene and Tulpehocken Sts. Built in 1859. Norman-Gothic style. *Grumblethorpe,* 5267 Germantown Ave. Built in 1744 as the county seat. *Wyck,* 6023 Germantown Ave. Built in 1690. Oldest house in Philadelphia. *Germantown Mennonite Meetinghouse,* 6121 Germantown Ave. First Mennonite meetinghouse here. Built in 1770. Library, museum, tours. Northeast of the Germantown area and just off Broad St., Rt. 611, is *Stenton,* 18th and Windrim Sts. Built between 1723 and 1730 by James Logan, aide to William Penn. Garden, colonial kitchen, barn.

 RELIGIOUS SITES: *St. John Neumann National Shrine,* 1019 N. 5th St. *Museum of American Jewish History,* 55 N. 5th St. *Judaica Museum,* Rodeph Shalom Synagogue, 615 N. Broad St. *St. George's Church Museum,* 235 N. 4th St. (Mother Church of American Methodism; oldest Methodist Church in continuous service in the country.) *National Shrine of Our Lady of Czestochowa,* North of Doylestown. (See Bucks County Chapter.) *Arch Street Friends Meetinghouse,* 4th and Arch Sts. (Built in 1804, still in use, it is the oldest Quaker meetinghouse in the city.) *Beth Sholom Synagogue,* Old York Rd. (Rt. 611) and Foxcroft Rd., Elkins Park. (Only public building in Philadelphia designed by Frank Lloyd Wright and only synagogue designed by Wright.) *Bryn Athyn Swedenborgian Cathedral,* Bryn Athyn, Montgomery County (north of the city on Rt. 232). Unique architectural blend of Gothic and Romanesque. *Cathedral of Sts. Peter and Paul,* Logan Square. (Center of Archdiocese of Philadelphia.) *Mother Bethel AME Church,* 419 S. 6th St. (First AME church; founded in 1787 by a former slave.) *Christ Church,* 2nd St. north of Market St. (George Washington and members of the Continental Congress worshipped here. Two signers of the Declaration of Independence buried here.) *Christ Church Burial Ground,* 5th and Arch Sts. (Benjamin Franklin buried here.) *Old Swedes Episcopal Church,* or *Gloria Dei,* 927 S. Water St. (Founded by Swedish settlers; city's oldest church; dates back to 1700.) *Chapel of the Four Chaplains,* 1855 N. Broad St. (Memorial to chaplains who went down with the *S.S. Dor-*

chester in 1943. Interfaith chapel.) *Old St. Mary's Church,* 244 S. 4th St. (Built in 1763; Commodore John Barry, "Father of the U.S. Navy," buried here.) *Burial Ground, Congregation Mikveh Israel,* Spruce and 9th Sts. (Graves of Haym Solomon, Revolutionary War financier, and Rebecca Gratz, probably model for Rebecca in Sir Walter Scott's *Ivanhoe.*)

 LIBRARIES. Every college, university and cultural institution has its own library, and books may be located in them through the *Union Catalogue* of the University of Pennsylvania. This catalogue lists every book in participating libraries by author, title and subject.

In the meantime, if you are just browsing you can visit the *Philadelphia Free Library* in Logan Square. Atop is the rare-book room, where you can see a cuneiform stone tablet recorded 4000 years before Christ—if you can prove that you can read it. The *American Philosophical Society,* 105 S. 5th St., has Benjamin Franklin's library and the books used by Thomas Jefferson to write the Declaration of Independence. The *Rosenbach Museum,* 2100 Delancey St., not only has the rare books of Dr. Rosenbach, who was the city's most celebrated book dealer, but his brother's collections of furniture and silver as well. The *Union League,* 140 S. Broad St., a very private club, has extensive collections of manuscripts and books pertaining to the Civil War. The *Library Company of Pennsylvania,* 1314 Locust St., was founded by Benjamin Franklin. The entire library of James Logan is housed here. Logan was a great colonial scholar and secretary to William Penn. *Civil War Museum and Library,* 1805 Pine St., has books pertaining to Abraham Lincoln and the Civil War.

 TOURS. In the **U.S. Mint,** 5th and Arch Sts., you will see the making and bagging of coins. This is the largest of the country's three mints.

Philadelphia's **City Hall** is larger than the U.S. Capitol and was fashioned after the Louvre in Paris (Broad and Market Sts.). There are guided tours through the Mayor's Reception Room, City Council Chambers, Caucus Room and Pennsylvania Supreme Court Chambers. A glass elevator takes you to the base of William Penn's statue.

The **Academy of Music** (Broad and Locust Sts.) has guided tours on certain Tuesdays from October to May. It is not only the home of the famous Philadelphia Orchestra but also a national landmark. Almost every President from Abraham Lincoln to Richard Nixon has spoken from its stage and all the greats of the musical world have appeared there. The building is acoustically perfect, fashioned after La Scala in Italy.

Masonic Temple, 1 North Broad St. One-hour tours. Closed holidays. This incredible building was built in 1873 and has seven lodge rooms, each in a different architectural period: Corinthian, Ionic, Italian Renaissance, Norman, Gothic, Oriental and Egyptian. In its museum is a Masonic apron embroidered by Madame de Lafayette and worn by George Washington when he laid the cornerstone for the U.S. Capitol building. Daily tours, but you need reservations.

INDUSTRIAL TOURS. Guided tours are offered by the *Bell Telephone Co.* Call its business office for tour information. The *Navy Yard,* League Island, may be visited by writing its Security Department. *Water treatment plants* may be visited to see how water is purified in the city's push-button plants.

SPECIAL-INTEREST TOURS. Your own special interests may lead you to the *Perelman Antique Toy Museum,* 270 S. 2nd St.; to *Lankenau Hospital Health Museum* at Lancaster and City Line, or the *Pennsylvania Hospital's Museum,* 8th and Spruce, to see a collection of Benjamin West, Peale and other artists, as well as rare books and artifacts. Other places of interest include the *Print Club,* and the *Buten Museum of Wedgwood.* To explore the *South Street Renaissance,* stroll down South Street, between 2nd and 7th Sts., and visit craft and antique shops, and ice cream parlors. Or, buy a rose from a mime artist in evening clothes. This recently changed area is known as "the Greenwich Village of Philadelphia."

Phone the *Philadelphia Convention and Visitors' Bureau* (568-6599) for information about special tours of Society Hill, historic sites, Black History and museums—by bus, car or on foot.

Centipede Tours (925-0250) offers seven different tours, including one by candlelight. Guides in colonial dress.

SIGHTSEEING. Visitors can see the attractions of Philadelphia in a variety of different ways. *Gray Line Tours* offers a variety of narrated sightseeing tours in air-conditioned, deluxe buses. *Philadelphia Carriage Tours* takes you through Philadelphia Colonial neighborhoods in restored nineteenth-century horse-drawn carriages. The *Fairmount Park Trolley Buses* use Victorian trolleys to take visitors through the Park, its museums, and attractions. *Rainbow River Tours*—narrated cruises up and down the Delaware River take off at Penn's Landing at the foot of South St. June-Sept. Great for children. For a truly spectacular view of the city, a great place to begin or end your visit is the observation deck at the Penn Mutual Tower, located at 6th and Walnut streets in back of Independence Hall.

GARDENS. Bartram's Gardens, 54th St. and Elmwood Ave., is the nation's first botanical garden, with the mansion of John Bartram, America's first botanist. A visit to the gardens is free, a fee is charged at the home to everyone 12 years or older. **Morris Aboretum,** Chestnut Hill, is a research center for the University of Pennsylvania. The **Schuylkill Valley Nature Center,** at 8480 Hagy's Mill Rd., has seven miles of trails, a wildlife reserve and nature museum. Handicapped accessible. **Longwood Gardens,** west of Philadelphia in Kennett Square (via U.S. 1), is the country estate of the late Pierre S. duPont, where there are 300 acres of flower beds, wooded paths, wildflower areas and conservatories. **Bowman's Hill State Wildflower Preserve,** Washington Crossing Park, Bucks County, contains wildflowers, marked trails and a lookout tower. **Tinicum Wildlife Preserve,** 86th and Lindburgh Blvd., offers trails, observation platform and canoe launch. The **Horticulture Center,** Belmont Ave. and Horticulture Dr. in Fairmount Park, has permanent and changing displays on site of Centennial Horticultural Hall. **Tyler Arboretum,** Rt. 352 north of Lima, contains 700 acres of rare plants and trees, 20 miles of trails and a fragrance garden for the blind.

MUSIC. Now that the **Academy of Music** has been air-conditioned, musical programs can be enjoyed throughout the summer, although the **Philadelphia Orchestra** itself may be playing at Mann Music Center in Fairmount Park or at Saratoga, N.Y., its summer home. At the *Academy of Music,* you can enjoy the *Philly Pops,* led by Peter Nero, symphony orchestras, operas, ballets and rock festivals. From Oct. to May there are concerts at **Civic Center Museum.** The *Mummers String Band* gives Tuesday night concerts (8 P.M.) at the **Mummers Museum** at 2nd and Washington Aves during the summer only. Children's concerts are given at the *Academy of Music* on five Saturday mornings from Nov. to May, 11 A.M. to noon, by the *Philadelphia Orchestra.* The **Robin Hood Dell East** stages top names in pop, jazz, gospel music, and ethnic dance nightly, July-Aug. The **Spectrum** hosts top recording stars. The *Tower Theatre* also features top recording entertainers. The **Philadelphia Folk Festival** hosts international performers and workshops in the folk-music world in nearby Schwenksville in Aug. Concerts are given regularly at The **Curtis Institute of Music,** 1726 Locust St.; The **Philadelphia College of the Performing Arts,** 250 S. Broad St.; The **Painted Bride Art Center,** 527 South St. and the **Electric Factory Concerts,** 18th and Lombard promotes rock, rhythm, blues, pop and jazz concerts (893-5252).

STAGE AND REVUES. Philadelphia has always been known as a good show town and Broadway-bound plays are tried out here. Many national road companies are booked into the city's three theaters, *Shubert, Forrest,* and *Walnut Street Theatre.* The *Valley Forge Music Fair* in nearby Devon has quality theatre. There is summer theatre at *Playhouse in the Park,* and the *Society Hill Playhouse.* The *Annenberg Center* is open from October through April, located on the University of Pennsylvania campus. There are a number of community and college theatre companies. Also, the world-famous *Pennsylvania Ballet* performs regularly in center city.

NIGHTCLUBS AND BARS. The old gag about spending a week in Philadelphia the other night is no longer valid. The city's swinging entertainment scene caters to those who enjoy the small, intimate bars and discotheques, as opposed to the giant nightclubs of bygone days. Among the popular spots are: **Stars** (2nd and Bainbridge Sts.) featuring jazz ensembles, singers, magicians, comedians, and amateur night on Weds.; **Artemis** (2015 Sansom St.)

which offers downtown's longest-running disco catering to an over-25 center-city **beaumonde** set; the **Bijou Cafe** (1409 Lombard St.) which offers an intimate club with big-name entertainers; **Grendel's Lair,** 500 South St., featuring off-Broadway reviews, jazz, and comedy acts. **élan** (in Warwick Hotel, 17th St. at Locust) has continental disco in elegant surroundings. Fine dining for breakfast, lunch, dinner—sophisticated, young professional clientele. **Doc Watson's Pub,** at 216 S. 11th St., is a popular place with the doctors and nurses from Jefferson Hospital and the actors and audiences from the Walnut and Forest Theaters. Also popular are **The Library, Palumbo's** and the **Windjammer Rooms** at the Marriot. Other popular bars include **Rick's Cabaret at Le Bistro, Downey's** and **Fran O'Briens.** Philadelphia's discos include **Second Story, Freckles,** The **News Stand** (1500 Market St.), **London's Restaurant and Bar, Ciao, Finnegan's Disco** (at the Philadelphia Hilton), and *Riply Music Hall* (6th and South Sts.).

 SPORTS. There's plenty for spectators in Philadelphia. In the fall, the *Philadelphia Eagles* and their National **Football** League opponents commit mayhem on each other in the new Veterans Stadium. Professional **basket-ball,** featuring the *76ers,* and college basketball, featuring the *Big Five,* come alive during the winter. Professional **hockey** (the *Flyers),* **boxing,** and **wrestling** are also very popular. In the summer, the *Phillies* play their home **baseball** games at the Vet. **Harness racing** may be enjoyed at Keystone, or at Liberty Bell, which also features **flat racing.** Philadelphia also hosts the *U.S. Professional Indoor Tennis Championships,* Jan. or Feb.; the *Penn Relays* in April; the *Dad Vail Regatta* in May; the *IVB-Philadelphia Golf Classic* in July; and the *Army-Navy Football Classic* held in JFK Stadium each December. Check newspapers for games at local colleges: The University of Pennsylvania, Villanova, Temple, LaSalle and St. Joseph's. The more active visitors may play **golf** and **tennis;** there are many courses and courts throughout the area. The Visitors Bureau can fill you in on this.

 SHOPPING. Philadelphia has such nationally known department stores as *John Wanamaker, Gimbel Brothers,* and *Strawbridge & Clothier.* Specialty shops such as *Nan Duskin* abound on Chestnut and Walnut Sts. in the midcity area. *Antique Row,* along Pine St., from Front to 22nd Streets, is a Mecca for buffs. *Flea markets* in the historic area operate weekends, spring to fall. A Sunday flea market is held on Independence Mall, complete with music, entertainment and food.

For those visitors who enjoy taking part of a city back with them, three shopping areas are a must. First is the recently opened 125-store *Gallery Mall* at 8th and Market Sts. *NewMarket Square* also offers unique shopping delights. *The Bourse,* a handsome mall on Fifth St. between Chestnut and Market Sts., features chic shops and ethnic restaurants.

 WHAT TO DO WITH THE CHILDREN. The *Children's Nature Museum,* a part of the *Academy of Natural Sciences,* allows exploration of fossil caves and dinosaur footprints, and has live animals. The *Franklin Institute and Science Museum* features displays explaining the latest developments in science and technology. *Please Touch Museum* (1910 Cherry Street) is a delight to young, curious children. The Zoo in Fairmount Park includes a children's section where the youngsters may pet and play with baby animals.

Or you may take the children for a summer boat ride along the Delaware River on the good ship *Showboat*. If you get tickets early enough, you may want to take your kids to the Philadelphia Ballet's annual Christmas production of Tchaikovsky's *Nutcracker Suite.* Children's concerts are given by the Philadelphia Orchestra both at the Academy of Music (at Broad and Locust Sts.) and at Robin Hood Dell in East Fairmount Park. *Temple University's* theatre department produces children's theatre on Saturdays, 1619 Walnut St., stage three. The *Perelman Antique Toy Museum,* 270 S. 2nd St., is a delightful visit for all. Also of interest to children are: Observation facilities at *Philadelphia International Airport, City Hall* and the *Penn Mutual Building* (510 Walnut St.); The *Fireboat Station,* Race St. at the Delaware River; the *historic ships* at Penn's Landing; the *Navel Shipyard;* and the *magicians and puppeteers* who perform at NewMarket in the summertime.

ONE-DAY SIDE TRIPS TO DELAWARE AND CHESTER COUNTIES

Heading west out of Philadelphia on U.S. 1, your first stop will be at the **Franklin Mint,** the world's largest private mint that has produced limited-edition commemorative coins and medals honoring over 3,500 persons, places and events. Glass-enclosed visitors' gallery permits viewing of the coining process. Tour begins with 30-minute film and ends at adjoining museum. Free.

Continue west on U.S. 1 to Rt. 202 and head north to the **Brinton 1704 House,** restored home of an early Quaker farmer. Note the indoor bake-oven, raised hearths and colonial herb garden. Back on U.S. 1 to the **Brandywine Battlefield** in Chadds Ford, site of the Revolutionary War battle. Begin at Visitors' Center; see original structure used by Lafayette and reconstructed headquarters of George Washington. Free.

Then continue west on U.S. 1 to **Brandywine River Museum,** an old grist mill that now houses works of many important American artists including N.C., Andrew, and Jamie Wyeth, Howard Pyle, Maxfield Parrish.

West on U.S. 1 for 1½ miles see the **Barns-Brinton House,** a restored tavern dating back to 1714. At Rt. 52 turn left to **Hillendale Museum** where, through dioramas and taped lectures, you will learn the story of the exploration of North America from a geographical viewpoint. Return to U.S. 1 and Kennett Square to visit **Longwood Gardens,** country estate of the late Pierre S. duPont, where there are 300 acres of flower beds, wooded paths, wildflower areas and conservatories enclosing four acres of heated indoor gardens. In the summer, Longwood Gardens features open-air theater, concerts, opera and fountain displays.

Also on U.S. 1, Kennett Square, is the **Mushroom Capital of the World.** Visit **Phillips Mushroom Museum** to learn about the process of growing mushrooms.

Now head back towards Philadelphia on U.S. 1 to Rt. 100. Turn left (north) onto Rt. 100 and continue one-quarter of a mile to the **John Chadd House,** a 1726 home that has been restored. (**Note:** While in this area, you may want to head south towards Wilmington, Del., to visit **Winterthur,** an extraordinary collection of American decorative arts, 1640-1840, amassed by Henry Francis duPont, and the **Hagley Museum,** a 19th-century industrial community, site of the original duPont Chemical Company.)

Heading north, via Rt. 100 or Rt. 202, plan to visit West Chester, known as "The Athens of Pennsylvania" because of its fine examples of Greek Revival architecture. The **Chester County Historical Museum** is located here at 225 High St. It contains exhibits of furniture, decorative arts and an important genealogical library.

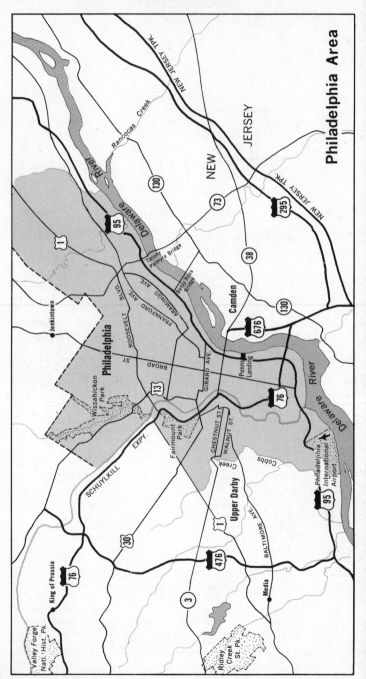

Philadelphia Area

If you plan to spend a full day in Chester County, you may go to any of the 16 public libraries in the county to borrow a cassette tape (and a cassette player, if necessary) which will guide you on a 90-mile tour. The tour begins in West Chester: Part I takes 2½ hours; Part II requires an additional 2 hours.

Returning to Philadelphia via U.S. 1, stop at the **Newlin Grist Mill** (U.S. 1 and Cheney Rd. at Concordville). This is a colonial grist mill, built in 1704 and restored to working order. A good spot here for hiking, fishing and picnicking. The next stop is **Tyler Arboretum**, Rt. 352 north of Lima, where you will find 700 acres of rare plants and trees, 20 miles of trails and a fragrance garden for the blind. Free.

The **Caleb Pusey House** (take Rt. 352 to Chester, at Widener College follow signs to Upland Ave.). Built in 1683, this was the home of William Penn's miller and it remains the only house in Pennsylvania visited by Penn. An 18th-century log house, a 19th-century schoolhouse and a museum are located here. Admission charge.

The **Colonial Pennsylvania Plantation** can be reached by taking Rt. 252 to Newtown Square and continuing for three miles on Rt. 3 to Ridley Creek State Park, Edgmont. This 200-year-old farm, is being restored and reconstructed to re-create life of a typical farm family in the late 1700s. Admission charge.

Back on U.S. 1, take Rt. 320 south to Wallingford to visit the **Thomas Leiper House**, a Georgian mansion constructed in 1785.

For additional information contact: Chester County Tourist Promotion Bureau, 33 West Market St., West Chester, Pa. 19380. (215) 431-6365.

Visitors' Council of Delaware County, 602 E. Baltimore Pike, Media, Pa. 19063. (215) 565-3677.

SIDE TRIPS TO VALLEY FORGE, READING, AND MONTGOMERY COUNTIES

After seeing Philadelphia, plan to visit "Valley Forge Country!" Begin with a tour of the National Historical Park which has been restored to show it as it was during the winter of 1777-78. At that time, Washington's ill-clad, poorly fed, badly supplied Continental Army suffered through the cold while General Howe and the British troops occupied Philadelphia. You may want to continue on to Reading, Pa. (known as the "Outlet Capital of the World") to a pair of reconstructed villages, a group of extraordinary historic buildings and some small museums that will give you a good idea of 17th and 18th century life among the Pennsylvania "Deutsch."

You can reach **Valley Forge National Park** by traveling west on the Pennsylvania Turnpike to the King of Prussia exit. Or leave the city on the Schuylkill Expressway and continue along Rt. 23 for about 15 miles.

Before beginning your tour of the 2,255-acre historic and recreational site, stop in at the *Visitors' Center* for a map and, if you wish, a rented cassette for your car. Bus tours of the park are available daily, April to October, and on weekends the remainder of the year.

A short distance outside the park, General Henry Knox's stone headquarters building still stands. Not far away is Lafayette's headquarters of yellow stucco and stone; then, General Lord Stirling's headquarters. Near Valley Creek you may visit the Washington Headquarters building, a pretty farmhouse of gray stone, heavy beams and wrought-iron hardware. It has been refurnished as it was in Washington's day.

The founding of the nation is vividly portrayed in a series of stained glass windows at Memorial Chapel, and the heraldry of the states is used as a theme for the paneled ceiling. Donations collected in 1926 from the first thirteen states provided funds for the acquisition of the chapel's carillon. Next to the chapel is the Valley Forge Park Museum containing mementos of Washington's encampment. There is also a Valley Forge Museum of American History, a memorial arch, reconstructed soldiers' huts and a field hospital. The old camp schoolhouse that served as a hospital during that long Valley Forge winter has been restored. In springtime this is a particularly lovely place to visit, for pink and white dogwood bloom in profusion.

The **Mount Joy Observatory,** a 75-foot tower, offers a splendid view of the surrounding countryside.

Just north of Valley Forge is **Mill Grove,** first American home of artist/ naturalist John James Audubon. Located in the **Audubon Wildlife Sanctuary,** six miles of marked hiking trails that wind through woods along the Perkiomen Creek. Many species of birds and wild plants.

One-quarter mile west of Valley Forge Park on Rt. 23 is the **Freedoms Foundation,** our nation's "Patriotic Headquarters," where our heritage of freedom is honored each year. The Visitors' Center features displays, exhibits and audio-visual programs of the country's history, heritage and the responsibilities of citizenship.

Also just west of Valley Forge are the **Wharton Esherick Museum,** former home of one of America's foremost sculptors and furniture-makers, and **Yellow Springs,** site of a popular 18th-century mineral water spa used by many famous early Americans. Today Yellow Springs is a center for the arts.

Heading northwest on Rt. 23, look for **St. Peter's Village** (just north of Knauertown), a restored Victorian village along French Creek that features an inn, stores and craft shops. Nearby is **French Creek State Park** where you can enjoy camping, hiking, fishing and boating.

Another restored village in this area is **Hopewell Village,** an old iron-making community. During the summer you can see demonstrations of mid-19th-century crafts and trades.

The **Daniel Boone Homestead** is located seven miles east of Reading. Frontiersman Boone was born here on Nov. 2, 1734 in a log house. That original building was replaced some time later with a two-story stone house. Nearby you can visit a blacksmith's shop, a smokehouse, a bank barn (an architectural rarity, unique to this Pennsylvania German region) and a restored log cabin.

Your next stop is Reading where dozens of *factory outlets* offer everything from clothing and high-style accessories to household goods, food and workbench tools. (Ask at any one of the outlets for a map that will direct you.)

Also in Reading you can drive up **Mt. Penn** to visit the **Japanese Pagoda** at the very top and get a spectacular view of the surrounding area. Built in 1908 in the style of the Shogun Dynasty, the pagoda was intended to be a resort but because no suitable access road could be built, it was sold and later donated to the city.

If you are continuing west, plan a stop at **Roadside America** in Shartlesville (25 miles northwest of Reading). This is a miniature village depicting rural U.S.A. The exhibit spans 200 years and contains 4,000 miniature figures, 2,250 feet of railroad and trolley track, 300 minute buildings and 650 tiny lights.

If you are heading back to Philadelphia, you may want to drive through Montgomery County to see some of the following:

Pottsgrove Mansion in Pottstown (Rtes. 422 and 663) is a distinguished Georgian home built in the 1750's by John Potts, wealthy ironmaster and founder of this industrial community. Also in Pottstown is **Pollock's Auto Showcase** where you can see exhibits of rare, pre-World War I cars, motorcycles and bicycles. (If things vehicular appeal to you, take a short side trip to Boyertown and the **Museum of Historic Vehicles** filled with cars, sleighs, wagons, stage coaches and fire trucks from 1763.)

Traveling north on Rt. 663, head for Pennsburg and the **Schwenkfelder Museum** (open by appointment only) which contains an extraordinary collection of household, farm and craft articles of the 18th- and 19th-century Pennsylvania Germans. If you happen to be in Green Lane (southeast of Pennsburg on Rt. 63 at the intersection of Rt. 29) on a Sunday, stop in at the **Goshenhoppen Historians' Folk Life Museum.** This is a small facility (open only on Sundays) offering exhibits on the history, customs and artifacts of early Pennsylvania settlers in this region.

Farther southeast (Rt. 63 to Rt. 113 north) is the community of Souderton with its **Mennonite Heritage Center** which features a collection of Mennonite art and history. Call for hours.

Off Rt. 63 in Lansdale is the **Morgan House,** birthplace of Daniel Boone's mother. (Open only by appointment.) Now take Rt. 363 south to Rt. 73 at Center Point for the **Peter Wentz Farmstead,** a restored colonial farmhouse used by George Washington before and after the Battle of Germantown. Craft demonstrations on many weekends.

Continue east on Rt. 73 to Bethlehem Pike to see **Hope Lodge** in Whitemarsh Township. This colonial Georgian mansion was built in 1721 by Samuel Morris. It served as a Revolutionary War headquarters for Gen. Nathaneal Greene. Also in this area is **Fort Washington State Park,** a 500-acre, wooded facility where you can hike and picnic. This was Washington's northern defense line against the British in 1777.

For additional information contact: Montgomery County Convention and Visitors' Bureau, Court House, Norristown, Pa. 19404. (215) 278-3558.

Berks County Pennsylvania Dutch Travel Assn., Washington Towers, Suite 3, 50 North 4th St., Reading, Pa. 19610. (215) 376-3931.

 HOTELS AND MOTELS in Philadelphia include several fine, old-fashioned establishments that still pride themselves on providing service in the traditional manner. Many newer hotels and motels have been built in recent years, not only in the downtown area, but in suburban or outlying areas as well. Fine accommodations can be found in all these areas also. A 6 percent state tax will be added to all hotel rates.

Double-occupancy rates in Philadelphia are categorized as follows: *Deluxe* $70 average, *Expensive* $60 average, *Moderate* $50 average, *Inexpensive* under $30.

Barclay. *Deluxe.* 237 S. 18th St. Old distinguished hotel on Rittenhouse Square. Personal service and quiet, dignified atmosphere. Good restaurant, cocktail lounge, parking ($3.50). Enjoys a loyal clientele. Baby-sitting service.

Bellevue Stratford. *Deluxe.* Broad at Walnut St. Newest luxury hotel with gourmet restaurant, supper club in prime center-city location. It contains 565 spacious rooms with 24-hour room service. Live music in 4 dining rooms.

Four Seasons. *Deluxe.* 1 Logan Square. Luxurious hotel with indoor pool, health club, outdoor café. Due to open in June 1983.

Franklin Plaza Hotel. *Deluxe.* Between 16th and Race Sts. just north of Penn Center. Brand new $48 million convention hotel. Pool, squash and tennis courts, jogging track, exercise rooms.

Hilton Inn Northeast. *Deluxe* 2400 Old Lincoln Hwy., Trevose. 16 miles northeast of Philadelphia, off U.S. 1 and ½ mile from Turnpike Exit 28. Pools, golf.

Hilton Hotel of Philadelphia. *Deluxe.* 34th St. and Civic Center Blvd. On the University of Pennsylvania Campus off Schuylkill Expressway. Indoor year-round pool. Top of the Hilton restaurant and Lounge. Minutes from center city.

Latham Hotel. *Deluxe.* 17th and Walnut Sts. Philadelphia's new luxury hotel has 150 rooms furnished in Regency "antiques." Every convenience: color TV, phone in bathroom, push-button refrigerators that dispense half-bottles of liquor, beer of all kinds—all recorded on bill downstairs. Baby-sitting service.

Marriott. *Deluxe.* City Line Ave. at Monument Rd. on Schuylkill Expressway. This large, attractively designed motor hotel has 750 rooms and 8 restaurants and cocktail lounges; free parking, indoor or outdoor swimming and sauna. Ice-skating rink available November to March. Live entertainment, weekend package plans, sitter list.

The Palace. *Deluxe.* 18th and Benjamin Franklin Pkwy. Attractive location. Health club.

Philadelphia Marriott Airport Inn. *Deluxe.* Philadelphia International Airport. Adjacent to the airport, free parking, shuttle service to all terminals, indoor pool, health spa, entertainment, two restaurants, meeting facilities. Baby-sitting service.

Sheraton Motor Inn. *Deluxe.* 9461 Roosevelt Blvd. 14 miles northeast on U.S. 1 and 6 miles south of Turnpike Exit 28. Pool, sauna, bar, cafe, airport bus.

Sheraton Valley Forge. *Deluxe.* First Ave. and Route 363, King of Prussia. 247 rooms; one mile north of Pa. Turnpike; 3 restaurants, nightclub and discotheque; racquet club with full health club and indoor pool; 2 movie theatres and shopping arcade, outdoor pool, florist, game room.

Stadium Hilton Inn. *Deluxe.* 10th and Packer, at Vet Stadium. Heated pool, airport transportation. Dining room and coffee shop.

Stouffer's Valley Forge Hotel. *Deluxe* Gulf Rd., King of Prussia. In-room movies, tennis, golf, entertainment, discotheque.

Valley Forge Hilton. *Deluxe.* 251 W. De Kalb Pike, King of Prussia. 250 guest rooms; excellent restaurants. Close to the Valley Forge Historical Park, Valley Forge Music Fair, and King of Prussia shopping area. Baby-sitting service.

The Warwick Hotel. *Deluxe.* 17th St. at Locust. Center city location. 170 rooms. Parking adjacent to hotel. Excellent restaurant and bar on lobby level; party facilities.

Adam's Mark. *Expensive.* City Line Ave. 515 rooms, 2 restaurants, 3 lounges, recreational facilities. Due to open in March 1983.

Franklin Motor Inn. *Expensive.* Parkway at 22nd St. This motel offers the greenery of the Benjamin Franklin Parkway, yet is only six blocks from city hall. Located in cultural belt of the Franklin Institute, the Philadelphia Museum, the Free Library and the Academy of Natural Sciences. Restaurant, pool and coin laundry. Baby-sitting service, cocktail lounge.

Hershey Philadelphia Hotel. *Expensive.* Broad and Locust Sts. 4-story atrium lobby, gourmet restaurant and terrace restaurant overlooking Academy of Music. 2 lounges, wine bar. Due to open in 1983.

Holiday Inn Airport South. *Expensive.* I–95 at Wanamaker Rd. High rise with 325 rooms. Restaurant, swimming pool, meeting rooms. Baby-sitting service.

Holiday Inn Independence Hall. *Expensive.* 4th St. at Arch. Large high-rise motel in historic area. Has 364 rooms, outdoor pool, cocktail lounge, restaurant and coffee shop. Free parking. Reservations are necessary, particularly in summer.

Holiday Inn Midtown. *Expensive.* 1305 Walnut St. High-rise motel in heart of city. Features heated swimming pool, restaurant, café and bar. Children under 12 free, crib free, cot $2. Free parking.

Holiday Inn Penn Center. *Expensive.* 18th St. at Market. Center city high-rise has 450 rooms, swimming pool, 3 restaurants, coffee shop, cocktail lounge, movie theater. Facilities for conventions, meeting rooms.

Penn Center Inn. *Expensive.* 20th St. at Market. This conveniently located downtown motor hotel has a drive-in, park and drive-out-yourself garage on the second and third floors (free). Swimming pool outdoors on 5th floor, coffee shop, cocktail lounge, restaurant. Baby-sitting service.

Philadelphia Centre Hotel. *Expensive.* 1725 John F. Kennedy Blvd. Located in center city. Near historical, sports, museums, and shopping sites. 860 superior rooms, parking, live entertainment, five restaurants. Baby-sitting service.

Sheraton Motor Hotel at Station Square. *Expensive.* On banks of Monongahela River. 297 rooms and a marina. Take boat to the new convention center, or to Three Rivers Stadium to watch the Pittsburgh Pirates. Fantastic view of downtown Pittsburgh.

University City Holiday Inn. *Expensive.* 36th and Chestnut Sts. 377 rooms; adjacent to Civic Center; on campus of University of Pa. and Drexel Univ., close to Medical Center, historic sites and U.S. Science Center. Two restaurants, cocktail lounge, baby-sitting service.

Alpine Inn Motor Lodge. *Moderate.* 650 Baltimore Pike. 1¼ miles east of Rt. 320, 12 miles west of Philadelphia. Pool, restaurant, entertainment.

George Washington Motor Lodge. *Moderate.* Turnpike Exit 25 and Rt. 422, Plymouth Meeting. Pool, golf, restaurant, entertainment.

George Washington Motor Lodge. *Moderate.* Rt. 202, King of Prussia, near Valley Forge. Pools, golf, restaurant.

George Washington Motor Lodge. *Moderate.* Rt. 611 and Turnpike Exit 27, Willow Grove. Two pools, sauna, golf, restaurant.

Hamilton Motor Inn. *Moderate.* 39th St. at Chestnut. Has 100 rooms, restaurant, cocktail lounge.

Holiday Inn. *Moderate.* Turnpike Exit 26 and Rt. 309, Fort Washington. Pool, entertainment, restaurant.

Holiday Inn Northeast. *Moderate.* 3499 Street Rd., Cornwells Heights, just south of Turnpike Exit 28, 18 miles northeast of Philadelphia. Pool, kennel, cafe, dancing.

Howard Johnson. *Moderate.* Rt. 202 from Turnpike Exit 24, King of Prussia. Pool, patios, 24-hour restaurant, movies, tennis, sauna.

Howard Johnson. *Moderate.* 11580 Roosevelt Blvd. 15 miles northeast of Philadelphia on U.S. 1 and 3 miles south of Turnpike Exit 28. Pool, cafe, free ice skating.

Philadelphia International Airport Motel. *Moderate.* Industrial Hwy. on State 29 at Airport. Has 300 rooms, swimming pool and café. Children under 12 free, crib free, cot $4.

Treadway Mohawk Motor Inn. *Moderate.* 4200 Roosevelt Blvd., near exit 28 from Pennsylvania Turnpike. Has 116 rooms, restaurant, café; children under 12 free, cot free. Sitter list.

Treadway Roosevelt Inn. *Moderate.* 7600 Roosevelt Blvd. Has 107 rooms, restaurant, café, bar. Children under 12 free; crib or cot free. Sitter list.

Howard Johnson's Motor Lodge of Horsham. *Inexpensive.* 15 mi. N of exit 27 from Pa. Tpke. About 100 rooms, restaurant, swimming pool, free parking.

HUB Budget Inn. *Inexpensive.* 7605 Roosevelt Blvd. Pool, restaurant.

International House. *Inexpensive.* 3701 Chestnut St. Near University of Pennsylvania.

Martinique Motor Inn. *Inexpensive.* 24th and Penrose Ave. Near stadiums and airport.

DINING OUT in Philadelphia, one experiences the various cuisines and gracious individuality proper to a city so proud of its heritage. The older restaurants serve a clientele that is comfortable and familiar with both the establishment and each other. The newer places, ringing the central business district, tend to be more informal and more concerned with contributing to the neighborhood ambience.

Restaurants are categorized on the basis of their own medium-priced full-course dinners, drinks, tax and tip excluded: *Deluxe* $20 average and higher, *Expensive* $15 average, *Moderate* $7.25–8.50 average and *Inexpensive* under $6.50 average. For a fuller explanation of these ratings, see *Facts at Your Fingertips* at the front of this volume.

EDITOR'S CHOICES

Rating restaurants is, at best, a subjective business, and obviously a matter of personal taste. It is, therefore, difficult to call a restaurant "the best," and hope to get unanimous agreement. The restaurants listed below are our choices of the best eating places in Philadelphia, and the places we would choose if we were visiting the city.

Le Bec Fin. We consider this restaurant a rare treat, and the best table in town. Only twenty tables are available in the small, elegant dining room, so reservations are a must. The food is the handiwork of an extremely talented, young master chef, and the Chicken Albufera is but one of his many masterpieces. The unexpected is the rule here, and the heights reached are often very impressive. *Prix fixe* dinner. 1312 Spruce Street. *French Cuisine*

Deja-Vu. Elegant service in a small, exquisite, French dining room. Naturally grown vegetables. Among the culinary delights prepared by the owner are Vegetable Terrine and Acidulee (filet of veal with lemon sauce). *Prix fixe* for 5-course dinner, $35. 1609 Pine Street. *French Cuisine*

The Frog. This is one of the best of the city's fine new crop of creative restaurants with a youthful atmosphere. The service is rather informal, but no less attentive. One of the 25 unusual entrées is bay scallops with pasta in champagne sauce. A spicy yoghurt and cucumber concoction is the most interesting of the soups. The menu is consistently adventurous and ever-changing. Average price for dinner (per person): $17. 15th and Locust. *Continental Cuisine*

Bookbinder's Seafood House. A cut above the other Philadelphia seafood emporium of the same name. The original family holds court here, which may account for the difference. This despite the fact that the other restaurant is called the "old, original." The food here is consistently top-drawer, and it is a happy, bustling institution. Oddly enough, the steaks served here are not bad either. Children's menus available. Average price for dinner (per person): $17. 215 South 15th Street. *Seafood*

OTHER RECOMMENDED RESTAURANTS

American-International

La Truffe. *Deluxe.* 10 S. Front St. Intimate, but casual atmosphere. Serves classic French cuisine, wine and cocktails, with an elegant flair. Gourmet specials—lobster thermidor and rack of lamb. Lunch and dinner.

The Commissary. *Expensive.* 1710 Sansom St. Upstairs, one will find a nice, noisy, and creative atmosphere garnished with distinctive dishes from all cuisines. Downstairs, there is a gourmet cafeteria with a bar, omelette kitchen, and cookbook library.

PHILADELPHIA

East Philly Cafe. *Expensive.* 200 South St. Comfortable and warm. Generous drinks.

élan. *Expensive.* At the Warwick Hotel, 17th and Locust Sts. Gourmet specials include boneless rack of lamb, shrimp élan.

Lickety Split. *Expensive.* 401 South St. Small and charming. Steaks, chops, salads and seafood.

London's Restaurant & Bar. *Expensive.* 114 S.12th St. Continental food. Saturday brunch. Upstairs is Hard Rock Café.

Arthur's Steak House. *Moderate.* 1512 Walnut St. An old Philadelphia standby and popular with the expense account and business crowd. Semi-á la carte. There's music and the surroundings are pleasant.

Cheese Cellar. *Moderate.* 120 Lombard St. Reminiscent of Old World wine cellar. Diners watch as fondues and omelettes are prepared.

City Tavern. *Moderate.* 2nd St. near Walnut. This is where signers of Declaration of Independence dined. Authentic 18th-century meals; spirits, entertainment.

Club Rittenhouse. *Moderate.* 256 S. 20th St. Small, intimate dining rooms on second and third floor. Nouvelle cuisine.

Downey's Pub. *Moderate.* 526 S. Front St. Interior was once part of a Dublin bank. Irish-American specialties, also steaks and chops. Pianist. (*Upstairs at Downey's* offers elegant dining and dancing.)

Friday, Saturday, Sunday. *Moderate.* 261 S. 21st St. Gourmet dishes served in romantic setting.

In Season. *Moderate.* 315 S. 13th St. American-Gourmet. Menu changes with equinox. Lunch menu features Danish open-face sandwiches, salads.

Le Bistro. *Moderate.* 757 S. Front St. Superb country French cuisine at reasonable prices served in the casual atmosphere of a 175-year-old colonial pub. Overlooking the river.

Judy's Cafe. *Moderate.* 3rd and Bainbridge Sts. Eclectic decor, ultra-casual. Imaginative menu. Salads with Oriental accent.

Moshulu. *Moderate.* Chestnut Mall at Penn's Landing. Dine aboard this old sailing ship at anchor. Plush Victorian decor. Maritime museum aboard.

October. *Moderate.* 26 S. Front St. Relaxed atmosphere, regional American cooking. Piano bar and lounge.

Periwinkle. *Moderate.* 115 S. 19th St. Tri-level bar and restaurant. Nightly jazz. American and Continental menu.

Rusty Scupper. *Moderate.* At NewMarket, Front St. between Pine and Lombard. Happy crowd. Salad bar, catch-of-the-day, seafood, beef. On riverfront.

Wildflowers. *Moderate.* 516 S. 5th St. Popular place for Sunday brunch.

The Down Under. *Inexpensive.* Concourse Level at #5 Penn Center. Candlelit tables, stockticker information, disco dancing, daily specials.

Holly Moore's Upstairs Cafe. *Inexpensive.* 123 S. 18th St. Entree salads, interesting sandwiches, homemade desserts.

The News Stand. *Inexpensive.* 15th and Market Sts., also at The Gallery, 900 Market St. Hot sandwiches, chili, bloody mary soup.

Robert's Cafe. *Inexpensive.* At "Robert's at NewMarket," Front and Lombard Sts. View of NewMarket.

Arab

Middle East. *Moderate.* 126 Chestnut St. Anybody can have a good time here. The lights are dim, the music hot and the belly dancers hotter. The food is authentic and rather good. There's raw kibbee (lamb), homus tahini (chick pea paste with garlic), baba ghanooj (spicy chopped eggplant) and many kebab (skewered meat) dishes. Finish it off with baklava and coffee.

Salloum's. *Moderate.* 1029 S. 10th St. Mid-Eastern food and vegetarian dishes. Small, intimate family restaurant one block from Italian Market.

Chinese

Fortune Cookie. *Moderate.* 106 Chestnut St. One of the city's newest. Top Cantonese food; there are 16 dishes on the menu. One recommendation is Seafood Worba—lobster, shrimp and crabmeat.

Hunan. *Moderate.* 1721 Chestnut St. Winner of Cordon Bleu Award. Spicey Hunan lamb, crisp duck.

Lotus Inn. *Moderate.* 1010 Race St. Pleasant atmosphere, comfortable surroundings. You may have to wait in line on a Sat. or Sun night. Good Cantonese cooking. They have a 90-minute special dinner that's excellent.

Trudie Ball's Empress. *Moderate.* 1711 Walnut St. Hunan and Szechuan dishes. Peking duck is house specialty.

Ho Sai Gai. *Inexpensive.* 1000 Race St. Mandarin, Szechuan and Cantonese specialties. Get there early—it gets crowded!

Imperial Inn. *Inexpensive.* 941 Race St. Head chef is native of China and prepares all manner of Mandarin, Szechuan and Cantonese foods.

Mayflower. *Moderate.* 220 N. 10th St., in Chinatown. A large menu that includes Mandarin, Szechuan and Cantonese cooking. If you like it hot, try the sauteed shrimps Szechuan.

Continental

Stouffer's, Top of Centre Square. *Expensive.* 1500 Market St. A special beef Wellington, plus steaks, seafood, and flaming desserts are served against a breathtaking view of the city. Live entertainment and dancing Tues.-Sat.

Under the Blue Moon. *Moderate.* 8024 Germantown Ave. In the lovely Chestnut Hill section. Unusual and delicious continental cuisine. Intimate, leisurely dining.

English

Dickens' Inn. *Expensive.* 421 S. 2nd St. Created in style of a 19th-century English inn with strong Dickensian associations. Fine wines.

French

La Camargue. *Expensive.* 1119 Walnut St. Cuisine and decor have captured country charm of France. Attentive service. Red snapper, lobster curry, rack of lamb.

Conversation, Cafe Pierre. *Expensive.* 1642 Pine St. Romantic French hideaway. Breakfast, lunch, tea and dinner. Sunday brunch. Fine wine cellar.

The Garden. *Expensive.* 1617 Spruce St. Elegant townhouse and romantic garden. Hearty French country cooking. Seafood a specialty.

La Panetiere. *Expensive.* 1602 Locust St. Classic French cuisine in an elegant setting. Winner of a "Holiday Award."

La Terrasse. *Expensive.* 3432 Sansom St. Open-air terrace (glass-enclosed in winter). Left bank atmosphere. Sunday brunch. Piano music nightly. At University of Pennsylvania campus.

Maureen's. *Expensive.* 11 S. 21st St. Nouvelle cuisine. Small, intimate. Features mostly interesting seafood dishes.

Le Champignon. *Expensive.* 122 Lombard St. In Society Hill. Fine French food at reasonable prices.

German

Hoffman House. *Moderate.* 1214 Sansom St. Elegant yet comfortable. Former carriage house. German specialties and fine game dishes.

Greek

Onasis. *Moderate.* 1735 Sansom St. Bouzouki player and grotto ceiling murals create Greek atmosphere. Authentic Greek dishes.

Indian

Siva's. *Expensive.* 34 S. Front St. Watch the master chef from Delhi perform the culinary art of preparing North Indian cuisine, including tandoori specialties and delectable breads.

Nandi's Chicken Tandoori. *Inexpensive.* 1621 Ranstead St. Indian fast food. Take out, eat in, deliveries.

Italian

Il Gallo Nero. *Expensive.* A small, cozy, Florentine restaurant which specializes in fine veal piccante and cannelloni. Delicious espresso.

Luigi's Trattoria. *Expensive.* 511 S. 2nd St. Northern Italian cooking—seafood and steaks.

Centi' Anni. *Moderate.* 770 S. 7th St. Dinner only. Warm atmosphere. Exceptional Italian fare.

Dante's. *Moderate.* 762 S. 10th St. Steamed mussels, eggplant parmigiana, manicotti, squid.

La Famiglia. *Moderate.* 8 S. Front St. Old recipes prepared by the Sena family.

Ristorante La Buca. *Moderate.* 711 Locust St. Regional style food with changing menus.

Villa de Roma. *Moderate.* 932 S. 9th St. In the heart of the Italian market. Good food, friendly service.

De Vinci. *Inexpensive.* 3007 Walnut St. Portions are king-sized, service good. They have one of the latest-closing kitchens in Philadelphia. Outside are sidewalk tables that set the decor. Downstairs—a wine-cellar atmosphere with candles and checkered tableclothes. Veal dishes are a specialty. For dessert—zuppa inglese.

Strolli's Bar. *Inexpensive.* 1528 Dickinson St., in South Philadelphia. Mr. Strolli's tender pasta and other home-cooked dishes exemplify the tradition of good inexpensive eating in the Italian section of South Philadelphia. Closed Sun.

Japanese

Kanpai. *Moderate.* NewMarket. Japanese steakhouse. Seafood, steak, tempura prepared at your table. Done with a flair. Much fun.

Mexican

Los Amigos. *Inexpensive.* 50 S. 2nd St. Authentic Mexican food. Generous portions. Live Mexican music on weekends.

Polynesian

Kona Kai. *Expensive.* Marriott Motor Hotel, City Line and Monument Aves. Specialties are seafood, curries and beef. Ambitious menu. Drinks are big and potent. Try Polynesian pork sauteed with pineapple and green pepper. Plenty of parking.

Portuguese

Cafe Lisboa. *Expensive.* 2nd and Pine Sts. at NewMarket. Old World setting. Portuguese menu includes seafood, paella, duckling and veal.

Seafood

Old Original Bookbinders. *Deluxe,* 125 Walnut St. One of the city's oldest, with a reputation going back to 1865. Select your own lobster from the tank. Other specialties: crabmeat, strawberry shortcake. Bar. Free parking.

The Fish Market. *Expensive.* 124 S. 18th St. Philadelphia's only gourmet seafood restaurant specializes in live Maine lobsters, sole Oscar, and crab quiche. The desserts are also exceptional, the atmosphere informally elegant.

Kelly's of Mole Street. *Inexpensive.* 1620 Ludlow St. Since 1901, popular for oysters and seafood.

Sansom Street Oyster House. *Inexpensive.* 1516 Sansom St. Neighborhood oyster house, good food—good service.

Spanish

Meson Don Quijote. *Moderate.* 110 Chestnut St. Old favorites such as paella and gazpacho plus some new Hispanic treats. Flamenco dancers and guitar music.

Thai

The Thai Royal Barge. *Inexpensive.* 23rd and Sansom Sts. Authentic Thai fare. Specialties include soft shell crabs, Thai salad. National award winner.

Fast Food Restaurants

Eden. *Moderate.* 1527 Chestnut St. Better than usual fast food cafeteria: Soups, quiche, stir-fry dishes. No frills.

Friendly's. *Inexpensive.* 600 Chestnut St. Close to Independence Park. Burgers, chicken, salad bar. Breakfast, lunch, early suppers.

RESTAURANTS OUTSIDE OF CENTRAL PHILADELPHIA

Chestnut Hill Area

Chiyo. *Moderate.* 8136 Germantown Ave. Interesting Japanese cuisine in intimate surroundings.

The Depot. *Moderate.* 8515 Germantown Ave. Running train is built right in. A 30-foot glass bar houses miniature train.

21 West. *Moderate.* 21 West Highland Ave. Omelettes featured at noon. Continental entrees for dinner.

Under the Blue Moon. *Moderate.* 8024 Germantown Ave. Unusual and delicious Continental cuisine. Intimate, leisurely dining.

City Line to Main Line

Benihana of Tokyo. *Expensive.* 2 Bala-Cynwyd Plaza, 333 E. City Line Ave. Dine in authentic country house, Japanese style. Food prepared at your table. Menu includes steak, chicken, lobster tail or shrimp.

General Wayne Inn. *Expensive.* 625 Montgomery Ave., Merion. This Main Line landmark was established in 1704. Both Washington and Lafayette stayed here on the same night. Seafood and beef are specialties.

Illusions. *Expensive.* 24 Merion Ave., Bryn Mawr. International foods are served. Magic performed at your table if requested.

Kona Kai. *Expensive.* At Marriott, City Line Ave. and Monument Rd. Specialties include elaborate Polynesian dishes, seafood and curries.

San Marco. *Expensive.* 27 City Line Ave., Bala-Cynwyd. Northern Italian dishes served in romantic setting of old Philadelphia mansion.

Sirloin and Saddle. *Expensive.* At Marriott, City Line Ave. and Monument Rd. Specialty is beef in candle-lit setting.

Top of the Line. *Expensive.* At City Line Holiday Inn, City Line Ave. and Monument Rd. Revolving roof top restaurant. Spectacular panoramic view from 23 stories up. Continental entrees.

The Greenhouse. *Moderate.* King of Prussia Rd., Radnor. Dine in the garden, the stables or in greenhouse. International menu.

Montgomery County

Coquille St. Jacques. *Deluxe.* 314 Old York Rd., Jenkintown. Exquisite French cuisine in intimate French restaurant.

Ristorante DiLullo. *Deluxe.* 7955 Oxford Ave., Fox Chase. Northern Italian food prepared with great care. See pasta being made. Quiet and elegant.

Tremont Hotel. *Expensive.* Broad and Main Sts., Lansdale. French food including sweetbreads, frog legs provencale, scallops.

Blue Bell Inn. *Moderate.* Skippack Pike (Rt. 73), Blue Bell. Continental cuisine. Extensive menu.

Coach Inn. *Moderate.* Off Rt. 309 at Pennsylvania Turnpike. (In the Fort Washington Industrial Park.) Dine in a restored railroad car. Victorian motif. Seafood, fowl, steaks.

Huong Restaurant. *Moderate.* 2651 Huntingdon Pike, Huntingdon Valley. Vietnamese dishes which have been influenced by both the Chinese and French.

Lakeside Inn. *Moderate.* Limerick. Restored 18th-century inn. Picturesque setting. Specialties are seafood and prime ribs.

Valley Inn. *Moderate.* 737 Huntingdon Pike, Huntingdon Valley. 200-year-old farm house. Family dining at noon; continental fare at night.

Collegeville Inn. *Inexpensive.* 4000 Ridge Pike, Collegeville. Smorgasbord with wide selection.

Beyond the Main Line

Coventry Forge Inn. *Expensive.* Coventryville. French cuisine. Inn built in 1717.

Joe's. *Expensive.* 7th and Laurel Sts., Reading. Local landmark dedicated to developing culinary qualities of the wild mushroom.

L'Auberge. *Expensive.* 503 W. Lancaster Ave., Wayne. Elegant dining. Specialties include souffles and mousses. French country atmosphere.

Stokesay Castle. *Expensive.* Hill Rd. and Spook Lane, Reading. Patterned after original Stokesay Castle in England. Menu features veal Cordon Bleu, beef Stroganoff, chateaubriand.

BUCKS COUNTY

Home of Artisans

Long a vacation spot for New Yorkers as well as for Philadelphians, Bucks County is full of important historic sites, artists' colonies, exceptional nature preserves, camp grounds, antique shops, recreational facilities, old inns, and modern restaurants. There are also lots of things to interest the children—including Sesame Place, mule-drawn barge rides, an old steam railroad, an Indian Village and even an annual re-enactment of Washington crossing the Delaware.

Bucks County is located northeast of Philadelphia and can be reached via I–95 or the Pennsylvania Turnpike to U.S. 1.

If traveling with children, plan to begin at **Sesame Place** in the Oxford Valley Mall. This new educational theme park, set on 15 acres, includes an indoor science and game pavilion starring the Sesame Street Muppets; 40 outdoor activities for the whole family, and a re-creation of the famous Sesame Street TV studio where the youngsters can perform and watch themselves on closed circuit television. Food service is available.

Now continue east on U.S. 1 to historic *Fallsington,* a pre-Revolutionary village where William Penn worshipped. See a primitive log cabin of the 17th century, two dozen 18th-century homes and the Victorian extravaganzas of the 19th century. Visit the three old meetinghouses at the center of town; the **Stage Coach Tavern** (1790); the

Schoolmaster's House (1758); and the **Burges-Lippincott House** (18th century).

Southeast of Fallsington, near Morrisville (named for Robert Morris, signer of the Declaration of Independence and the Constitution), is **Pennsbury Manor,** a re-creation at the site of William Penn's country manor house. This self-supporting plantation located (in Penn's words) "along the Delaware in a wilderness 25 miles above Philadelphia" has its own bake and brew house, a smoke house, ice house, stone stable, orchards and garden. **Summerseat,** on Ridge Ave., was Washington's headquarters during December, 1776.

Heading northwest from Pennsbury Manor, plan to visit colonial *Newtown* with its handsome 18th- and 19th-century homes. Begin at the **Court Inn,** Court St. and Centre Ave. (open Sundays and by appointment). This is a restored colonial tavern, now headquarters for the local historical society. Arrange to take a walking tour through town. You may want to lunch at the **Temperance House,** 5 South State St. When opened in 1772, fine food and safe lodging were available, but no ale. Today there is still fine food and lodging plus a well-stocked bar. Don't miss the **Hicks' House** on Penn St., home of Edward Hicks, 19th-century sign painter and primitive artist best known for his paintings of "The Peaceable Kingdom."

While in the Newtown area plan to visit the **Octagonal Schoolhouse,** just off Rt. 232 in Wrightstown, and the **Wilmar Lapidary Museum** on Rt. 232 and Pineville Rd., Pineville. (The museum is closed in January and February.)

Now back east to the Delaware River where your next stop will be **Washington Crossing State Park.**

It was from this site, on Christmas night in 1776, that Washington and 2,400 of his men crossed the Delaware River, surprised the mercenary Hessian soldiers and captured Trenton. A tall granite shaft surrounded by 13 cedar trees marks the point from which the soldiers embarked that snowy night. Visit the **Thompson-Neely House,** a handsome farmhouse where Washington met with his generals just before the crossing. At the southern section of the park in the **Memorial Building** is Emmanuel Leutze's famous painting "Washington Crossing The Delaware." Descendants of men who made that crossing often come to gaze upon the painting and point out the resemblance between themselves and the soldiers in the boat. It's a vain and useless exercise! Leutze was in Düsseldorf, Germany, when he painted the figures. For models he used either young men from villages along the Rhine River or American artists living abroad.

The huge painting is at the back of the stage and resembles the opening scene of a wide-screen epic. The story of the crossing is told by recording: Washington's victory at Trenton, followed by the successful Battle of Princeton, gave new hope to the Continentals. Up until that point the British had had their way with the Americans and a victory was badly needed to bolster morale.

(If you happen to be in this area on Christmas Day, plan to attend the annual re-enactment of Washington's crossing at the Park early Christmas afternoon.)

In the northern section of the Park are the *graves of America's first Unknown Soldiers,* a *wildflower preserve* and a *grist mill* that furnished flour to the Americans during the 1776 encampment.

To the north, along the beautiful River Road (Rt. 32), you will come to *New Hope,* a small community of fine art galleries, book shops, antique stores, restaurants, outdoor cafes and one of the country's oldest and most famous theaters—**The Bucks County Playhouse**—housed in a remodeled 18th-century mill.

Flowing through New Hope is the *Delaware Canal,* built in 1831. Rides on the canal are offered on mule-drawn barges for a small fee. Also see the **Logan Inn,** in operation since 1732 (and reputed to house a friendly ghost!). Visit the **Parry Mansion,** built in 1784, now a museum.

You can follow the River Road (Rt. 32) northward out of New Hope for a beautiful and leisurely ride along the picturesque Delaware River and the canal. You will see a number of 18th-century homes, historic mills, old inns and perhaps an artist or two painting at easels set up on the river bank.

At Lumberville, stop to see the old canal locks. Between Point Pleasant and Uhlerstown you can meander away from the river to see five of the county's 13 remaining **covered bridges.** (The Bucks County Historical-Tourist Commission, 152 Swamp Road, Doylestown, Pa. 19047, can provide a list of all 13 covered bridges with directions to each.)

Near Upper Black Eddy examine the **"Ringing Rocks,"** left in an open field by great glaciers. These stones actually "ring" when hit with a hammer.

Now turn back toward New Hope. When you reach the little town, going south on Rt. 32, turn right onto Rt. 202.

Peddlers' Village is just west of New Hope in *Lahaska.* This is an unusual complex of 42 shops and restaurants and seasonal events. Also in this area are two wineries:

The **Bucks County Vineyards and Winery** (3 miles west of New Hope on Rt. 202) offers tours of the winery, museum and tasting room. The museum contains original costumes of many Broadway stars.

The **Buckingham Valley Vineyard and Winery** (south of Doylestown on Rt. 413) is one of Pennsylvania's first limited wineries. Wine is produced here in the traditional Old World method.

At nearby *Doylestown* (reached on 202) is **Fonthill,** an odd stone-and-mortar structure built between 1914 and 1916 by Dr. Henry C. Mercer, then curator of American and Prehistoric Archeology at the University of Pennsylvania. It is a chateau-like building, its rooms ornamented with colored tiles and its roof made of bright red tiles (Dr. Mercer was a potter and tile-maker as well as an archeologist). Don't miss the **Mercer Museum** (described as "the most complete record of early American artifacts") with its collection of more than 40,000 tools and machines used in America before 1820. There are also dugout canoes, Colonial furniture, cider presses and a Conestoga wagon.

Also visit the **Moravian Pottery and Tile Works** built by Dr. Mercer to house his tile manufacturing operations. It was here that Mercer, while trying to recapture the lost German art of tile-making, created a process that brought a new dimension to the ancient art with his now-famous and unique Mercer Picture Tiles.

Just outside of Doylestown is the **National Shrine of Our Lady of Czestochowa** (pronounced Shen-sta-hov-a), at Iron Hill and Ferry Rds., erected by Polish-Americans in honor of the patron saint of Poland. The shrine, dedicated by President Lyndon B. Johnson in 1966, is maintained by the Pauline Fathers, and is open for tours.

Heading north on Rt. 313, look for the crossroads community of Dublin, then turn west (left) onto Dublin Rd. toward **Green Hills Farm** in *Perkasie,* home of Pearl S. Buck, the late Pulitzer and Nobel Prize-winning author. Now a National Historic Landmark, visitors may tour Miss Buck's home, see the desk where she wrote "The Good Earth," and stop in at the big red barn where the Buck Foundation for Amer-Asian children is headquartered.

Return to Rt. 313 and go north to *Quakertown,* formerly a settlement established prior to 1710, to see **Liberty Hall,** 1237 W. Broad St., where, it is claimed, the Liberty Bell was hidden on its way to Allentown in 1772. (Open by appointment.) Also in Quakertown is the **Burgess-Foulke House,** 26 N. Main, home of the town's first mayor and now a museum and headquarters of the local historical society. If you have lunch at the **Liberty Bell Bakery and Delicatessen,** 1313 N. Broad and adjacent to the Burgess-Foulke House, ask to see the restaurant basement, a *country store museum.*

Now head west on Rt. 663, crossing the Pennsylvania Turnpike, to *Geryville* on the Geryville Pike. Issued its first liquor license in 1745 (by the British Crown), the **Geryville Inn and Publick House** is where Fries Rebellion was plotted in the late 1700s. On Friday and Saturday nights, this restaurant is the scene of local "boom-ba" playing. (A "boom-ba" is a spring-based stick outfitted with all manner of cowbells, tambourines, drums and horns.)

This northern section of Bucks County boasts one dozen *camping grounds.* Nine of them are privately owned and the remaining three (Tinicum, Tohickon and Lake Towhee) belong to the county. The County Historical-Tourist Commission can provide a list of the facilities and accommodations.

Also, along the Delaware River—at Riegelsville, Point Pleasant, Upper Black Eddy, Tinicum, Lumberville, New Hope and Washington Crossing—you will find *canoes* for rent. At Nockamixon State Park, near Quakertown, canoes and *rowboats,* as well as *paddle, sail* and *pontoon boats* may be hired. At Nockamixon you may bring your own *motor boat,* if under 10 horsepower.

CONVERTING METRIC TO U.S. MEASUREMENTS

Multiply:	by:	to find:
Length		
millimeters (mm)	.039	inches (in)
meters (m)	3.28	feet (ft)
meters	1.09	yards (yd)
kilometers (km)	.62	miles (mi)
Area		
hectare (ha)	2.47	acres
Capacity		
liters (L)	1.06	quarts (qt)
liters	.26	gallons (gal)
liters	2.11	pints (pt)
Weight		
gram (g)	.04	ounce (oz)
kilogram (kg)	2.20	pounds (lb)
metric ton (MT)	.98	tons (t)
Power		
kilowatt (kw)	1.34	horsepower (hp)
Temperature		
degrees Celsius	9/5 (then add 32)	degrees Fahrenheit

CONVERTING U.S. TO METRIC MEASUREMENTS

Multiply:	by:	to find:
Length		
inches (in)	25.40	millimeters (mm)
feet (ft)	.30	meters (m)
yards (yd)	.91	meters
miles (mi)	1.61	kilometers (km)
Area		
acres	.40	hectares (ha)
Capacity		
pints (pt)	.47	liters (L)
quarts (qt)	.95	liters
gallons (gal)	3.79	liters
Weight		
ounces (oz)	28.35	grams (g)
pounds (lb)	.45	kilograms (kg)
tons (t)	1.11	metric tons (MT)
Power		
horsepower (hp)	.75	kilowatts
Temperature		
degrees Fahrenheit	5/9 (after subtracting 32)	degrees Celsius

PRACTICAL INFORMATION FOR BUCKS COUNTY

 HOW TO GET THERE. Bucks County is located northeast of Philadelphia and can be reached via the Pennsylvania Turnpike, Exits 26–29. From Philadelphia take I–95 for a quick trip; U.S. 1 or Rt. 611 for slower travel through the city.

 HOW TO GET AROUND. *Shun-Pike Tours,* 100 S. County Line Rd., Telford. Mini-bus day trips and specialized tours (covered bridges, gardens, old homes, etc.). Also limosine service to Philadelphia Airport and train stations.

TOURIST INFORMATION. *Bucks County Historical-Tourist Commission,* 152 Swamp Road, Doylestown, Pa. 18901.

SPORTS. *Liberty Bell* and *Keystone Racetracks.* Both in the southeast area on the Philadelphia border.

LIBRARIES. *David Library of the American Revolution,* River Rd., Washington Crossing. *Historic Langhorne Association Library-Museum,* 160 W. Maple Ave., Langhorne. *Spruance Library* (of the Bucks County Historical Society), at Mercer Museum, Pine St., Doylestown.

For price categories of hotels, motels and restaurants in this region, see *Practical Information* in the first chapter of this book.

 HOTELS AND MOTELS. BENSALEM: Holiday Inn Northeast. *Moderate.* 3499 Street Rd. Just off Turnpike Exit 28. Pool, Kennel, cafe, dancing. Near Keystone Racetrack.

BRISTOL: Imperial 400. *Moderate.* Rt. 13 and Turnpike. Breakfast, lunch, dinner. Cocktail Lounge. Entertainment Fri. and Sat. nights.

DOYLESTOWN: Court House Motor Inn. *Expensive.* 625 N. Main St. Continental breakfast. Dinner from 5 P.M.

ERWINNA: Golden Pheasant Inn. *Deluxe.* River Road, north of Pt. Pleasant. Continental breakfast until noon. Dinner. Closed Mondays, January 1 to February 14. Old country inn along Delaware River.

LUMBERVILLE: Black Bass Hotel. *Deluxe.* River Road north of New Hope. Old country inn. Continental breakfast, lunch, dinner; Sunday brunch. Cocktail lounge and bar.

1740 House. *Deluxe.* River Road north of New Hope. Country Inn, private balcony or terrace, between Canal and River. Breakfast buffet included with room. Dining room open to public for dinner. Card room, canoeing on Canal, tennis, pool.

NEW HOPE: Hacienda Inn. *Expensive.* 36 W. Mechanic St. Continental breakfast, lunch, dinner. Walking distance to New Hope attractions.

Holiday Inn. *Moderate.* Route 202. All meals, cocktail lounge. Entertainment nightly. Discounts to senior citizens and children.

QUAKERTOWN: George Washington Motor Lodge. *Moderate.* Route 1. Breakfast, lunch, dinner. Cocktail lounge, entertainment nightly. Pools, golf, bowling.

Quakertown Motel *Moderate.* Rt. 663. Breakfast and lunch to 1 P.M. Swimming pool.

TREVOSE: Hilton Inn Northeast. *Deluxe.* 2400 Old Lincoln Highway. All meals, cocktail lounge, entertainment nightly, indoor and outdoor pools, exercise equipment, sauna. Racquetball nearby. **Best Western.** *Moderate.* West Broad St., off Rt. 309. Restaurants, shopping nearby.

WARRINGTON: Warrington Motor Lodge and Restaurant. *Moderate.* All meals, cocktail lounge, bar.

 DINING OUT IN BUCKS COUNTY. Price categories are: *Deluxe* $20 and higher; *Expensive* $15 average; *Moderate* $7.25–$8.50 average; *Inexpensive* under $6.50 average. For a fuller explanation of categories, see *Practical Information* in the first chapter of this volume.

DOYLESTOWN: Conti Cross Keys Inn. *Deluxe.* Rts. 611 and 313. Colonial atmosphere, gourmet dishes, extensive menu.

Grandaddy's Restaurant. *Expensive.* Rt. 611 south of Doylestown. Renovated barn with Continental menu.

ERWINNA: Golden Pheasant Inn. *Deluxe.* River Road north of Pt. Pleasant. Candle-lit solarium. Pheasant, veal, rack of lamb.

HATFIELD: Century House. *Moderate.* Rt. 309.

HOLLAND: Mill Race Inn. *Moderate.* 183 Buck Rd. Charming old mill converted into a restaurant.

LAHASKA: Cock'n Bull. *Expensive.* Rt. 263. At Peddler's Village. Sophisticated.

LUMBERVILLE: Black Bass Hotel. *Deluxe.* River Road north of New Hope.

Cutaloosa Inn. *Deluxe.* River Road north of New Hope.

1740 House. *Deluxe.* River Road north of New Hope.

NEW HOPE: La Bonne Auberge. *Expensive.* At Village 2. Fine French menu.

The Inn at Phillips Mill. *Expensive.* North River Road.

Canal House. *Moderate.* 30 W. Mechanic St.

Chez Odette. *Moderate.* South River Road. A barge stop in 1794.

Hacienda Inn. *Moderate.* 36 W. Mechanic St.

Logan Inn. *Moderate.* 10 W. Ferry St. at Main St.

NEWTOWN: Lavender Hall. *Moderate.* Rt. 532.

Temperance House. *Moderate to Inexpensive.* 5 South State St. Opened in 1772.

Goodnoe Farm Dairy Bar. *Inexpensive.* Rts. 413 and 532. Full meals—but ice cream is the specialty.

Temperance House. *Moderate to Inexpensive.* 5 South State St. Opened in 1772.

PENNSBURG: Geryville Publick House. *Moderate.* Geryville Pike. Issued first liquor license in 1745 (by British Crown); Fries Rebellion was plotted here.

PERKASIE: Lake House Inn. *Expensive.* 1100 Old Bethlehem Pike.

PIPERSVILLE: Brugger's Pipersville Inn. *Moderate.* Rts. 413 and Old 611. Country inn serving Continental specialties. Antique-laden diningroom.

QUAKERTOWN: Sign of the Sorrel Horse. *Expensive.* Old Bethlehem Road.

Benetz Inn. *Moderate.* Rt. 309.

Trainer's Restaurant. *Moderate.* Rt. 309.

RIEGELSVILLE: Riegelsville Hotel and Restaurant. *Moderate.* 10-12 Delaware Road.

SPINNERSTOWN: Spinnerstown Hotel. *Moderate.* Old Rt. 663 and Spinnerstown Road.

WARRINGTON: Vincent's Warrington Inn. *Moderate.* 1373 Easton Rd. at Bristol Rd.

THE POCONOS

The Four Seasons Playground

The Pocono Mountains resort area is a vast playground of some 2,400 square miles in northeast Pennsylvania. Dotted with lakes, mountains, streams and fine hotels, the Poconos offer fishing, championship golf courses, swimming, skiing, hunting and outstanding camping opportunities.

For hikers, the Appalachian Trail passes through the Poconos, from Delaware Water Gap to Wind Gap and from Wind Gap to Lehigh Gap. For skiers, there are fifteen areas throughout the four-county section.

And for honeymooners, the Poconos offer a unique contribution to tourism—the special "honeymoon resorts," luxurious hostelries off-limits to all but newlyweds. The Poconos have long been known as the world's Honeymoon Capital. In fact, there's a Pocono Mountains Honeymoon Center in Stroudsburg.

"Pocoño," as one might imagine, is an Indian name, and means "a stream between the mountains."

Simply as a scenic attraction, the Poconos are hard to surpass, whether in June when the laurel is blooming, or in fall when the foliage is red and gold above the roaring waterfalls.

Only a few hours' drive from Philadelphia or New York, the Poconos are a popular retreat for Eastern city dwellers, easily reached by car, bus, train or plane. The motorist will find many excellent roads criss-crossing the area: State 611 and the northeast extension of the Pennsylvania Turnpike run north and south; I–80 crosses the Poconos from east to west, and so do State 940 Route 33 and I–84.

A good spot to begin a tour of this colorful region is at Delaware Water Gap, the famous scenic entrance to the Poconos. Located at a bend of the Delaware River easily reached on I–80 from New York or State 611 from the south, the gap is a deep, tree-covered gorge that attracts visitors throughout the year. It is especially beautiful in the fall, when the autumn hues are brilliant, and in the spring, when the mountain laurel on the nearby hillsides is ablaze with blossoms.

Three miles from the Gap is the lively resort area of the Stroudsburgs, one of the Poconos' leading tourist centers. North of Stroudsburg, off State 611 at Tannersville, is Big Pocono State Park, where you can get a superb view of the area from the top of Big Pocono Mountain, Camelback Ski Area and Alpine Slide. The scenic drive up to the summit is well supplied with picnicking sites. Camelback is the center of one of the most popular ski resorts in the area.

Another magnificent view can be had from Poconos Knob at nearby Mount Pocono, another leading resort center.

There are many scenic side roads throughout the area. From Mount Pocono you can dip south to Naomi and Pocono Lakes, or head northeast to Cresco, on 191. From Cresco to Mountainhome (home of the summer Pocono Playhouse), a turn off at State 390 leads us to scenic Buck Hill Falls, near Canadensis, and up to the splendors of the Promised Land State Park, which has excellent camping facilities. Promised Land is the center of the Pocono big game country, and some of the wild deer have become tame enough to wander into picnic areas for a snack. Lake Wallenpaupack, Pennsylvania's biggest man-made lake, is about 10 miles north of Promised Land. A great center for water sports and one of the most popular Pocono resort areas, this lovely lake is a man-made creation, formed in 1924.

From Lake Wallenpaupack, let's swing east on US 6 to Milford, a charming town on the banks of the Delaware. Nearby, beneath the bluffs at Coykendall's Pool, thousands of swallows make their summer home every year from April to August. Continuing down the Delaware on US 209 we soon reach Dingman's Ferry and the waterfalls of Child's State Park, where you can take a swim in the pools below the falls. Farther south, just a bit before the town of Bushkill, is another splendid group of waterfalls, the Bushkill Falls, the "Niagara of Pennsylvania."

Four seasons of activities make the Poconos a beautifully relaxing and invigorating vacation experience. Information on the National Recreation Area is available from the National Park Service, U.S. Department of the Interior, Interstate 80, Columbia, New Jersey 07832. The Recreation Area maintains an information station at Kittatinny Point near Delaware Water Gap.

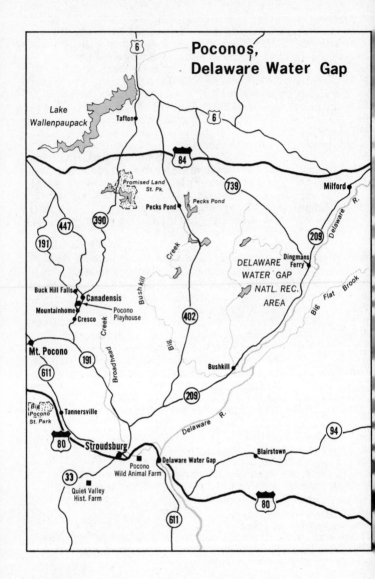

Poconos,
Delaware Water Gap

PRACTICAL INFORMATION FOR THE POCONOS

HOW TO GET THERE. By bus: *Greyhound, Martz Trailways* and *Pocono Mountain Trails* have direct service through the Poconos.

By air: *USAir, Eastern* and *United* fly to Allentown and Wilkes-Barre/Scranton, the airports closest to the Poconos. Some of the larger resorts maintain limousine service from the airports; airport limousine and automobile rental service are available.

By car: The northeast extension of the Pennsylvania Turnpike and Route 611 run north and south and Interstate 80 and 84 cross the Poconos from east to west as does State 940. Driving time is approximately 90 minutes from New York City and about 2 hours from Philadelphia.

TOURIST INFORMATION. The *Pocono Mountains Vacation Bureau* has maps, brochures and all the information a traveler might require. Anyone with a special interest such as hunting, fishing, skiiing or camping should mention it when requesting information or publications. The address is: Box K, 1004 Main Street, Stroudsburg, Pa. 18360. Phone: (717) 421-5791.

NATIONAL AND STATE PARKS. Delaware Water Gap National Recreational Area, near Stroudsburg, is at the 1,200-foot-deep gorge formed by the Delaware River cutting through the Kittatinny Mountains. There are trails and spectacular overlooks.

Big Pocono State Park, near I–80 in Tannersville, has Camelback Ski Area on its 1,300 acres. The chair lift at Camelback also operates in the summer for hikers and sightseers.

Tobyhanna, on State 423 near Mount Pocono, 4,000 acres with woods and water sports. Tent and trailer sites are available.

Gouldsboro, 10 mi. N of Mount Pocono on State 611, has a 270-acre lake with a boat rental facility and camping.

Promised Land, 12 mi. S of Hawley on State 390, has 2,300 acres, water sports and campsites.

White Haven State Park, on State 940 in White Haven, has 15,000 acres. There are water sports, camping, trailer sites and a sewage disposal station.

Bruce Lake Park, in Pike County, offers hunting on its 2,300 acres.

George W. Childs Park, in Dingman's Ferry, contains 154 acres with facilities for picnicking, fishing and hiking.

CAMPING OUT. Some of the finest camping in the country can be found in the beautiful Pocono Mountains where the surroundings are clean and smog-free. Whether a camper is seeking a quiet, escape-type experience or prefers lots of activities and sightseeing, the Poconos offer campgrounds to suit every taste. There are more than twenty-five private campsites with facilities for tents and recreational vehicles. At least fifteen campgrounds stay open all year to accommodate winter campers. In addition, the Poconos is one of the few areas which provides storage of campers during the week for visitors who wish to camp out on weekends.

Camp Charles, on Blue Mountain Drive, Bangor, is near the Appalachian Trail. There are 25 tent sites in a secluded area. Nearby are a recreation hall, store, laundry and bath house. There are also 85 trailer sites.

Fern Ridge KOA Campground, located on Route 115 at exit 43 of I–80 in Blakeslee, is only three miles from the Pocono International Raceway. Open all year.

Bernie's Camp-In, on Route 209 in Dingman's Ferry, has tried to maintain a rustic atmosphere with a minimum disturbance to the natural environment. Campers who enjoy boating will find it ideally situated near the Delaware River.

Timothy Lake Camp Resort, R.D.6, Box 50 P.E. in East Stroudsburg, has 220 sites and offers trailer storage. A family campground with deluxe facilities, it is open all year, and pets are welcome.

Jim Thorpe Campground, located on the Lentz Trail in Jim Thorpe, has wooded campsites nestled in a mountain valley. Fishing enthusiasts will find outstanding trout fishing nearby at Mauch Chunk and Beltsville Lake. It is near the area where the Bavarian Festival is held.

Yogi Bear Jellystone Camp Resort, located one-half mile from Lake Wallenpaupack, one mile off Route 590W, is situated on 54 acres and has a 6-acre lake. This resort is open all year with four-season activities.

Otter Lake Camp-Resort, near the junction of State 402 and U.S. 209 in Marshalls Creek, is situated on 150 acres with a 60-acre lake and borders on a state forest. Four tennis courts are available in addition to other facilities including a swimming pool, movies, free firewood, store and laundry. This resort is open all year—from July through Labor Day. There is a five-night minimum stay.

Driftstone on the Delaware, on River Road near State 611 in Mount Bethel. This campground makes good use of the river; there are canoes for rent and a boat launching ramp for campers who bring their own boats. Explore their 20-acre island. There are a laundry and hot showers.

Mount Pocono Campground, located near the junction of State 196 and 611 in Mount Pocono, adjoins the 4,500-acre Devil's Hole Gameland. With its 2,000 foot elevation in the center of the Poconos, this campground has a breathtaking view. There are 140 sites for both tents and recreational vehicles.

Scotrun Park Campground is near State 611 in Scotrun. Situated high in the Poconos, the spacious sites give everyone a feeling of privacy. A mountain stream flows through the park and is stocked with trout. Firewood is free. There are hot showers and a laundromat.

PVP Pocono Vacation Park, on Shafer's School House Road in Stroudsburg, is open throughout the year, and all sites have full hook-ups. There is a live dance band every Saturday night.

Nearly every camping site in the Pocono area has electricity and water. For more information on campgrounds in the area, write to the Pocono Mountain Vacation Bureau.

STAGE AND REVUES. The **Pocono Playhouse** in Mountainhome, from June through September, has summer theatre with Broadway plays and musicals starring Hollywood, television and stage personalities. The **Shawnee Playhouse,** located at Shawnee-on-Delaware, is open all year. **East Stroudsburg State College** has recitals, revues and one-act plays. The **Milford Playhouse** also presents summer theatre.

SPORTS. The Pocono area has a total of 118 slopes and trails for *downhill skiing*. All 15 Pocono ski areas are equipped with snow-making facilities. The major areas are: **Big Boulder, Camelback, Jack Frost, Shawnee** and **Tanglewood.** All facilities include fully staffed ski schools, rentals and lodge activities. Beginners' experiences will be as enjoyable as the experts, who will find slopes to challenge their skiing ability. (See chapter on sports for more detailed information.) Sixty radio stations throughout the East give daily *Pocono Sno Bunny* reports about Pocono skiing conditions.

Many areas in the Poconos have expanded to accommodate the growing demand for *cross country skiing.* Each area offers miles of scenic trails, reasonable rentals and guided tours. Cross country skiing can be enjoyed at **Tanglewood** ski area, **Pocono Manor, Buck Hill Inn, Mt. Airy Lodge, Tamiment, Shawnee Mountain, Fernwood, Masthope Ski Area, Mt. Tone, The Lodge at Split Rock,** and **Pocono Hershey.** In addition, **Pack Shack Adventure,** located in Delaware Water Gap and the **Tobyhanna Sports Camp** in Tobyhanna have acres of scenic trails.

State Park lands and privately owned *snowmobile* trails are available to Pocono visitors. Many of the resorts in the Poconos offer snowmobiling. Other winter sports include *ice-skating, sledding, tobogganing, sleigh rides* and *ice-fishing.*

Whitewater rafting, fishing and *hunting* are excellent in the Poconos. These activities are fully described in the chapter on sports.

The less-crowded mountain facilities allow *golfers* to spend more time enjoying their favorite sport and little or no time waiting to tee off. Recently referred to as the "Myrtle Beach of the North," the Poconos offer over 30 courses from early spring to late autumn. Some of the more well-known golf courses in the area are the **Pocono Hershey Resort, Shawnee Inn, Tamiment, Mt. Airy Lodge, Penn Estates,** and **Buck Hill Inn and Golf Club.** Tournaments held in the Poconos are the *Buck Hill Invitational* in August, the *Ladies PGA Tournament* at Pocono Manor in August, the *Danny Kaye Invitational* at Tamiment.

Because of the popularity of *tennis,* more and more resorts are adding additional courts, lighting them for night play, and building indoor facilities. Some campgrounds have recently installed tennis courts. Tennis tournaments are held at the major resorts and clubs. Many resorts offer tennis packages.

Horseback Riders will be delighted with the miles of rambling woodland trails, scenic views and crisp, clean mountain air. The major resorts offering horseback riding are **Fernwood in Bushkill, Shawnee Inn, Pocono Palace, Pocono Hershey, Mount Airy Lodge, Pocono Manor Inn** and **Tamiment.** Other riding stables are **Carson's** on Rt. 611, one mile south of Mount Pocono, **Double W Farm Resort** in Honesdale, **El-J Riding Stable** in Cresco, the **Malibu Dude Ranch** in Milford, **Fox Run Stables** in Tannersville, **RJD Stables & Riding Center, Inc.** in Lake Ariel, and **Saw Creek Stables** in Bushkill.

Day and overnight *canoe trips,* instructions and rentals are offered. Some of the facilities will arrange for pickup and delivery of canoes. Most of these places request reservations. Canoe trips and rentals are provided by **Adventure Tours** in Stroudsburg, **Chamberlain Canoe Rentals** in Minisink Hills, **Doe Hollow Canoe Rentals** in Bangor, **Pack Shack Adventures** and **Water Gap Canoes** in Delaware Water Gap, **Northland Canoe Outfitters** in Marshall's Creek, **Point Pleasant Canoe Rentals** in Bushkill, and **Kittatinny** in Dingman's Ferry.

The unique *Pocono International Raceway* has a 2.5-mile, tri-oval track that draws hundreds of thousands of spectators to the area annually. Fans enjoy seeing the top names in auto racing here. Two 500-mile events highlighting the season are the **Pocono 500** for USAC Indy Champ cars and the **Stock Car 500** for NASCAR Daytona Type Stock Cars. Additional events include *Go-cart racing, motorcycle racing* and *modified stock car races.* Fans are urged to order tickets well in advance. The address is: Box 500, Mount Pocono, Pa. 18344.

For further information about your favorite sport, write to the Pocono Mountain Vacation Bureau, Box K, 1004 Main St., Stroudsburg, Pa. 18360.

SHOPPING. Unique shops featuring handcrafted items can be found throughout the Poconos. **Scrimshaw,** hand-thrown **pottery, Early American crafts, baskets, miniatures, furniture** and **jewelry** can be found at *Bendixen's* in Pocono Summit, *Calico Craftsman* in Stroudsburg, *Colony Village* in Canadensis, *Holley Ross Pottery* in Cresco, *House of Baskets* in Gilbert, *Huttens Hut* in Pocono Pines, *Pocono Mountain Woodcrafters* in Canadensis, *Sciota Craft Shop* in Scotia, *Stony Holly Pottery* in Tannersville and *The Woodworker* in Bartonsville. The *Pocono Candle Shop* in E. Stroudsburg and *American Candle* in Bartonsville sell **candles** of every size and shape. They also offer demonstrations in candle making.

A large selection of **artificial flowers, plants,** and **trees** can be found at *It's Unreal* in Mountainhome. They specialize in silk and dried flowers and do custom arrangements in your own container. Another interesting shop in Mountainhome is *The Other Woman,* with seven rooms containing **fabric, dried flowers, pillows, paintings, antiques** and **clothing.**

WHAT TO DO WITH THE CHILDREN. *Winona Five Falls and Nature Trail* is part of *Poconos Magic Valley Park* in Bushkill. The park also has thrilling rides, including "The Screamin' Demon" rollercoaster, live shows and a petting zoo. *Rainbow Falls,* located in Moon Valley Park in Milford, is a good place for younger children, who can tour *Old McDonald's Farm* and *Storybook Land* at the same time. Adventurous children of all ages will enjoy both the *Alpine Slide* and water slide at the *Camelback Ski Area.* After a scenic chairlift ride up Big Pocono Mountain, thrill to the 3,200 foot ride down the alpine slide. *Claws 'n' Paws Wild Animal Farm* in Lake Ariel is an animal lovers delight. Besides wild animals, which can be seen close up, there is a large petting area with tame deer, llamas and lambs to feed and hug. Other attractions the children will enjoy are: *Memorytown U.S.A.* in Mount Pocono, *Pennsylvania Dutch Farm and Frontier* in Mount Pocono, *Pocono Indian Museum* in Bushkill, *Shawnee Place* in Shawnee. *Pocono Snake Country* in Marshalls Creek and *Quiet Valley "Living" Historical Farm* in Stroudsburg. One can see candy being made at *Callie's Candy Kitchen* in Mountainhome. They specialize in all kinds of fresh fruits dipped in chocolate; visitors are treated to free samples.

POCONO WINTER CARNIVAL. This popular annual event is held the last week in February and the first week in March. All kinds of ski races, including cross-country, are held. Tobogganing and skating parties with hayrides, bonfires and free refreshments are offered to guests at the various resorts. Visitors can also enjoy dog sled races, torchlight ski parades and fondue parties. Many ski areas have free videotaping clinics for the serious skiier. Other activities during carnival time are the Pennsylvania Special Olympics (for handicapped and retarded children), hosted by Shawnee Ski Area and Fernwood Resort in Bushkill, snowmobile races and ski fashion shows. Early reservations are suggested for this time period. The Pocono Mountains Vacation Bureau can supply a listing of scheduled events.

HONEYMOON CAPITAL OF THE WORLD. Each year, more than 275,000 couples spend their honeymoon in the Poconos. The honeymoon resorts offer a total package that includes accommodations, activities, gourmet meals, a social director and a honeymoon picture album. Accommodations are luxurious and many include sunken heart-shaped bathtubs, private pools in the room, saunas for two, whirlpool baths and beds in all sizes and shapes.

Resorts catering to honeymooners and couples are: *The Summit* in Tannersville, *Stricklands Mountain Inn and Cottages, Mt. Airy Lodge, Pocono Gardens Lodge* and *Paradise Stream Honeymoon Resort* in Mount Pocono, Penn Hills and Analomink. Also, *Cove Haven* in Lakeville, *Birchwood* in E. Stroudsburg, *Pocono Palace* in Marshalls Creek and *Wayne Newton's Tamiment* in Tamiment.

HOTELS AND MOTELS in the Poconos offer so many types of accommodations and plans at each of the large resorts that prudent vacationers will want to examine them in detail by sending for brochures. The categories used for the survey in this section are, for double occupancy: *Super Deluxe* over $70, *Deluxe* $60 average, *Expensive* $50 average, *Moderate* $35 average and *Inexpensive* $30 and lower.

ANALOMINK

Penn Hills. *Deluxe.* Routes 447 and 191. 4 mi. N. of Stroudsburg. Indoor pool and ice skating rink. Entertainment nightly. Cocktail lounge and night club. All sports and facilities. Honeymoon and couples-only resort.

BARTONSVILLE

Heritage Motel. *Inexpensive.* State 611, 5 mi. N. of Stroudsburg. Lawn games, picnic area and swimming pool recommend this small inn.

BUCK HILL FALLS

Buck Hill Falls Inn and Golf Club. *Deluxe.* One mi. NE of State 191, off State 390. This famous resort nestles in a famous setting. On its extensive grounds, sportsmen enjoy 27 holes of golf, tennis, riding, swimming, fishing in a nearby river and skiing in winter. The inn has its own lifts and snow-making equipment. Restaurant, room service, bar, movies, concerts and other entertainment during the summer.

BUSHKILL

Wayne Newton's Tamiment. *Deluxe.* Tamiment, between US 6-209 and State 402. Spacious grounds include: a 90-acre lake; ten tennis courts, lighted for night-time play; winter snow sport areas and a skating rink. Indoor sports facilities include a large pool, tennis courts, racquet ball courts and fully equipped spas for men and women. Excellent food and top-flight entertainment.

Fernwood. *Expensive.* US 209, 1½ mi. SW of town. Golf, tennis, private lakes, swimming pool, horses, entertainment, ski area with school and rentals, snowmobiling and gift shops. Restaurant and bar.

Pocmont. *Expensive.* West off US 209 in Bushkill. Suites with sunken tubs and king-size beds, indoor and outdoor pools, saunas. Sports program includes boating and horseback riding. A golf course is nearby. In winter, there's a ski slope. Restaurant and bar, dancing and entertainment.

CANADENSIS

The Overlook Inn. *Deluxe.* Dutch Hill Rd., 2 mi. off Rt. 447. The atmosphere is warm and friendly in this beautiful 19th-century country inn. Superb cuisine.

Laurel Grove Inn and Cottages. *Moderate.* Within easy walking distance of the village, this establishment has a 9-hole golf course and all-weather tennis facilities. Heated pool, rec room, live music.

Linder's Hillside Lodge. *Moderate.* State 390. 1 mi N. of town. One of the newest in the area, it's in an attractive woodland setting. Motels and cottages available. Tennis courts, golf nearby. Entertainment and dancing, coin laundry, rec room and a heated swimming pool.

Daniels Top-O-The Poconos Resort. *Inexpensive.* Spacious grounds, pool, lake with canoes, trout stream, tennis, Indoor swimming pool with sauna and hot tub.

CRESCO

Crescent Lodge. *Deluxe.* State 191 at State 940. Tennis, other indoor and outdoor games. Golf, riding and skiing nearby. New lounge and nightclub.

Pocono Gardens Lodge. *Deluxe.* Paradise Valley. Paying special attention to honeymooners, it has Roman baths, sunken tubs, log-burning fireplaces. There are an indoor pool, horseback riding, water sports and skiing. New lounge and nightclub.

Naomi Cottages. *Moderate.* State 390, 1 mi. N. of town. In a secluded area, this motel has tennis, shuffleboard and a rec room; early check-out time.

Lazy Rock Lodge. *Inexpensive.* Informal atmosphere. Motel and cozy, secluded cottages, with fireplaces, beneath tall pines. Pool, all activities.

DELAWARE WATER GAP

Glenwood Hotel & Resort Motel. *Moderate.* Social directors and children's counselors. Large pool, tennis, archery, boating, night club.

Howard Johnson's Motor Lodge. *Moderate.* Near exit 53 from I-80. Heated pool, cocktail lounge. Fishing, hunting, golf, skiing nearby.

Delaware Water Gap Motor Lodge. *Inexpensive.* Exit 53 of I-80. Located at entrance of Delaware Water Gap National Park. Motel rooms and housekeeping cottages. Swimming pool and wading pool for children.

EAST STROUDSBURG

Birchwood. *Super Deluxe.* A couple's resort with private, completely separate deluxe chalet suites with jacuzzi whirlpool baths, fireplaces and color TV. Tennis, 3 lakes, winter sports. This resort has its own airport.

Sky-Hi Lodge. *Moderate.* Lodges, cottages and motel-type accommodations. Swimming pool, private lake, social director. Golf nearby.

Sunset Hill Resort. *Moderate.* Informal, friendly atmosphere. Snack bar, teen-age room, pool, all sports.

Winona Falls Lodge. *Moderate.* Rt. 209, 1 mi. S. of Bushkill. Small, quiet resort with relaxing atmosphere. Swimming pool. Located in the waterfall area of the Pocono Mountains.

Paramount Motel. *Inexpensive.* US 209 Business. This in-town establishment is next door to a restaurant and provides a pool and some games. Good place to locate in the Poconos if your interest in the area is exploring rather than resort living.

GREENTOWN

White Beauty View Resort. *Expensive.* On Lake Wallenpaupack. Has 65 modern cottages, sandy beaches, all water sports, cocktail lounge, toboggan chute, orchestra. Skiing nearby. American-European plan. There is a 25 percent reduction before June 30 and after Sept. 4.

HAWLEY

Woodloch Pines. *Expensive.* An outstanding resort. Excellent food. 4-season sports. Entertainment.

Tanglewood Motor Lodge. *Inexpensive.* On Star Route 2. All rooms present a spectacular view of Lake Wallenpaupack. Swimming, boating, fishing, cocktail lounge.

MILFORD

Milford Motel. *Moderate.* ¼ mi. E. of town on Rts. 6 and 209. Heated pool, playground. Free coffee in your room. Lawn games.

Malibu Ranch. *Inexpensive.* A ranch vacation on 1,000 scenic acres. Unlimited horseback riding all year. Tennis, boating, indoor pool, rifle range, cocktail lounge and entertainment. Winter activities include skiing, snowmobiling and ice skating.

Moon Valley Park Housekeeping Cottages. *Inexpensive.* Cozy cottages along brooks in a country setting, ½ mile from town. Free access to "Storybookland Farm." Fishing, pool, waterfalls on premises.

MOUNT POCONO

Mount Airy Lodge. *Super Deluxe.* Near Scotrun exit from I–80. New sports palace with indoor tennis courts, indoor ice skating rink, indoor and outdoor heated pools, shows and dancing every night. Year-round sports facilities.

Paradise Stream. *Super Deluxe.* For couples only. Each accommodation has its own swimming pool and sauna and fireplace. Entertainment nightly, pool, tennis, miniature golf, skiing, snowmobiles, night club.

Strickland's Mountain Inn and Cottages. *Super Deluxe.* Honeymoon and couples-only resort. Award-winning skytop chalets and various suites. Three pools, free golf, tennis, summer and winter sports. Night club and cocktail lounge.

Hawthorne Inn and Cottages. *Deluxe.* W. of State 611, 1 mi. S. of town. Pool, tennis, playground, golf, riding, cellar bar. Open June 22 to Sept. 4.

Memorytown Homestead and Motor Lodge. *Moderate.* Between State 611 and 940. Cottages, motel, canopy beds, fireplaces, indoor and outdoor pools, summer and winter sports, farmhouse restaurant, tavern, saloon. Gift village. Restored pioneer homestead.

POCONO MANOR

Pocono Manor Inn. *Deluxe.* State 314, 2 mi. W. of town. Year-round 3,100-acre resort "atop the Poconos." 36-hole golf course, indoor pool, skiing (with snowmakers), skating rink, tennis, riding. Early American decor is charming. Dancing and entertainment.

SCOTRUN

Brookdale-On-The-Lake. *Super Deluxe.* NW of town, a mi. W. of State 611. Brick cottages with fireplaces, rooms in the lodge. A 12-acre lake with swimming, boating, fishing, sailing. Pitch-and-putt golf, tennis. Open Apr. to Nov.

Fern Rock Cottages. *Inexpensive.* Lakeview housekeeping cottages on 7 acres of beautiful woodland. Pool, 6-acre lake and brook for swimming, boating and fishing. Away from highway noise. Laundromat on premises.

SHAWNEE

Shawnee Inn. *Deluxe.* Off US 209, 3 mi. NW of Delaware Water Gap. Six tennis courts, 27 holes of golf, indoor and outdoor swimming, canoeing. Major new ski area featuring Jean-Claude Killy Ski School. Excellent European cuisine.

SKYTOP

Skytop Club. *Deluxe.* Off State 390. Golf, tennis, swimming pool, riding, fishing, artificial ice skating pond, rec room.

STROUDSBURG

Sheraton Pocono Inn. *Expensive.* 1220 W. Main St. Indoor courtyard with pool, sauna, gift shop, rec room, indoor putting green, coffee shop, restaurant, cocktail lounge.

Best Western Pocono Inn. *Moderate.* 700 Main St. 100 rooms. Restaurant, cocktail lounge, room service from the bar. Coffee shop.

Hillcrest Farms Resort. *Moderate.* Off Rt. 611 at Bartonsville. Family-oriented resort with day camp, wading pool and ponies for children. Tennis, all sports, indoor pool.

Bush's Golf Course and Cottages. *Inexpensive.* Furnished housekeeping cottages. Private 5-acre lake for swimming, boating and fishing. Nine-hole golf course, swimming pool and recreation hall.

SWIFTWATER

Swiftwater Inn. *Expensive.* State 611 at State 314. Built in 1778, this offers 18th-century charm with 20th-century comfort in 40 rooms. Heated outdoor pool, trout stream, wooded parklands and pathways.

Antlers Lodge and Cottages. *Moderate.* Off State 611, E. of town. A 34-acre resort with cottages decorated in Early American style. Pool, miniature golf, fishing, boating, tennis, winter sports.

Chestnut Grove Resort. *Moderate.* Family-type resort featuring 3 types of accommodations—from the deluxe main lodge to lakeside cottages. Pool, lake, tennis, cocktail lounge, entertainment.

Holiday Glen. *Moderate.* Small, informal resort with individual cottages and A-Frame chalets. Entertainment, ski areas, golf courses and night clubs only minutes away.

TANNERSVILLE

The Summit. *Super Deluxe.* At exit 45 from I–80. One of the newest resorts in the area, this has a honeymoon or couples-only policy. Every villa has its own enclosed sun deck, hexagonal bed, sunken bath and wood-burning fireplace. All sports, indoor and outdoor pools, sauna. Entertainment, dining room and cocktail lounge.

Hill Motor Lodge. *Moderate.* At exit 45 of I–80. Pool, restaurant, and cocktail lounge. Free golf to guests weekdays at nearby 18-hole golf course.

Penn's Wood Motel and Cottages. *Inexpensive.* Only 3 miles from Camelback ski area. Pool, 24-hour service.

WHITE HAVEN

Pocono Hershey Resort. *Deluxe.* At exit 42 of I–80. Indoor and outdoor Olympic-size pools, golf course, tennis and skeet shooting, horse and bike trails, cocktail lounge, nightly entertainment. Private balconies, sauna. Convention facilities up to 1,100.

Holiday Inn, Pocono-Lake Harmony. *Expensive.* ½ mi. E. of I–80 Exit 42 and Pennsylvania Turnpike Exit 35. Holidome Fun Area, putting green shuffleboard and sauna. Two excellent restaurants, cocktail lounge, live entertainment.

Lodge at Split Rock. *Expensive.* Four mi. from Pocono exit, NE extension of Pennsylvania Tpke. Fifty rooms in new lodge, 50 units in cottages on Lake Harmony. All seasonal sports. Skiing on grounds. Big Boulder Ski Area 1½ mi. away; Jack Frost Ski Area 4 mi. away. Family rates available. Cafe, bar. Rustic atmosphere.

 DINING OUT in the Poconos means one thing above all else—Pocono Mountain trout, the specialty of many restaurants in this area. In addition to trout, of course, are many other foods associated with Pennsylvania, including attempts at Pennsylvania Dutch cuisine, though the limitations here are not the same thing as the original dishes to be had around Lancaster. The vast, recent growth of hotels, motels and inns in the area has resulted in a similar proliferation of restaurants, and you can now get almost any kind of dish. US highways, such as 6 and 209 are dotted with truck stops and these are at their best around breakfast time.

Price categories for the region are: *Deluxe* $20 and higher, *Expensive* $15 and higher, *Moderate* $7.25–8.50 and *Inexpensive* $6.00 or lower. These prices include first course or soup, entree and dessert. Not included are drinks, tip and the Pennsylvania 6% food tax. For a more complete explanation of price categories, see *Facts at Your Fingertips* in the first chapter of this book.

BANGOR

Selecta. State 191. *Expensive.* The specialty is *rijstafel,* the traditional "rice table" of Indonesia. Open weekends only, by reservation.

BUSHKILL

Fernwood Gaslight Lounge Restaurant. *Moderate.* On US 209, 1½ mi. SW of town. Dinner, music, dancing and entertainment nightly.

CANADENSIS

Pump House Inn. *Super Deluxe.* State 390 at Skytop Rd. French provincial cuisine includes roast rack of lamb Persille. They have their own wine list and enjoy a good reputation in the area.

The Overlook Inn. *Expensive.* Dutch Hill Road, 2 mi. off Route 447. Gourmet dining in a 19th-century inn with superb service and an 18-entree menu. Reservations appreciated. Open all year.

Pine Knob Inn. *Moderate.* Charming country inn built before the Civil War. Tennis, pool and trout stream.

CRESCO

Crescent Lodge. *Deluxe.* Over 30 entrees to choose from. Junction of Rts. 191 and 940. Popular family dining spot.

Linders Hillside Lodge. *Moderate.* State 390, 1 mi. N. of town. Open at mealtimes only from Easter to Nov. 1. The restaurant is part of the resort and has the standard menu.

Triano's Italian-American Restaurant and Cocktail Lounge. *Inexpensive.* Homemade lasagna, manicotti, fettucini Alfredo, linguini with clam sauce, veal dishes, soups, appetizers, hoagies and subs.

EAST STROUDSBURG

Pepe's. *Deluxe.* Eagle Valley Mall junction of Business 209 and 477. A favorite with the locals, who like its Early American charm. Complete luncheon and dinner menus, cocktails from the carriage pub.

The Alternative. *Expensive.* Business Route 209. Gourmet Chinese and Polynesian cuisine, excellent steaks, seafood. Cocktail lounge, banquet facilities.

Albinos. *Inexpensive.* 228 Washington St. Italian, American and seafood. Cocktails from Yankee bar. Shrimp special served daily from 2 P.M.

GREENTOWN

White Beauty View Resort. *Deluxe.* State 507, Lake Wallenpaupack. Dining room open to public. Specializes in Italian and American Cooking. Spectacular, expansive view of the lake from dining rooms and cocktail bar.

MOUNTAINHOME

Diamond Jim's. *Expensive.* State 390. Reflects the splendor of the Gay Nineties, and serves lobster, lobster tails, prime sirloins and filet mignon. One block from Pocono Playhouse, with large parking area. Closed Tues. Reservations in summer.

Mountainhome's Own Country Inn. *Expensive.* Seafood, steaks and chops. Special smorgasbord for groups of 50 or more.

MOUNT BETHEL

Charlemagne. *Expensive.* Sunrise Blvd. Fireside dining in a medieval country setting. American and continental cuisine.

The Glenside-Pa. Dutch Restaurant. *Moderate.* Route 611. Hearty, good quality food. Family-style meals with homemade pies for dessert. Open for breakfast, lunch and dinner every day except Monday.

MOUNT POCONO

Johnnie's Pocono Summit Inn. *Expensive.* Two mi. W. of blinker light at Mt. Pocono. Italian cuisine, steaks, chops and seafood. Lobster tail is a house specialty.

Country Manor Inn/Country Breadboard. *Moderate.* State 611, ¼ mi. N. of Pocono Village Mall. Family restaurant and bakery in an Early American setting. Open for breakfast, lunch and dinner. Children's menu and senior citizen's discount.

Highland Inn. *Moderate.* State 611. Features home-cooked food. Rustic fire-side lounge, private dining room for groups. Opens at noon.

Tinker Hollow Ale House. *Moderate.* Mount Pocono Mall. Complete lunch-eon and dinner menus. Sandwiches served till 2 A.M. Cozy barnsiding and denim interior.

SCIOTA

Round Table Restaurant. *Expensive.* Rt. 209. Classical gourmet restaurant. Private dining room available.

STROUDSBURG

Sheraton Pocono Inn. *Deluxe.* At exit 48 of I–80. Elegant atmosphere. Authentic ship's bar. Fine service and cuisine in Three Fathoms Restaurant. Enjoy a refreshing tropical drink at Gazebo Bar in enclosed garden next to indoor pool. Banquet facilities to 225.

Beaver House. *Moderate.* 1001 N. 9th St. (State 611, 1 mi. N. of town). Six dining rooms. Maine lobsters, shore dinners, steaks. Cocktails. Open at meal-times only.

House of Ming. *Moderate.* State 611, 1 mi. S. of town. Tasty Chinese and American food, specializing in Cantonese food. Saturday night special is prime ribs of beef.

Historic Henryville House. *Inexpensive.* State 191 at 715, 6 mi. N. of town. Authentically restored Victorian inn. Museum rooms open to public. All food and pastries prepared on the premises.

SWIFTWATER

Fannucci's. *Expensive.* Rt. 611. Italian-American Cuisine. Superb cocktail service. Open seven days a week.

Hickory Valley Farm Stores and Restaurants. *Inexpensive.* On State 611. Smoked turkey, ham, bacon and similar foods. Treat yourself to ham and eggs served in the pan.

TANNERSVILLE

Smuggler Cove-Restaurant and Lounge. *Deluxe.* Rt. 611. Just 10 minutes from Camelback Ski Area. Seafood and steaks, salad bar. Rustic decor, copper bar.

Hill Motor Lodge and Train Coach Restaurant. *Moderate.* At exit 45 off Rt. 80. Authentic railroad dining cars and cocktail lounge. Open seven days a week.

The Inn at Tannersville. *Inexpensive.* Exit 45 off I–80. Char-broiled steaks, chops and seafood. Dinner served till 1 A.M. daily, 11 P.M. Sunday. Outdoor beer garden, open air market.

LANCASTER COUNTY

Pennsylvania Dutch Country

Lancaster County—heart of the Pennsylvania Dutch Country—boasts about being "200 years ago," yet it is only 90 minutes from Philadelphia (via the Pennsylvania Turnpike, west to Exit 21, then Route 222 to Route 30). It is here that you will find the "Plain People," the Old Order Amish who still use horse-drawn buggies and dress as their families have dressed for centuries and who refuse to use electricity or telephones.

Lancaster County is also the home of more liberal religious sects who wear somewhat more modern clothing and drive black, chrome-less cars.

These people are descendents of the fundamentalist groups who accepted William Penn's invitation to join his "Holy Experiment" by emigrating from religious persecution in Europe to settle in Pennsylvania. The Mennonites came in 1683 and the Amish followed in 1727.

Today the Old Order Amish, or "House Amish" (so-called because they worship in each other's homes) and the more liberal "Church Amish," live in Lancaster County along with the New and Old Order Mennonites. You will be able to distinguish between members of the two groups: The Amish drive gray buggies with slightly rounded roofs; the buggies of the Old Order Mennonites are painted black and have flat roofs. Also, the Mennonite women wear small, white net prayer caps at the backs of their heads, while the Amish women wear large, black bonnets.

(*Important:* Some members of these Old Orders do not believe in having their pictures taken. They consider photographs to be "graven images" forbidden by the Bible. So always ask permission of your subject before taking out your camera.)

While in Lancaster County plan to sample the food of the Pennsylvania Dutch (really Pennsylvania "Deutsch," meaning German). There are the traditional chicken-and-corn soup, shoofly pie, scrapple, schnitz and funnel cakes.

You can ride in an Amish buggy and on a steam railroad (perhaps in the very coach you saw in the movie "Hello Dolly"). You can visit farmers' markets, replicas of Amish homes and farms, go to the oldest pretzel bakery in the country to twist your own pretzel and, finally, tour an 18th-century monastery.

The recommended first stop is at the **Pennsylvania Dutch Visitors Information Center,** 1799 Hempstead Rd., just off the Rt. 30 bypass, east of Lancaster City. Here you can see a 36-minute film about the area, the people and their customs. Also pick up a map of Lancaster County and, if you wish, inquire about the tape-recorded tour guides available for in-car use.

The city of **Lancaster** (west on Rt. 340) is claimed to be the oldest inland city in the United States. It was founded in 1718 and served as the country's capital for a single day when the Continental Congress met here on September 27, 1777 as it was fleeing the British in Philadelphia. This was the home of Robert Fulton, inventor of the first, commercially successful steamboat, and of James Buchanan, only U.S. President born in Pennsylvania. It was in this area that the "Kentucky" rifle and the Conestoga wagon were developed.

Ninety-minute walking tours of this attractive city—with its attractive streets and crooked alleys—can be arranged at 15 West King St. (Tours scheduled Monday through Saturday, 10 A.M. and 1:30 P.M.; on Sunday at 1:30 P.M. only. Not available January through March.)

Lancaster's 246-year-old **Central Market** on Penn Square should not be missed. (Open Tuesday and Friday.) Visitors can sample Lebanon bologna, scrapple and smierkase. The latter is a gamey but tasty local cheese, rather like cottage cheese. Other markets are the **Southern,** 106 S. Queen St. (open Saturday except holidays) and **Meadowbrook** on Rt. 23, one-half mile west of Leola (open Friday and Saturday). The **Fulton Opera House,** 12 N. Prince St., was built in 1852 and is claimed to be one of the oldest in inland America. Sarah Bernhardt, John and Ethel Barrymore played here. Tours available.

Before leaving Lancaster City, take a short (1½ mile) ride west on Rt. 23 to **Wheatland.** Built in 1828, this was the home of President James Buchanan. Tour guides in period costumes will lead you through this restored house, decorated and furnished in pre-Civil War style. (Open daily, including Sunday, April 1 to November 30, 10 A.M. to 4:30 P.M.) You can also take a side trip (four miles south of Penn Square in Lancaster City) to see **Rock Ford,** a 1793 plantation and home of General Edward Hand, Revolutionary War commander and member of the Continental Congress. In this authentically furnished home, visitors can see and touch the original structural elements that were seen and touched by General George Washington when he visited his fellow officer here. On the site of the original barn at Rock Ford Plantation is the **Rock Ford-Kaufmann Museum,** filled with folk artifacts from the mid-18th to the mid-19th centuries. See early Pennsylvania pewter and copper ware; carved wood; plain and decorated tin ware; examples of "fraktur"—the colorfully ornamented birth and marriage certificates of the Pennsylvania Dutch; and a representative collection of furnishings. (Open April through November, Tuesday through Saturday, 10 A.M. to 4 P.M.; Sunday, noon to 4 P.M. Special evening candlelight tours are conducted periodically and on request from tour groups.)

Now you can begin an eastward loop to discover dozens of historic and recreational sites.

Leave the City of Lancaster on Rt. 340 east to Mt. Sidney Rd. then turn left to the **Folk Craft Museum** where you can visit a 1762 "log haus," a restored 1831 country store and a display of Pennsylvania Dutch antiques. Back to Rt. 340, jog right and then left to continue south on Witmer Rd. At Rt. 30 you will be at the **Amish Farm and House,** replica of a typical Old Order Amish farm that is actually in operation. A hostess-lecturer will lead your tour and answer your questions. (Summer: Daily, 8:30 A.M. to 8 P.M.; Spring and fall: 8:30 A.M. to 5 P.M.; Winter: weekends only, 8:30 A.M. to 4 P.M.) Allow at least an hour and a half to tour the house and farm.

Just west, on Rt. 30., is the **Amish Homestead.** This is not a replica but a 200-year-old-home, occupied by an Amish family. Guided tours of the house and 71-acre farm are available seven days a week.

 Dutch Wonderland, a 44-acre theme park filled with rides, amusements, shops and places to eat, is on Rt. 30 between Amish Homestead and Amish Farm. Also on the Road is the **National Wax Museum,** featuring historical figures and events.

Back on Rt. 30, head southwest to Kinzer and the **Rough and Tumble Engineers' Historical Association.** Here you will find home, farm and industrial tools and machinery of bygone days. (Open Monday through Saturday, 10 A.M. to 5 P.M. from April through October; Saturdays only the remainder of the year.)

Heading west for a short distance, take Wolfrock Rd. south to Rt. 741. Then turn right and look for two attractions: The **Railroad Museum of Pennsylvania** and the **Strasburg Steam Railroad.** (Turn right off Rt. 30 onto Paradise Lane for the **Toy Train Museum.**)

The Railroad Museum of Pennsylvania features locomotives and passenger cars dating from 1875, audio-visual exhibits and artifacts. (May through October, daily 10 A.M. to 4:30 P.M., November through April, 10 A.M. to 4 P.M.) The Toy Train Museum exhibits examples of many manufacturers dating from the 1880s to the present and three large layouts. (Open daily, 10 A.M. to 5 P.M., May through October; also some weekends and holidays in the winter.) The Strasburg Steam Railroad provides a 45-minute, nine-mile round trip to Paradise (Pennsylvania) in late 19th-century coaches pulled by various antique locomotives.

As you continue west on Rt. 741, you will see the **Eagle Museum** with its "Kentucky" rifles (actually a misnomer because the rifles were developed in Lancaster, Pennsylvania, and should have been called "Pennsylvania rifles!"). Also see the museum's collection of early china, pewter, toys and weapons. (Open seven days a week, April-October.)

Your next stop is the **Hans Herr House** (Rt. 741 west to fork; take Rt. 222 to Hans Herr Drive). Built in 1719, this is an outstanding example of medieval Germanic architecture. There are guided tours of this authentically restored house, grounds and museum of farm implements and tools. (April through October, 9 A.M. to 4 P.M.; November through March, 10 A.M. to 3 P.M.)

Farther south on Rt. 222, near the Maryland border, is the **birthplace of Robert Fulton,** who was an artist and the inventor of the first commercially successful steamboat. Fulton's miniature portraits are reputed to be among the finest produced in this country. His family moved to the city of Lancaster about 1766, a year after he was born. In 1965 the Commonwealth of Pennsylvania acquired Fulton's birthplace to restore and refurnish it. Today it represents a home of Fulton's lifetime. One area of the house contains exhibits depicting the inventor-artist's life and accomplishments. (Open Memorial Day through Labor Day, Saturday only, 11 A.M. to 4 P.M., Sunday, 1 P.M. to 5 P.M.)

The area around Lancaster City has a **100-year-old brewery,** several **wineries** and **America's oldest operating distillery.** The Pennsylvania Dutch Visitors Information Bureau can provide a map and directions for reaching each one. Also in Lancaster County is the **Phillips Lancaster County Swiss Cheese Company** in Gordonville (via Rt. 772), where tours show how Swiss cheese is still being made in 300-gallon copper kettles—exactly as it was made years ago.

While visiting the wineries in the northwest corner of the county, plan to stop at **Donegal Mills Plantation** (Rt. 141 to Musser Rd., then left on Trout Run Rd.) Guided tours of the old mansion, a miller's house, bake kitchen and mill. (Easter through Columbus Day, Tuesday-Saturday, 10 A.M. to 4:30 P.M.; Sunday, 1–5 P.M. Open Columbus Day through Easter, Tuesday-Thursday, 11 A.M. to 2 P.M.; Friday and Saturday, 11 A.M. to 2 P.M. and 6 P.M. to 9 P.M.; Sunday 12:30 P.M. to 3:30 P.M.

On Rts. 501 and 772 in Lititz, Pa., you will discover the **Julius Sturgis Pretzel House,** billed as "America's oldest commercial pretzel bakery." Founded in 1861, it has been restored as a museum. See the pretzel-making demonstrations and try your hand at pretzel-twisting. "Diplomas" are awarded to the best twisters! (Open Monday through Saturday, 9 A.M. to 5 P.M.) Return on Rt. 772 to Rt. 501. This will take you south to Valley Road in Neffsville. Turn left for Landis Valley and the **Pennsylvania Farm Museum.** Here you can learn about the history of rural Pennsylvania through exhibits (some 250,000 items have been assembled) and demonstrations. Begin at the Orientation Building, then visit a re-created tavern, a gun shop, barn, blacksmith shop and a group of mid-19th-century buildings that includes a restored schoolhouse, a country store and a farm house. (Open Tuesday-Saturday, 9 A.M. to 5 P.M.; Sunday, noon to 5 P.M.)

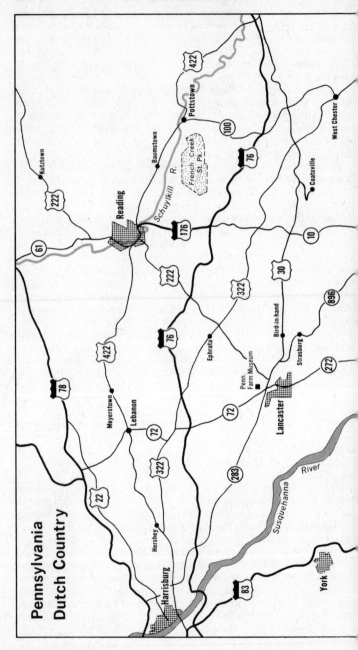

Pennsylvania Dutch Country

On Rt. 272 head northwest to **Ephrata Cloister,** a German monastic settlement of the Seventh Day Baptists. It was founded in 1732 by Conrad Beissel who, with a group of followers, sought to serve God in medieval fashion through lives of austere self-denial and pious simplicity. The original log and stone buildings have been extensively restored and include the chapel, the Sisters' House, a bake house and Beissel's log house. Begin with an orientation film that explains how the Sisters slept on boards with wooden blocks for pillows and how the low doorways taught humility. Note that after the Battle of Brandywine this religious commune became a military hospital for the patriotic forces. The Cloister is open weekdays, except Monday, 9 A.M. to 5 P.M.; Sunday, noon to 5 P.M.

On Saturdays and some Sundays during the summer months, Ephrata Cloister is the setting for a musical drama depicting life as it was in the community of Beissel's followers during the late 18th century.

PRACTICAL INFORMATION FOR LANCASTER COUNTY

HOW TO GET THERE. By Car: From the Pennsylvania Turnpike, Exits 20, 21 or 22. Then head towards Lancaster City. From Harrisburg, Rt. 283. From Baltimore, Rt. 272.

TOURIST INFORMATION. *Pennsylvania Dutch Visitors Information Bureau,* 1799 Hempstead Road, Lancaster, Pa. 17601. *Mennonite Information Center,* 2209 Mill Stream Rd., Lancaster, Pa. 17604.

SIGHTSEEING TOURS. *Conestoga Tours,* 825 E. Chestnut St., Lancaster, Pa., 17602. *Dutchland Tours,* Box 265, Bird-in-Hand, Pa., 17505. *Brunswick Tours,* 2034 Lincoln Highway East, Lancaster, Pa., 17602.

 INDUSTRIAL TOURS. Anderson Bakeries, Rt. 340, Lancaster: Tour a commercial pretzel bakery and retail store. **Lancaster County Winery,** Rawlinsville Rd., Willow Street. Tour the vineyards, wine processing rooms and cellars. **Woodstream Corp,** 69 N. Locust St., Lititz. A sporting-goods and pest-control equipment plant. Group reservations, required. **Nissley Vineyards,** Bainbridge. Wine-tasting follows winery tour. Groups of 15 or more adults should call in advance. In Nottingham, visit **Herr's Potato Chips,** where potato chips and pretzels are made. **Susquehanna Glass Co.,** 731 Avenue H, Columbia. See a glass cutter at work in factory store. **Weaver Poultry,** 403 S. Custer Ave., New Holland. Tour of fried chicken production center plus a multimedia presentation. Group reservations requested.

 SHOPPING. Throughout the Lancaster County area you will find *factory outlets* specializing in *shoes, apparel, accessories* and *glassware.* A brochure, available at the Pennsylvania Dutch Visitors Bureau, lists each one with directions for getting there.

 HOTELS AND MOTELS in Lancaster County offer many types of accommodations. Pennsylvania Dutch cooking is a specialty of the area. There are also farms offering a unique vacation experience through living and working on a farm and experiencing the special pleasures of these hospitable people. The categories in this section may change due to increases in prices, but for this guide's purposes the following rates apply, for double occupancy: *Super Deluxe* over $70, *Deluxe* $60 average, *Expensive* $50 average, *Moderate* $35 average and *Inexpensive* $30 and lower.

LANCASTER

Host Farm and Corral. *Super Deluxe.* 2300 Lincoln Highway (US 30). This resort has four pools (two Olympic size), 27-hole golf course, tennis courts and tennis pro, horseback riding and instruction and many winter sports as well. Food and bar. There are saunas, health clubs and top-name entertainers.

Holiday Inn (East) *Deluxe.* Hempstead Rd. & Rt. 30. Restaurant, pool. Pets permitted.

Brunswick Motor Inn. *Expensive.* N. Queen St. and E. Chestnut St. Located right in the heart of the city. Free garage, indoor pool, free coffee in rooms, entertainment and dancing except Sunday.

Cherry Lane Motor Inn. *Expensive.* 84 N. Ronks Rd., 6 mi. E. of town. There's a heated pool and recreational facilities. A cafe that closes at 9:30 P.M. is half a mile away.

Howard Johnson's. *Expensive.* In Denver, on US 222 near exit 21 from Pennsylvania Turnpike. Coin laundry; some waterbeds.

Sheraton-Lancaster Resort. *Expensive.* Rt. 272 North Oregon Pike. Restaurant, indoor and outdoor pool. Pets permitted.

Treadway Resort Inn. *Expensive.* 222 Eden Rd., just N. of crossroads between U.S. 30 and 222. Pool, sauna, health club, children's program. Also rec room, movies, wading pool.

Harvest Drive Farm Motel. *Moderate.* Clearview Rd. & Harvest Dr. R. D. 1, Gordonville. Motel on a working farm. Restaurant.

Manheim Motel. *Inexpensive.* 670 Lancaster Road.

 DINING OUT in Pennsylvania Dutch territory means enjoying many regional dishes, prepared carefully and with tender loving attention. Many restaurants offer "family style" dining, with long tables accommodating as many as fifteen diners. You can choose from a six- or seven-course meal, including such specialties as wiener schnitzel, pork and sauerkraut, marvelous pastries. And you can even go for a carriage ride after dinner. For mid-priced dinners on each menu (sometimes, family-style, menus are not even necessary), the following categories apply: *Deluxe* $20 and higher, *Expensive* $15 and higher, *Moderate* $7.25–8.50 and *Inexpensive* $6.00 and under. These costs include hors d'oeuvres or soup, entree and dessert. They do not include drinks, tax or tip.

ADAMSTOWN. Ed Stroudt's Black Angus Steak House. *Deluxe.* Rt. 272. Steak and prime ribs are the specialty.

BIRD-IN-HAND. Plain and Fancy Farm. *Expensive.* Family style, Pennsylvania Dutch menu.

Amish Barn. *Moderate.* Family style, Pennsylvania Dutch food.

Bird-in-Hand Restaurant. *Inexpensive.* Home cooking.

BROWNSTOWN. Brownstown Restaurant. *Inexpensive.* Home cooking.

DENVER. Zinn's Country Diner. *Inexpensive.* Pennsylvania Dutch food.

EAST PETERSBURG. Haydn Zug's. *Deluxe.* 1987 State St. Gourmet dining.

EPHRATA. Family Time Restaurant. *Moderate.* Rt. 322. Smorgasbord and menu dining.

GORDONVILLE. Harvest Drive Farm Restaurant. *Inexpensive.* Rt. 1. Family style, Pennsylvania Dutch.

INTERCOURSE. Stoltzfus Farm Restaurant. *Expensive.* Family style, Pennsylvania Dutch.

Deitsch-Shier Restaurant. *Moderate to inexpensive.* Rt. 772. Pennsylvania Dutch food.

LANCASTER. Lemon Tree. *Deluxe.* 1766 Columbia Ave. Gourmet dining.

Bernhardt's. *Expensive.* At Brunswick Motor Inn, Chestnut and Queen Sts.

Copper Kettle. *Expensive.* At Brunswick Motor Inn, Chestnut and Queen Sts.

Glass Kitchen at the Willows. *Expensive.* 2425 Lincoln Hwy. East. Pennsylvania Dutch food.

Willow Valley Farms. *Inexpensive.* 2397 Willow St. Pike. Pennsylvania Dutch menu and smorgasbord.

MT. JOY. Groff's Farm. *Expensive.* Intimate, family-style dining.

RONKS. Miller's Smorgasbord. *Expensive.* Smorgasbord, Pennsylvania Dutch.

SMOKETOWN. Good 'n Plenty. *Moderate.* Family style, Pennsylvania Dutch.

STRASBURG. Washington House. *Moderate.* At Historic Strasburg Inn. Pennsylvania Dutch fare and smorgasbord.

Hershey Farm Restaurant. *Inexpensive.*

GETTYSBURG

A Living Battlefield

Gettysburg National Park is undoubtedly the most famous Civil War monument in the state, perhaps in the nation. It was here, on July 3, 1863, that the greatest artillery battle ever held on this continent was fought.

The Battle of Gettysburg began on July 1, 1863. General Robert E. Lee had marched his army up the Valley of the Shenandoah, across the Potomac, through Maryland and into Pennsylvania. His hope was to take Harrisburg and then Philadelphia, but he and his host were met at Gettysburg by the Union army under General George C. Meade. For three days the relentless fighting went on and when the last shot had been fired, one man out of every four of the 159,000 who took part in the engagement had been killed or wounded or was missing. The Union army had taken the worst the Confederates could inflict on them—and the Blue line held. Lee was forced to retreat; his hopes for victory now were dashed; the tide had turned.

Within a few weeks of the battle, it was decided to make a cemetery on seventeen acres of the battlefield, bought by the State of Pennsylvania for that purpose. Today, the *Gettysburg National Military Park* covers more than sixteen thousand acres. On November 19, 1863, at dedication ceremonies, President Lincoln spoke a few words that became immortal and known around the world as the *Gettysburg Address.*

Practically all of Gettysburg is a museum. There are regular guided bus tours of the battlefield that leave the terminal near US 15 and US 140. At the Visitors' Center, designed by Philip Neutra, a cyclorama portrays Confederate General Goerge Pickett's charge up Cemetery Ridge. After hours of furious gunfire, the Union guns had become silent and the Confederates assumed that they were out of ammunition. Not so. A barrage of artillery and musket fire ripped apart the advancing line of men in gray; the attackers were forced to retreat, with heavy casualties.

A new feature of the Gettysburg experience began in 1980 with the opening to the public of the **Eisenhower Farm.** The home depicts their lives in Gettysburg from 1955 to 1969. Visitors to the country estate find a modified Georgian home with 15 rooms preserved and protected by the interpretive staff of the U.S. National Park Service. Every effort is made to provide an unhurried, enjoyable experience while maintaining the dignity of the Eisenhower home.

This is the only home the Eisenhowers owned in their 52 years of married life. The Eisenhowers lived in 37 places in 35 years, but this is the place they called home. Mamie once said, "I long to unpack my furniture some place and stay forever."

The Park Service has refrained from overdeveloping the site, and is keeping the home just as it was during the time it was occupied by President and Mrs. Eisenhower.

After entering the house through the front door, visitors are directed to the living room at the north end of the house. Next, they see the glass-enclosed porch—Eisenhower's favorite room. Before heading upstairs, they view the formal dining room. The wallpaper in the upstairs hallway bears the insignia of each state. Many of Eisenhower's paintings hang here. Visitors also see the guest rooms and the maid's room. Returning downstairs, as they pass through the den, the exposed beams, salvaged from an original log structure on the farm, can be seen. The tour ends with a visit to Eisenhower's office, more often used for farm business than for matters of state.

From June till October on weekends you can ride the Gettysburg Steam Railroad (tel. 334–6932). Another family attraction is the Miniature Horse Farm, 5 miles west of Gettysburg off Route 30 (tel. 334–7259).

An interesting side trip begins on US 30, which goes to York, the capital of the American colonies from September 1777, to June 1778. At the **Codorus furnace,** built in 1765, weapons were forged for General Washington. The pamphleteer Thomas Paine lived briefly in 1778 at 438–40 Codorus Street. The house is now a private residence. While in York, visit **Lauck's Farm and Craft Museum,** with exhibits of Early tools, and the **Historical Society of York County,** which has fine displays of Early American life. Particularly interesting is the restoration of the York village square as it looked in 1776, including a taproom and apothecary shop.

Leaving York, take I–83 to **Harrisburg, the state capital.** When the legislature is in session, this is, of course, a bustling city, but there are always—even at that time of year—pleasant, quiet walks that may be taken along the banks of the Susquehanna River, or through the lovely rose gardens and the formal Italian garden. The Italian Renaissance **capital building** is considered by many to be the finest in the nation. It was completed in 1906; the dome rises to a height of 272 feet and was modeled after St. Peter's in Rome. Its marble staircase was inspired by the Paris Opera House. One also should stop at the new cylindrical **William Penn Memorial Museum,** which has exhibits of natural history, an art gallery and a planetarium. Next to it is the **Archives Tower,** with records dating back as far as 1681. The home of the city's founder, John Harris, is at 219 South Front Street and contains various documents of local history.

Another interesting trip might be made to **Carlisle,** a city rich in Colonial lore, located about fourteen miles west of the state capital of Harrisburg via US 11. This attractive, 250-year-old town was the locale of a number of significant historic events when America was young. Even today, Carlisle reflects this era of gracious 18th-century living in its lovely gardens and row upon row of authentic Colonial homes, beautiful Georgian doorways and village squares. It is also the home of a college which bears the name of its founder, John Dickinson, one of three Carlisle men who signed the Declaration of Independence. The others were James Wilson and George Rose. The town was established as an Indian trading post in 1720. In July 1775, Col. William Thompson led the first regiment of riflemen to join Washington's army in Boston. In 1776, **Carlisle Barracks,** America's second oldest military post still in existence, was established. Today, it houses the Army War College belonging to the U. S. Government and has been used in various capacities since 1757. See the Cavalry station used in the Civil War and barracks that were abandoned, then taken over by Capt. Richard Pratt. The **Hamilton Library** at 21 N. Pitt St. contains early newspapers, historical documents and souvenirs of early days. Historical lectures are presented on the third Thursday of winter months at 7:30 P.M.

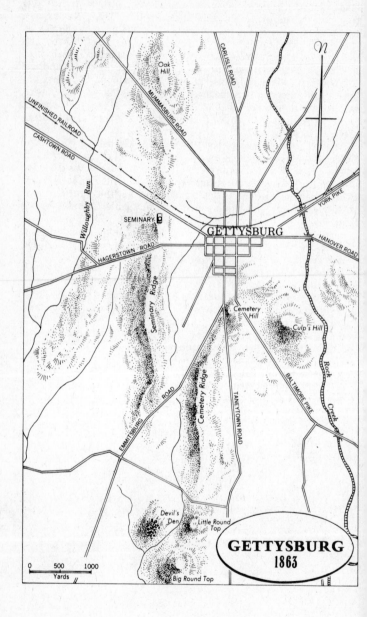

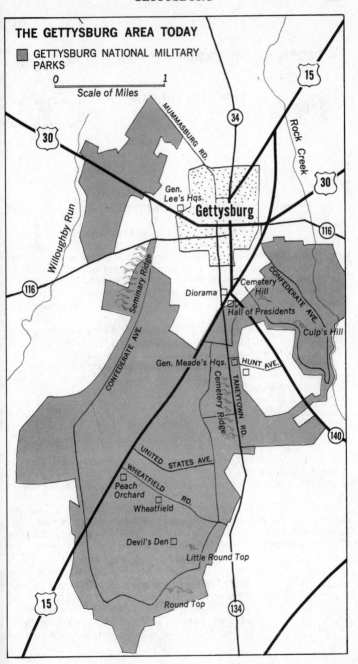

THE GETTYSBURG AREA TODAY

GETTYSBURG NATIONAL MILITARY PARKS

0   1
Scale of Miles

PRACTICAL INFORMATION FOR GETTYSBURG

HOW TO GET THERE. By bus: *Greyhound* and *Trailways* have direct service to Gettysburg.

By air: Most major airlines fly to Harrisburg, Baltimore and Washington, the airports closest to Gettysburg.

By car: From the *Pennsylvania Turnpike,* take US 15 south for 28 miles. US 30 crosses Gettysburg in an east-west direction.

TOURIST INFORMATION. The Information Center of the Gettysburg Travel Council is located in the *Historic Western Maryland Railway Station.* It was built in 1858 to serve as Gettysburg's railroad terminal. Although extensive renovations were made to the interior, the exterior of the building remains much the same as it did when President Lincoln visited Gettysburg in 1863. Friendly hostesses provide visitors with free information and literature on all attractions, restaurants and lodging facilities in and around Gettysburg. The address is: Gettysburg Travel Council, 35 Carlisle St. Gettysburg, Pa. 17325. 334–6274

TOURS. For a free walking tour of historic downtown Gettysburg or a 36-mile driving tour of scenic Adams County, stop at the Gettysburg Travel Council Information Center for maps and further information.

Gettysburg Bus Tour Center. Hollywood actors have recorded "The Battle of Gettysburg" which accompanies the 35-mile, 2-hour tour in an air-conditioned bus. Main terminal on Baltimore St. 717–334–6296.

Association of Gettysburg Battlefield Guides. You can take a guide in your own car for an informative, pleasant tour. Licensed guides at Lincoln Square, 1½ mi. W. on Rt. 30 and at Park Service Visitor Center. 717–334–9876 or 334–1124.

CC Inc. Auto Tape Tours. Hear historic 3-day battle vividly re-created in your own car. Rent player and tape at *National Civil War Wax Museum.* Bus. Rt. 15 south. 717–334–6245.

Helicopter Tours. Unobstructed, spectacular views of the battlefield. 3 mi. S. on Bus. Rt. 15.

Eisenhower National Historic Site. Tours of President Eisenhower's Gettysburg farm and home. Limited visitation on a first-come, first-served basis. Free tickets distributed at 8:A.M. at the National Park Visitor Center. Tour duration 90 minutes. Modest fee for shuttle bus service to the farm.

NATIONAL PARKS. Gettysburg National Military Park surrounds the town of Gettysburg at the junction of US 30 and 15 and 140 about 7 miles north of the Maryland border. It comprises the battlefield on which, on July 1, 2 and 3 of 1863 was fought—one of the bloodiest and most decisive battles of the Civil War. Here, too, is the spot on which President Abraham Lincoln delivered his most famous speech, the *Gettyburg Address,* on November 19, 1863. The park covers 25 square miles and has almost 30 miles of roads through the fighting area. Monuments, markers, tablets of granite and bronze and 400 cannon in battle positions are located on the field. Battlefield guides, licensed by the National Park Service, conduct 2-hour tours to all the points of interest, describing the troop movements and highlights of the battle. Tours are also available in air-conditioned sightseeing buses that supply the sounds of battle and a dramatized description in stereophonic sound. A helicopter service is also available which gives the tourist a superior view of the battlefield. Tours are also available at the *Gettysburg Wax Museum.* A **Park Visitors Center,** located on US 15 and State 134, features many instructive exhibits and dioramas in a large museum, as well as a 356-foot cyclorama painting of *Pickett's Charge.* The center is open 8–5 P.M. daily and is free, but adults pay 50¢ admission to the cyclorama. During June, July and August there is a free *Campfire Program* in the amphitheater in *Pitzer's Woods.* It is held nightly at dusk, weather permitting, and features a brief talk on the Civil War soldier and a 45-minute MGM film, *The Battle of Gettysburg.* Boy Scouts of America offer a special Gettysburg Merit Badge patch for scouts completing a ten-mile historical hike.

  MUSEUMS AND GALLERIES. In Gettysburg, site of the largest battlefield shrine in America, you may tour the Gettysburg National Military Park, six miles by seven miles, and also visit countless museums unlike any in the world. There are some privately owned museums, for which there is an admission charge. Begin your tour at the Visitor Center. See the electric map-orientation program; a *Cyclorama Center* features sound-and-light program of Pickett's charge. The *Gettysburg Battlefield Tower* has a dramatic sound program in a sky capsule. The *National Civil War Wax Museum,* Bus. Rt. 15 S. has an audio-visual presentation of the entire Civil War. The *Hall of Presidents,* at the main gate of the *National Cemetery* on US 140, has life-size figures in wax of all the presidents. *General Lee's Headquarters,* Rt. 30 W, 7 blks., houses a collection of Civil War relics. The *Lincoln Train Museum* offers a "ride" with Lincoln in sound, sight and motion. The *Lincoln Room* downtown on Lincoln Square, records the "Spirit of Lincoln" where he wrote his Gettysburg Address. The *Gettysburg Battle Theatre* presents a film and diorama, "America at Gettysburg," and the *Jennie Wade House* pays tribute to the only citizen killed during the battle, with a tape of the poignant story.

 STAGE. The *A. Lincoln Place Theater* is a unique one-man live theater performance portraying the life and times of President Abraham Lincoln. James A. Getty, who bears a striking resemblance to Lincoln, is the operator of the daily live theater program. The 35-minute program covers the life of Lincoln—his childhood days in Kentucky, his early political life in Illinois, the Lincoln-Douglas debates and his role as America's Civil War President. The theater has been nominated for the Travel Industry Excellence Award.

SHOPPING. The *House of Bender,* on Lincoln Square, has a large line of **gifts, souvenirs, greeting cards** and a free display of Civil War firearms. *Codori's Toy Store and Bavarian Gift Shop,* on 19 Barlow St. off N. Stratton St., has German **handmade nutcrackers, dolls, antique toys, Hummels, ornaments** and **Swedish gifts.** *Mr. Ed's,* on Rt. 30, 8 mi. W. of Gettysburg, has nine rooms to browse. **Candy shop,** restaurant, Indian Trading Post, **souvenirs** and **gifts.**

WHAT TO DO WITH THE CHILDREN. When the children tire of playing the passive role of observers, they will enjoy: *Allen's Kartway,* where they can ride in buddy-seat karts (small children ride with parents) around a ½ mile paved course. On Rt. 94, Carlisle Pk. Hanover, 2 mi. S. of Rt. 30. Hours: 1–10 P.M. Tues, thru Sun. 10 A.M. to 10 P.M. Sat. Closed Mondays. *Gettysburg Miniature Horse Farm.* Some of the smallest horses in the world are on display and in training. Indoor arena, rides, snack bar and picnic area. On Rt. 30 W. off Knoxlyn Rd. In *Gettysburg Game Park,* children can roam among the tame deer, llamas and sheep and observe monkeys, bears, lions and tigers. On Rt. 116, Fairfield, *Ski Liberty Alpine Slide* has, in addition to the thrilling slide, a restaurant, swimming pool and grass skiing.

SEASONAL EVENTS. May is the month when the *Blue Grass Festival* is held. This three-day event features stars of the Grand Ole Opry and several regional bands. There are contests and prizes for visitors. Also held in May are the *Apple Blossom Festival, Square Dance Round-Up* and *Memorial Day Parade,* followed by services in the Gettysburg National Cemetery. **June:** The *Gettysburg Horse Show,* at the South Mountain Fairgrounds, 10 mi. NW of Gettysburg on Rt. 234. *New Oxford Outdoor Antique Show,* 10 mi. E. of Gettysburg on Rt. 30, featuring arts, crafts, antiques and entertainment. *Authentic Civil War Encampment,* a free two-day event that features musket and cannon firing, camp tours, calvary drill and a camp visit by "President Lincoln," who reviews the federal troops. You will see troops on guard duty, washing clothes, cooking and drilling, while the doctor examines those reporting for sick call. There are also a court martial of a camp offender and off-duty activities. All the soldiers will be pleased to answer questions, show pieces of equipment and pose for photographs. In addition, a concert played with original Civil War instruments, is performed. **July:** Anniversary of the Battle of Gettysburg, The *Fireman's Festival.* Activities include a parade, all-day flea market and a fireworks display. *Civil War Relic and Collectors Show,* featuring a display of American Civil War relics at the Sheraton Inn, 5 mi. S. of Gettysburg on Bus. Rt. 15; free lectures from leading experts in the field of collecting. **August:** *Littlestown Good Old Days Celebration,* a flea market with music and entertainment. On Rt. 97 at Littlestown. **September:** *South Mountain Fair,* an extensive display of agricultural exhibits plus live entertainment held at the South Mountain Fairgrounds, 10 mi. NW of Gettysburg on Rt. 234. *Historic Gettysburg Marathon.* Events include a 26-mile, 385-yard marathon and a fun-run of approximately 3 miles. Entry forms can be obtained by writing to Gettysburg Area Chamber of Commerce, Gettysburg 17325. *Gettysburg Outdoor Antique Show,* held in downtown streets of historic Gettysburg and featuring approximately 180 antique dealers and their displays. **October:** *Apple Harvest Festival.* The highlight of this event is the crowning of Miss Apple Queen USA. Other attractions include apple butter boiling, an old cider press, ox roast, chicken barbecue, free steam engine rides, shingle mill, bus tours of the orchards, arts and crafts displays and many apple desserts. **November:** *Anniversary of Lincoln's Gettysburg Address.* This annual celebration is a brief memorial service in the Gettysburg National Cemetery.

CAMPING OUT. There are private campgrounds throughout the state; most have facilities for both tents and travel trailers. Campgrounds range from merely an open space to pitch a tent to elaborate facilities including movies, churches, organized social activities, in fact, all the amenities of a resort. The Travel Development Bureau publishes a *Pennsylvania Campground Association Guide* that lists over 100 private campgrounds. Write: The Travel Development Bureau, Department of Commerce, 206 S. Office Building, Harrisburg, Pa. 17120.

A-O.K. Campground. 49 acres, centrally located near Visitor Center. Hot showers, elec. & water, pool, laundry. 717–334–1288.

Artillery Ridge Campground. 50 acres with pool, hayrides, fishing, playground, gameroom, store, bike and paddleboat rentals, firewood, laundry. Camping with horses. Battlefield bus and tape tours. Rt. 134, one mile S. of Nat'l Park Visitor's Center. 717–334–1288.

Colonel's Creek Campground and Cottages. Cool mountain comfort along shady stream. Hook-ups, cottages, fishing. US 30, 12 miles W. of Gettysburg. R.D.2, Fayetteville, Pa. 717–352–8938.

Drummer Boy Camping Resort, 100 acres, 300 shaded sites for family camping. Pool, fishing, lake, mini golf. 1½ miles E. of Gettysburg on Rt. 116 at US 15 R.D. 5, Gettysburg, Pa. 17325. 717–642–5713.

Gettysburg Campground. 240 sites in wooded area along the banks of Marsh Creek. 35 full hook-ups, 30 drive throughs. Hot showers, laundromat, playground, rec. hall, swimming pool, dump station, snack bar, general store. 3 miles W. of Gettysburg on Pa. Rt. 116. 717–334–3304.

Gettysburg KOA Campground. Quiet, wooded setting. Pool, laundry, store. Full hook-ups, tent sites. Nitely historical program. Battlefield bus and tape tours. R.D. 3, Gettysburg, Pa. 17325. 717–642–5713.

Granite Hill Family Campground & R.V. Resort. Complete family camping. Hook-ups, tennis, hayrides, mini golf, pool. 6 miles W. Rt. 116. 717–642–8749.

Hershey's Fur Center Campground. Lake swimming, life guards and sand beach, open and wooded sites, hook-ups, dump station, flush toilets, hot showers, playground, walking trails, grocery, laundry. ¼ mile S. of Jct. US 15 on Rt. 94. 717–528–4412.

Quality First Acres, featuring a farm vacation, has individual cottages on 197 acres with swimming, horseback riding, tennis, basketball, hunting, fishing and game room. Farm animals include poultry, hogs and cattle. Cottages are heated, have bedrooms, living room, color television, bath and fully equipped kitchens. 20 minutes from Gettysburg in East Berlin. 717–259–0101.

Round Top Campground. Wooded sites, dump station, playground, pool, tennis, rec. building. R.D. 1, Jct. US Bypass 15 and Pa. 134, 3 miles S. of Gettysburg. 717–334–9565.

Welcome Traveler Camp Site. Hiking trails adjacent to Battlefield. Ten sites, restrooms, laundry. Pool, playground. 1½ miles S. on Rt. 140. 717–334–9226.

HOTELS AND MOTELS in the Gettysburg area range from *inexpensive* under $30, through *moderate* $35 average, to *expensive* $50 average.

Gettysburg Motor Lodge. *Expensive.* 380 Steinwehr Ave., US 15 Bus. 1 mile S. of midtown. This motel may charge extra during big college events such as graduations. It has a heated pool and newsstand; a cafe is next door, coin laundry a block away.

Holiday Inn. *Expensive.* 516 Baltimore St. US 140 at US 15 Bus. Swimming pool, suites available. College events may occasion a 2-day minimum. There is a ramp for guests with wheelchairs.

Howard Johnson's. *Expensive.* 301 Steinwehr Ave. US 15 Bus. Practically across the street from the Holiday Inn, this offers a sun deck and some private patios, as well as a heated pool.

Sheraton Inn-Gettysburg. *Expensive.* 5 mi. S. on US 15 Bus. Facilities include indoor heated pool, sauna, entertainment, beauty shop, par-3 golf, tennis and lawn games. 28 rooms with balconies.

Stonehenge. *Expensive.* Baltimore Pike US 140. Just S. of downtown, it has a pool with snack and drink service and a sauna. Entertainment enlivens the bar on weekends; the restaurant is open 11 A.M. to midnight in summer, from 4 P.M. other seasons.

College Motel. *Moderate.* 345 Carlisle St. In town, 3 blocks N. of center square on Bus. Rt. 15, opposite Gettysburg College, near major attractions. Air conditioned, pool, color TV, phones.

Gettysburg TraveLodge. *Moderate.* 10 E. Lincoln Ave. US 15 Bus. As usual, this is the least expensive in town among the big motel chains. Heated pool, cafe one block away.

Hi-Way Manor Motel. *Moderate.* 1 mile E. on US 30, ¼ mile W. of US 15. Family units available, air conditioning, TV, picnic and play areas. Away from city noise, but close to all attractions. RD 4, Box 34, Gettysburg 17325.

Blue Sky Motel. *Inexpensive.* 4 miles N. on Rt. 34. Comfortable rooms with air conditioning and TV. Pool, picnic and play area. RD 6, Gettysburg.

Criterion Motor Lodge. *Inexpensive.* 3 blocks N. on US Bus. Rt. 15 at 337 Carlisle St. Comfortable rooms in a convenient downtown location. Tours arranged.

Heritage Motor Lodge. *Inexpensive.* Junction Bus. Rt.15 and 140. Located in the heart of the historical and museum area.

Homestead Motor Lodge. *Inexpensive.* R.D. 5, 2 miles E. on Rt. 30, ¼ mile W. of US 15 bypass. 10 units, each with guest-controlled electric heat and air conditioning.

Home Sweet Home Motel. *Inexpensive.* Bus. Rt. 15, opposite Government Visitor Center. 41 clean, modern units with guest-controlled heat and air conditioning, color TV. Adjacent to museums and main entrance to the battlefield.

Lincolnway East Motel. *Inexpensive.* 1½ miles E. on US 30 ½ mile W. of US 15 bypass. Cable TV, picnic areas. Will arrange tours.

Penn Eagle Motor. *Inexpensive.* 1½ miles E. of Lincoln Square on US 30. Attractive accommodations, swimming pool. Plant and craft shop.

Perfect Rest Motel. *Inexpensive.* 4½ miles S. Bus. Rt. 15. Country surroundings near National Park. Close to leading sites. Pool, large family rooms. RD 2 Box 64, Gettysburg, Pa.

Quality Inn Larson's. *Inexpensive.* 401 Buford Ave. US 30. Next door is the house where General Lee stayed during the Civil War battle here. Larson's offers a pool, putting green, bar and dining room. Beautifully landscaped. Dutch Pantry kitchen.

Rainbow Motel & Efficiencies. *Inexpensive.* 3 miles N. on Rt. 34. 10 complete housekeeping units and one family unit for 8, all at ground level. Air conditioning, separate parking area for campers, pond, pines, senior citizen discounts.

Stuart's Motel and Coffee Shop. *Inexpensive.* 4 miles S. on Bus. Rt. 15, adjacent to the International Village. Modern rooms with guest-controlled heat and air conditioning. Large pool and playground.

DINING OUT in Gettysburg encompasses several regional influences; cosmopolitan, Pennsylvania Dutch, Oriental, European, and hints of the Midwest and Dixie. For medium-priced dinners on each menu, the following categories apply: *Expensive* $15 average, *Moderate* $11 average, *Inexpensive* $6.00 or lower.

Dobbin House. *Expensive.* 89 Steinwehr Ave. 1776 Restaurant and Tavern. Fine food served in the candlelit glow of history. Reservations advised.

Dutch Pantry Restaurant. *Expensive.* 8 blocks west on US 30. Country cooking prepared according to original Pennsylvania Dutch recipes. Famous for farm-style desserts.

Farnsworth House Dining. *Expensive.* 401 Baltimore St. Civil War house open for indoor and garden dining. Food and cocktails served in authentic Civil War atmosphere.

The Lamp Post Restaurant. *Expensive.* 301 Carlisle St. Four dining rooms in Early American atmosphere. Serving breakfast, lunch and dinner. Specialties: giant sizzling steaks, country ham, variety of seafood.

Dutch Cupboard Restaurant. *Moderate.* 523 Baltimore St. Pa. Dutch food featuring Schnitz un Knepp, Sauerbraten, Schmier Kaes, apple butter and Shoofly pie.

Elby's Big Boy Family Restaurant. *Moderate.* Bus Rt. 15 S. Steinwehr Ave. Menu ranges from sandwiches to steak dinners. Children's menu, carry-out service.

Fuji-Ya Restaurant. *Moderate.* 44 Steinwehr Ave. Fine Oriental cuisine: Chinese, Japanese and Korean dishes. Imported Oriental beer, wine and sake. Oriental music, cocktail lounge.

Hickory Bridge Farm. *Moderate.* Rt. 116 W. from Gettysburg, then N. to Orrtanna. Farm-style dinners served in old barn. Two meats, many vegetables, corn fritters, and dessert for one price.

Jennie Wade Village Kitchen. *Moderate.* Gettysburg Tour Center. Home-style cooking. Breakfast, lunch, dinner, snacks. Also outdoor dining when weather permits.

Stonehenge Country Buffet, Restaurant & Lounge. *Moderate.* Adjacent to tower. All you can eat. Steamship round of beef, baked ham, chicken, fish, vegetables, salads and desserts. Breakfast, lunch and dinner.

Gettysburg Battle Theatre Cafeteria. *Inexpensive.* 571 Steinwehr Ave. Gettysburg's only cafeteria catering to groups and individuals.

Lincoln Diner. *Inexpensive.* One block N. of Lincoln Square in historic downtown Gettysburg. Fine food, fast service, daily specials.

PITTSBURGH

The "Renaissance City"

Pittsburgh owes its origin to its strategic, dramatic location at the juncture of three rivers. Young George Washington of Virginia, then a 21-year-old major in the British army, noticed the assets of the site when, en route to Fort Le Boef in 1753, he paused at the fork where the Allegheny and Monongahela Rivers meet to form the Ohio. Washington gazed long at the land between, then praised it as "extremely well situated for a fort."

That is what it soon became. The British and French struggled for control of the area before and during the French and Indian War; by November 25, 1758, the British prevailed. The French abandoned their Fort Duquesne and General John Forbes raised the British flag and re-named the place in honor of England's Prime Minister William Pitt. Fort Pitt, at war's end, became Pittsborough and then Pittsburgh.

As the city plunged headlong into industrialism, it gained its share of detractors. When British novelist Charles Dickens visited, he called it "hell with the lid off." The nickname "Iron City" in the 19th century gave way to "Smoky City" in the 20th. Its own Mayor David Lawrence once described Pittsburgh as "the dirtiest slag pile in the United States." And when architect Frank Lloyd Wright visited for the first time in 1935, he observed, "It would be cheaper to abandon it and build another real one."

126

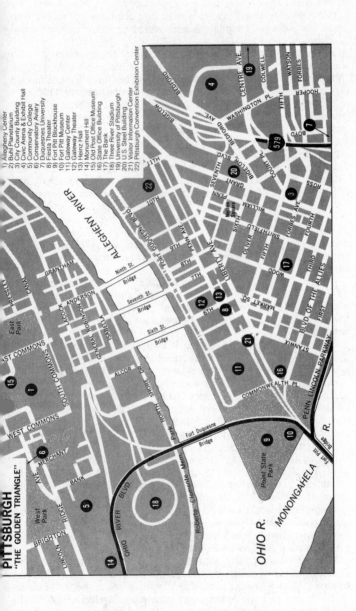

PITTSBURGH
"THE GOLDEN TRIANGLE"

1) Allegheny Center
2) Buhl Planetarium
3) City County Building
4) Civic Arena & Exhibit Hall
5) Community College
6) Conservatory Aviary
7) Duquesnes University
8) Fiesta Theater
9) Fort Pitt Blockhouse
10) Fort Pitt Museum
11) Gateway Center
12) Gateway Theater
13) Heinz Hall
14) Monument Hill
15) Old Post Office Museum
16) State Office Building
17) The Bank
18) Three River Stadium
19) University of Pittsburgh
20) U.S. Steel Building
21) Visitor Information Center
22) Pittsburgh Convention Exhibition Center

That is almost exactly what happened. The "Smoky City" and "slag pile" of yesterday was transformed into what is often called the "Renaissance City" of today—a city virtually reborn after an extensive and imaginative $3 billion renovation that combined the talents and resources of the city's capitalists, philanthropists, politicians and urban planners.

The result is a city that leaves a distinct impression on the traveler's mind. Industrial power and technology are still concentrated here (although with many tough anti-pollution laws), but this is a multi-faceted city of gleaming skyscrapers, green parks and picturesque hills.

Throughout Pittsburgh and Allegheny County, there are 1,700 bridges. It is also a city defined by its rivers and the tremendous activity generated by the nation's busiest inland port.

The renaissance begins, appropriately enough, at the origin of the city: "The Point," where two rivers meet to form the third. By the early 20th century, the land on which young Washington once stood had become a huge slum of crumbling warehouses and abandoned buildings. On a total of 59 acres of land, everything was razed except one building. Now, beautiful **Point State Park** occupies 36 acres, an expanse of greenery adorned by a giant computer-directed fountain at the tip of the Point (symbolizing, it is said, the joining of the rivers). Nor was the past forgotten: the blockhouse from the original Fort Pitt remains standing, and **Fort Pitt Museum** was erected to commemorate the city's history.

On the remaining 23 acres of razed ground arose **Gateway Center,** an area of six skyscrapers of gleaming steel and glass, promenades, a plaza of fountains, trees and abundant flowers and shrubs—over 100 varieties, in fact. Thus, from a former slum has come quite a renaissance indeed—modernity, beauty, recreation, and history.

The same sort of revitalization is evident throughout the Golden Triangle, as the city's downtown area (shaped by the two rivers meeting at a point) is called. **Market Square,** with its open-air food stalls surrounding a green mall—an area of colorful sights and often exotic scents—is undergoing a massive facelift. It will soon be home for a 40-story reflective glass tower designed by Philip Johnson. A short distance northeast is **Mellon Square,** another lovely oasis of trees, fountains and waterfalls, ingeniously perched atop six levels of underground parking facilities.

Nearby are all sorts of evidence of Pittsburgh as pioneer: the 30-story **Alcoa Building** is the first skyscraper to be sheathed in aluminum; on **Smithfield Congregational Church** is the first aluminum steeple ever raised; the striking **U.S. Steel Building,** triangular-shaped and 64 stories high, is the world's second largest office building completely structured with exposed beams. The modern **Civic Arena** features a retractable dome—three times as large as St. Peter's in Rome. It can fold up within itself in under three minutes.

If the new is impressive, so, too, is the ingenuity applied to adapting the old. Just across the river from the Golden Triangle is **Three Rivers Stadium.** Once a salvage yard, it is now the home of the world champion **Pirates** and the Super Bowl champion **Steelers.** Back in the downtown area, the **Bank Center** at 4th and Wood is a turn-of-the-

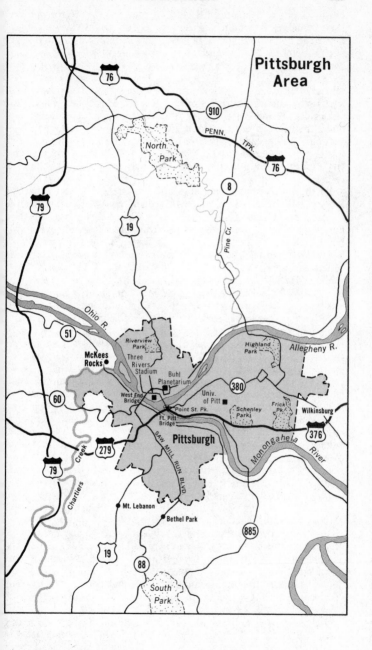

century landmark transformed for modern use. In five restored buildings, including a former bank and its vaults, is a modern complex, opened in 1976, with shops, offices and restaurants. The ornate and elegant detailing of the buildings is a fascinating counterpoint to the contemporary activity now within.

Equally ingenious is **Station Square** on West Carson St., a ten-minute walk across historic Smithfield Bridge from downtown. This amazingly varied 40-acre complex along the Monongahela includes among its attractions: a display of antique railroad cars; a modern hotel; the nation's last remaining Bessemer converter; a large restaurant built within the former P & LE Railroad terminal, plus assorted specialty shops inside the old railroad freight house—probably the city's most striking recent example of what is often called "adaptive re-use."

Pittsburgh's cultural attractions display the same adaptability. **Heinz Hall** at Sixth St. near the Allegheny River is created from a restored movie theater built in 1926 (no ordinary movie theater is this, but a magnificent Renaissance-style structure). Thus, an old movie house is now a concert hall—a worthy home for the renowned Pittsburgh Symphony Orchestra and host for numerous concerts, operas, ballets and musicals.

Heinz Hall is named for the founder of the giant food-packaging corporation famous for its 57 varieties. Many of the city's landmarks—museums, parks, buildings—were inspired and funded by the families of those who helped create the city's industrial, commercial and financial might a century ago or the original tycoons themselves, especially Henry J. Heinz (who began his career selling vegetables from a home garden). Others include: Andrew Carnegie, the steel and railroad wizard; Henry Clay Frick, coke manufacturer; and Andrew Mellon, banker. A more modern Mellon, Richard King, has exerted such influence on the city's renaissance that some dub Pittsburgh "the Mellon Patch."

This heritage of civic-minded men of wealth is especially apparent in Oakland, the section of the city where arts and science are most intensely focused. Names of the famous tycoons are ever-present among the cultural resources here: **Carnegie-Mellon University, Heinz Memorial Chapel, Henry Clay Frick Fine Arts Building** and more. However, not everything here bears a philanthropist's name. This area is home to the **University of Pittsburgh,** the **Pittsburgh Playhouse,** the **Stephen Foster Memorial,** WQED (America's first community-sponsored TV station), **St. Paul's Cathedral,** and **Phipps Conservatory** with its botanical wonders.

Nor, incidentally, does "Golden Triangle" refer to any literal gold or wealth of the city donors. It comes instead from one of Pittsburgh's misfortunes. When fire raged through the city in 1845, the mayor came down to the Point—from which the rivers form a triangle—viewed the damage and tried to summon optimism. "We shall make of this triangle of blackened ruins a golden triangle whose fame will endure as a priceless heritage," he predicted.

Quite in contrast to the Golden Triangle's gleaming modernity or the sophisticated cultural ambience of Oakland, the hills north and south of downtown are crowded with the colorful homes of ethnic neighborhoods, reflecting the authentic flavor of German, Italian and Polish-American shops and restaurants. The northside has also protected and restored residences dating back to the 1800s, when it was a separate city. Old Allegheny, as the region is known, has had loving attention from the Pittsburgh History and Landmarks Foundation. Cultural resources are plentiful here, too; **Buhl Planetarium,** the **Allegheny Observatory** and the **Aviary Conservatory** are nearby, and are easily accessible by the 6th, 7th or 9th St. bridges from downtown.

The southside hills are steeper. From **Mt. Washington's** glorious height, you'll see the entire area spread below, beautiful by day or evening. Two railway inclines, the **Duquesne** and **Monongahela,** provide novel ways to climb. There are observation decks at the top for panoramic views.

But wherever you look—north, south, or down to the Golden Triangle—you will not see any of those famous steel plants, even though both steel and coal are still basic to the city's economy; in fact, almost one-fifth of the nation's steelmaking is within a 50-mile radius. But the steel plants have moved beyond the city limits, and only one, Jones and Laughlin, remains within the city.

Under the leadership of the present mayor, Renaissance II is rapidly taking place. Four new skyscrapers, a new subway into downtown from the South Hills, a new East Busway that will take 90,000 riders to downtown Pittsburgh on a 21-minute ride along the Conrail right-of-way, commercial development and beautification of the north side of the Allegheny River from the Heinz plant to Three Rivers Stadium, highlight the impressive new developments.

Charles Dickens and Frank Lloyd Wright would hardly recognize the place, but it's a safe prediction that if they returned as tourists, they, too, would be delighted with the Renaissance City.

PRACTICAL INFORMATION FOR PITTSBURGH

HOW TO GET THERE. By car: I–79 runs north-south through Pittsburgh, and the Pennsylvania Turnpike (I–76) runs just north of the city.

By air: The Greater Pittsburgh International Airport, 14 mi. from town, via Parkway West, is served by numerous airlines including *American, United, TWA, Northwest, Eastern, Nordair, Delta, Piedmont* and *PeoplExpress. USAir.* USAir's Allegheny Commuter flights provide service to many cities in Pennsylvania. *Vee Neal* and *Cumberland Airlines* provide commuter service to Latrobe.

By train: Pittsburgh is on the *Amtrak* line. The station is at Liberty and Grant Sts.

By bus: The *Greyhound* terminal is at 11th St. and Liberty Ave., near the railroad station. *Trailways* is at 210 Tenth St. Among the numerous other lines running to Pittsburgh are *Lake Shore Lincoln Coach* and *Grove City, 88 Transit Lines,* and *Beaver Valley Motor Coach.*

HOW TO GET AROUND. By bus: The minimum fare is 60¢, but it varies for different zones in the city. Get a map of the routes and zones from the Port Authority at Wood Street, downtown. There is a weekend fare, 10 A.M. Sat.-4 A.M. Mon., providing unlimited rides on the PAT system for $3.25 for four people.

By taxi: Cabs are expensive here: $1 to start the meter and $1 per mile.

From the airport: *Yellow Cab* manages the limousine service at the airport. The fare is $5 downtown. The same trip in a taxi will cost you approximately $25. There are only four buses per day from the airport. Marked "Airport Red Flyers," they will take you downtown.

TOURIST INFORMATION. Pittsburgh Convention and Visitors Bureau, 200 Roosevelt Bldg., can answer any questions you might have: 281–7711. Additional information about other points of interest in Pittsburgh or Allegheny County can be obtained at the *PCVB Visitor Information Center,* Gateway Center, downtown, 412–281–9222. Hours: Mon.-Fri. 9:30 A.M.-5 P.M., Sat. and Sun., 9:30 A.M.-3 P.M. Closed Sundays, Nov. thru March.

MUSEUMS AND GALLERIES. In his well-known book on the city *(Pittsburgh: the History of an American City),* author Stefan Lorant observes that the 19th-century residents here cared little for art or letters. This could scarcely be said today. Pittsburghers work prodigiously to make events like the *Three Rivers Arts Festival* and the *International Poetry Forum* the justly acclaimed successes they are. Universities and institutes sponsor valuable museums and are impressive cultural centers. For the tourist, a varied choice of museums attests to the city's cosmopolitan taste for art and respect for its own history.

In a lovely landscaped setting, the **Frick Art Museum** at 7227 Reynolds St. displays its exquisite collection of French, Italian and Flemish Renaissance paintings, an 18th-century period room, Italian Renaissance bronzes, Flemish tapestries, rare Russian silver. The Italian Renaissance-style building also has an elegant concert hall where lectures, movies and chamber music concerts are given free of charge.

Carnegie Institute at 4400 Forbes Ave., established by Andrew Carnegie, is less an "institute" than a cultural world unto iself. In its *Museum of Natural History* over 10,000 objects are on display—birds, mammals, wildlife, Indian artifacts—with seven million more items available for research. Known also as "home of the dinosaurs," its Dinosaur Hall has, among other wonders, a rare 20-foot skeleton of a fang-tooth dinosaur *(Tyrannosaurus rex)*. The museum's new Information and Orientation Center has special audio-visual displays.

The second major museum here—the **Museum of Art**—includes the new *Heinz Galleries* for special exhibitions, the new **Alisa Mellon Bruce Galleries,** and the **Sarah Scaife Galleries,** heralded as an "unflawed paradise" where an atmosphere of airy spaces suffused with natural light provides a delightful setting for viewing the museum's permanent collection. It is a collection distinguished by many masterpieces of French Impressionist, Post-Impressionist and 19th-century American art, along with choice old masters and contemporary works.

Besides its two museums, this Institute also houses a lecture hall, **Museum of Art Theater** and the **Carnegie Music Hall** (not to be confused with Carnegie Hall in New York City).

The **University of Pittsburgh** is another multi-cultural world. The **Henry Clay Frick Fine Arts Building** at Schenley Plaza houses the Lochoff Collection: copies of fine Renaissance frescoes, rare Chinese porcelain, Italian Renaissance bronzes, ancient tapestries, furniture and paneling—all in a series of galleries surrounding a glass-etched cloister. As part of the University's Fine Arts Department, the museum also features changing exhibits and a reference library. It is open from September to early April.

The **Cathedral of Learning** is justly billed as the nation's only skyscraper college. A unique 42-story-high Gothic structure, Pittsburghers affectionately dubbed their skyscraper university "the inverted mineshaft." An attraction for tourists is a huge Commons Room surrounded by the unique **Nationality Classrooms.** Gifts to the University from ethnic groups of Allegheny County, these 19 rooms were meticulously designed and lavishly furnished by artists and architects from the nation each room represents. They span the globe, from Eastern Europe (Czechoslovak Classroom, Hungarian, Lithuanian, Polish, Romanian, Russian, Yugoslav) to Western Europe (Irish, Italian, German, Greek, Norwegian, Swedish, Scottish, English, French), to Asia (Chinese), the Mideast (Syria-Lebanon) and all the way to the New World. An Early American Room depicts a colonial home of the 1600s. Not only display rooms, these classrooms are used daily for teaching. They are admired by thousands from around the world each year. Tours (reservations are needed) are conducted by Quo Vadis, student volunteer guides trained in the history and culture of the countries. In the Visitors' Center in the Commons Room, a 35-minute narrated slide presentation, "The Story of the Nationality Rooms," is shown upon request (Telephone 624–6000 for details). Nearby, a **Gift Center** carries hand-crafted items from over 30 countries.

Adjacent to the Cathedral of Learning, and also part of the University, is the **Stephen Foster Memorial,** built to honor the American songwriter and Pittsburgh native. Born in the Lawrenceville section on July 4, 1826, Foster in his brief life (he died at age 38) wrote 235 songs, including such classics as "Old Black Joe," "My Old Kentucky Home," "Beautiful Dreamer," and "O Susanna." He died in New York after a fall from a lodging house in the Bowery, with just 38 cents in his pocket and the lyric of a song that began, "Dear hearts and gentle people. . . . " His lonely, impoverished death is quite in contrast to the tribute of the $250,000 memorial in his native city. It houses thousands of exhibits on Foster's life and music and on American music in general. It is said to be the most extensive memorial to a musician ever created.

Off campus, but not far from the Stephen Foster Memorial, is the **Historical Society of Western Pennsylvania** at 4338 Bigelow Blvd. Here is a fascinating collection of Early American glass—goblets, decanters, and other glassware, and an impressive array of weaponry, including muskets, guns, and swords. There are also other artifacts of early Pittsburgh, even the first piano in the city, ordered in 1791 by Fort Pitt's commander for his daughter. The museum also displays paintings, antique furnishings, portraits, surveying equipment, manuscripts. Its library and archives comprise a hefty 12,000 books dealing with this period. Here, too, nature devotees can get guide booklets to two historic trails in the region, the French and Indian and the Roads to the Forks.

Also for history buffs is the **Old Post Office Museum** at 1 Landmarks Square, Allegheny Center, so named because this domed Italian-Renaissance building, erected between 1894–97, was the former North Side Post Office. Now it is a museum dedicated to the history of Allegheny County, with crafted artifacts, agricultural exhibits, mannequins dressed in 18th- and 19th-century attire, toys of the past, and re-created old shops. For restful enjoyment there's also a garden court and fountains.

Soldiers and Sailors Memorial Hall, 5th Ave. and Bigelow Blvd., also focuses on the Allegheny region, with displays of flags, weapons, uniforms, Civil War relics. And, in the huge auditorium, the Gettysburg Address is inscribed above the stage.

When you're ready for a shift from history to modernity, from artifacts of the past to creations of the present, the **Arts and Crafts Center,** 6300 5th Ave., provides an interesting glimpse of the art scene in the city today. Its exhibits change monthly, and paintings, sculpture, ceramics, jewelry and fabrics are all on display. The Center even-handedly gives attention to local artists from all ranges of the artistic spectrum—all the way from representation to op and pop art.

Those who enjoy gallery hopping will find quite a variety in Pittsburgh, as evidenced by the following sampler:

The Clay Place, 5600 Walnut Street.
Ivy School of Art Gallery, Perry Hilltop, University Ave.
Allegheny County Courthouse Gallery, 119 Courthouse, Grant St.
Kingpitcher Gallery, 303 S. Craig St.
Pittsburgh Plan for Art, 407 S. Craig St.
Russian Images, Ltd., The Bank Tower, 307 Fourth Ave.
Wunderly Galleries, 901 Liberty Ave.
Selma Burke Art Center, 6118 Penn Circle South.

HISTORIC SITES. Long before the "Smoky City" became the modern "Renaissance City" it is today, Pittsburgh was a fort—the largest inland fort in what would later become the United States. The modern visitor can retrace some of that early history at **Point State Park.** In the park, the **Blockhouse of Fort Pitt,** built by British Colonel Henry Bouquet in 1764, is the oldest building still standing in the city and the only one pre-dating the American Revolution. A typical frontier-style blockhouse, it has holes in the wall for long muskets to fire upon invaders. Near the historic blockhouse is **Fort Pitt Museum,** a reconstruction on the exact site of the Monongahela bastion of Fort Pitt. The triangular building, first opened in 1967, depicts the history of the Point until 1800. Displays include scale models of the three French and Indian war forts at the Point—Prince George, Duquesne and Pitt; dioramas depicting major events in the city's founding; reconstructed rooms; artifacts from the French and Indian War; and varied exhibits on early frontier life. On Sundays at 2:30 P.M. from mid-June until Labor Day, the Royal American Regiment parades at the Point with fifes, muskets, drums, cannons. The paraders wear authentic reproductions of General John Forbes' British Regulars as they re-create the sights and sounds of the British army of the 18th century.

Quite in contrast to war forts and military memorabilia is **Old Economy Village,** just a few miles north of Pittsburgh at Ambridge. This is the site of the Harmony Society's unique experiment in utopian communal living from 1825 to 1905. The Society was founded by a group of pious German Lutherans who fled their native Duchy to escape religious persecution. Led by weaver George Rapp, whom they revered as a prophet, they settled on a piece of land he purchased here, deeded all their property to the Society, and led lives of "harmony," work, and celibacy. And they prospered—in shoes, cotton, wool, wines and farming. For a time the Society was the leading industrial community in the West.

As restored in meticulous detail by the Historical Commission, Old Economy Village today occupies 6.7 acres of the original 20, a two-block area with 17 original and restored buildings that look exactly as they did in the Harmony Society's heyday. Wander along the streets today and you'll see the *Great House* where Father Rapp lived in far more splendor than his followers; the huge *Feast Hall* where "love feasts" were shared; the *craft shops* —the tailor's, barber's, cobbler's; the *Great Kitchen* where meals for 800 were prepared; the *wine cellar* with huge wine casks; the *Langenbacher House,* a typical house where members lived like brothers and sisters; and the *Grotto,* a lovely formal garden with wines and arbors. *St. John's Luthern Church,* completed in 1831, is also here. The *Center for the History of American Needlework* is at 14th and Church Sts. The village is open daily except holidays. Admission 75¢, free to children and those over 65.

Tour-Ed Mine in Tarentum (R.D. #2, Bull Creek Rd.) is a look at another sort of history. Here you'll see the details of an underground coal mine, a saw mill, an old company store, and a log house dating from 1789.

Perhaps surprising to find in rugged Western Pennsylvania is **Hartwood,** the Mary Flinn Lawrence Estate at 215 Saxonburg Blvd. It is a huge (629 acre) restoration of an English Tudor estate. It takes two hours to tour the mansion, the riding stables, and the formal gardens. In December, a special feature is the Old English Christmas tour of the estate, bedecked in all its old-world glory. Reservations needed for guided tours. Admission $2; $1 to those over 60; 50¢ for children under 14.

Quite in contrast to a lavish Tudor mansion is **Neill Log House** at East Circuit and Serpentine Rds., back in the city at Schenley Park. It is one of three confirmed 18th-century buildings in Pittsburgh. It was built by a farmer in the late 1700s and restored much later by the Mellon Foundation after an exhaustive dig that yielded thousands of artifacts. Open daily except Monday; free.

TOURS. Not only are there a variety of sightseeing attractions in the "Renaissance City," but also a variety of ways to see them—by boat, bus, limousine, or even by unique mountain-climbing railway cars more steeply inclined than the famed cable cars of San Francisco.

By boat: In a city of three rivers, there is a full program of cruises. *Gateway Clipper Fleet,* at the Sheraton Motor Hotel at Station Square on the South Side, operates two-hour cruises on all three rivers. *Gateway Clipper, Gateway Party*

Liner, River Bells and *Liberty Belle* sail daily, April to October. Phone 355–7980 for rates and schedule. For youngsters, the *Good Ship Lollipop* is a special attraction. Dinner-dance cruises for adults.

By bus or limousine: Port Authority of Pittsburgh offers a guided bus tour daily of downtown, Oakland, Civic Center and North Side. Call 231–5707 for price and information.

Pittsburgh Panorama, Inc. operates limousine tours, full or half day, for families or small groups (station wagons and vans are available, too). Tours cover city highlights in general, or are geared towards special interests (Arts and Crafts, Melting Pot, Camera Angles and others). Call 731–6044.

America Tours International, Inc. conducts a three-hour city tour, All Around the Town, a combined bus plus cruise tour on the *Gateway Clipper* or special excursions. Also *Creative Convention Services,* 741–5400, *Passport to Pittsburgh Tours,* 281–0686 and *Triangle Tours,* 561–6818.

By railway cable: For a unique do-it-yourself tour that gives a glimpse of Pittsburgh as it was in 1877 plus a spectacular view of the modern city, take a ride on Pittsburgh's two remaining "inclines," the *Duquesne* and the *Monongahela.* These compact cable railways, once described as "elevators climbing a mountain," climb the steep slopes west of the Monongahela River all the way to the top of Mt. Washington. It was the ingenuity and determination of the city's German immigrants that led to these inclines. When they settled on "Coal Hill," as Mt. Washington was then called, and worked in the steel mills below, they saw no reason to trudge wearily and daily up and down the steep grade. They found a solution by building "steilbahns" modeled on Germany's alpine cables.

The Monongahela was the city's first incline (eventually there were 17). Affectionately known as "Old Mon," it was inaugurated May 28, 1870, with 900 riding on the first day. By the second day, riders numbered over 4,000; by the year's end, 218,000 had ventured a journey. Today, "Old Mon" carries nearly half a million commuters and tourists from its base on West Carson Street up the 640 feet of railway track to Mt. Washington. At the top is an observation deck for enjoying the panoramic view of the city below.

If you're so inclined, don't limit yourself to the 60¢ ride on "Old Mon;" for the same fare you can also ride the Duquesne Incline, repaired and restored in 1963 and now operated as a devoted and non-profit enterprise by the Society for the Preservation of the Duquesne Heights Incline. Here you ride in cars with the original handcarved cherry panels and birdseye maple trim, amber glass transoms, and handsome old hardware. The cars still have the cable drum and wooden-tooth drive gear of the original installation, operating since 1877. The only concession to modernity is that the car is now powered by electricity, not steam. Waiting rooms contain exhibits and mementos of the past and this incline, too, has an observation deck at the upper section after the 400-foot jaunt.

Station for the "Old Mon" incline is on West Carson St. near the Smithfield Bridge. It operates Monday to Saturday until 12:45 A.M.; Sundays and holidays until midnight. Phone 231–5707. The Duquesne Inclined Plane lower station is also on West Carson St., SW of Fort Pitt Bridge; the upper station is 1220 Grandview Ave. Phone 381–1665.

 PARKS AND GARDENS. In the heart of the city is the 456-acre **Schenley Park** with a lake, playground, picnic area, miniature golf course in summer, skating rink in winter, nature trails and a bandstand. A highlight here is **Phipps Conservatory,** a huge botanical conservatory: 2½ acres under glass, 13 major greenhouses that form a tropical forest of exotic plants with rare blooms. The orchid collection is famous, the Southern-style garden is charming, and special shows to display spring and fall flowers in full bloon are held daily both day and evening.

The nature lover will delight in **Frick Park** at Beechwood Blvd. and English Lane, with its 499 acres of unspoiled nature trails, and a **Nature Museum** at 2035 Beechwood Blvd.

In the center of **Riverview Park** (two miles north on U.S. 19) is the **Allegheny Observatory** at 159 Riverview Ave., a renowned observatory for research in astronomy, maintained by the University of Pittsburgh. It offers slides, movies, and a tour of the Conservatory to adults and to children accompanied by adults.

Besides the city's 25 parks (not to mention 45 smaller parks, 60 recreation centers and 27 swimming pools), there are five county parks: **South Park, North Park, Boyce Park** and **Settler's Cabin Park,** *Hartwood*—easily accessible and offering varied recreational facilities: *golf, swimming, tennis, picnic areas, bridle paths, bicycle trails, ballfields, fishing* and *boating.* For information call 355–4251.

MUSIC. The **Pittsburgh Symphony Orchestra** is in its 12th season at renowned Heinz Hall for Performing Arts, 600 Penn Ave. (downtown). This world-renowned aggregation can be enjoyed during the fall, winter and spring seasons. It features its own brilliant conductors and international guest artists. Tickets and information available at Heinz Hall. The **Pittsburgh Opera,** also at Heinz Hall, combines local operatic and musical talents with celebrated stars appearing in best-loved operas through fall, winter and spring seasons. Performances are given on Thursday and Saturday nights. Heinz Hall is also home for the **Pittsburgh Ballet Theatre,** as well as for top-caliber theatrical and musical productions by outstanding performers. In summertime, the **Civic Light Opera Association** offers a good selection of musical comedies, operettas, revues and other attractions at Heinz Hall.

STAGE AND REVUES. Pittsburgh has several theaters. The **Pittsburgh Public Theater** performs at the Allegheny Theater, and **Heinz Hall** has a Broadway Theater Series. Also **City Theater Company, Carnegie-Mellon University Theater Company** and **Theater on the Green** at Hartwood. Occasional revues, such as the Ice Capades, are staged in the city's giant Civic Arena. **Pittsburgh Playhouse** in Oakland offers additional shows. Summer stock companies give performances at the **White Barn Theater, Little Lake Dinner Theater,** the **South Park Conservatory Theater,** and **Robert Morris Colonial Theater.** All are located within a short drive of downtown.

BARS. Since Pittsburgh has almost 500 thousand people, and 2 million in its metropolitan area, there are hundreds of bars and cocktail lounges to suit every taste and pocketbook. There are a few outstanding ones to interest visitors, among them: **The Tin Angel,** 1204 Grandview Ave. (atop Mt. Washington), tel. 381–1919, reached by "incline" railway and streetcar, or by car, has no entertainment, but prides itself on the breathtaking view of downtown Pittsburgh hundreds of feet below. Dinner by reservation only from 6 to 9 P.M., limited to sizzling sirloin steak. Open until 1–2 A.M. daily except Sun. Small, intimate place, advisable to phone in advance for a window table.

Frankie Gustine's Bar and Restaurant, 3911 Forbes Ave., is a sports hangout run by the former Pittsburgh Pirate baseball star who is now a basketball coach. Its walls are plastered with pictures of Gustine and baseball stars he played with in his long career. Open 10–1:30 A.M., closed Sun.

The Encore, 5500 Walnut Street, in the Shadyside area. Here is a loud and lively spot, situated in the artistic quarter of the city, there is some semblance of Latin Quarter ambiance.

Encore II, 629 Liberty Ave., is handsomely decorated and offers good food and good jazz. This is a cool club where well-dressed night owls strut. Live music Tues.-Sat., with a special jazz matinee on Saturday.

Happy Landing, Kossmann Bldg. downtown. Disco and restaurant.

Heaven, 6th Ave. near Fulton. Theater, disco-restaurant, dancing.

Old Allegheny, Roosevelt Bldg., downtown. Features good jazz entertainment.

Library, The Bank, downtown. If disco is your taste, this is the place.

The Rusty Scupper, The Bank, downtown. One of Pittsburgh's more popular drinking spots.

 NIGHTCLUBS. Many of Pittsburgh's nightclubs featuring entertainment are located in the suburbs and a bit farther out of town, reached by good highways. Quite a number of them feature acts and stars from Broadway and Hollywood. Here are a few of Pittsburgh's most popular clubs:

The Marriott Inn, 101 Marriott Drive, in Greentree, has live entertainment nightly and a discotheque.

Cross Gates Inn, Forbes Avenue at McKee Place, also offers top-level entertainment.

Holiday House, US 22 in Monroeville, boasts top show biz personalities in two floor shows nightly.

 SPORTS. Pittsburgh has been a great sports community ever since it played host to the first World Series in 1903. Today, **Three Rivers Stadium,** 600 Stadium Circle, is home of the National League Pirates and the Steelers of professional *football.* (For sports enthusiasts who are also tourists, there's a **Sports Hall of Fame** open April to December, and tours April through August; phone 323–5040 for information) The NHL Penguins, the indoor *soccer* team and the Spirit both play in the **Civic Arena,** the amphitheater in the **Golden Triangle** that accommodates 17,500 people. Professional *boxing, wrestling* and *hockey* are also frequent attractions here. With the city's universities—Pitt, Carnegie Mellon and Duquesne—holding sports events throughout most of the year, sports fans are kept quite busy.

As for those preferring participatory sports, Allegheny County is said to have more *golf* courses than any other county in the nation. Public and private *swimming* pools dot the landscape, and some of the best *ski* resorts in the East are along Laurel Ridge, some sixty miles southeast of the city. Closer is **Boyce Park Ski Area,** eighteen miles east of town. For those even more adventuresome, *white-water rafting* is at nearby Ohiopyle on the Youghiogheny. And for more standard fare, the county parks offer a wide range of possibilities, from *fishing* to *horseback riding* to *hiking* trails.

SHOPPING. Pittsburgh has four main department stores: *Gimbels* at 6th and Smithfield; *Joseph Horne Company* at Penn and Stanwix; *Kaufmann's* at 5th and Smithfield and *Saks Fifth Avenue* at 513 Smithfield. Stores are open 10 A.M. until 5:30 P.M., and until 9 P.M. on Monday and Thursday.

The city has also an assortment of specialty shops scattered throughout the areas both downtown and beyond. *Trevi* in Shadyside is an interesting boutique. The *Studio Shop* at 210 South Highland Ave. carries a vast and varied selection of imported **house furnishings.** This is the ideal place for gift shopping or for seeking something unusual for your own home. *The Theater* is a center of fine specialty shops and several restaurants.

But for specialty shops in a most unusual environment, head for the *Bank Center* at 4th and Wood, where five landmark buildings have been converted into a complex of contemporary shops (restaurants and offices are here, too). Even more unique are the *Freight House Shops* at Station Square, thriving in the old freight house of the P&LE Railroad. It's a setting so remarkable it's worth a trip even without the shopping—easily accessible by a short walk or on one of the many trolleys and buses serving the area.

Those looking for quality **works of art** will be delighted, even amazed, by the reasonable prices at the *Arts and Crafts Center,* 6300 5th Ave. **Paintings** and **sculpture** are also for sale (or rent) at *Pittsburgh Plan for Art,* 407 South Craig St. And one unusual aspect of *Kaufmann's* department store is its art gallery, with a good collection of contemporary **paintings, graphics** and **sculpture.**

For those who like to do their shopping outdoors, Pittsburgh's *Flea Market* is open every Sunday from 10 A.M.-4 P.M. from May thru November (weather permitting). It is located at the Common Market across from the Allegheny Center. *Keystone State Grand Flea Market* on Penn Ave., downtown, in the Strip District. Pittsburgh's *Farmers Market* is at the same location and is open on Mon., Wed., and Fri., July thru November. *Artists at Work,* just above Keystone State Market, shows artisans making crafts.

If you are lucky and resourceful—it takes both in this case—you may find a way to buy some *Pysanky,* the Ukrainian **hand-decorated Easter eggs,** bearers of good luck, good health and love, which are still made by some of the older Ukrainians in and around Pittsburgh. They are beautifully decorated by a tedious process of applying wax and dye, and constitute a prized possession. Other unusual and interesting things may sometimes be purchased at church or club fairs or sales—embroidered tablecloths and bureau covers, handsewn aprons, handsome Christmas wreaths or centerpieces for a holiday table. The *Fabulous Fun Free Fairgrounds Festival,* at the South Park Fairgrounds, offers a showcase of **arts, crafts, antiques, collectibles,** and **homemade items.** Every Sat. and Sun. 9 A.M.-5 P.M.

Allegheny Center Mall, on the North Side, has eighty stores and restaurants. *Sears* is presently the largest store. There is indoor parking for 2,800 cars, free for the first hour. In the complex there are an 8- and a 13-story office building, 4 high-rise apartments, and town houses.

Century III Mall in West Mifflin is the area's largest mall.

Monroeville Mall, directly out the Parkway East, has shopping facilities of practically all varieties, and restaurants for casual or leisurely dining. Its most engaging feature is a large glass-enclosed ice rink, where shoppers may dine at *Di Pomodro's* with a view of the skaters.

North Hills Village on McKnight Rd. offers a variety of shops and restaurants.

South Hills Village Shopping Center, Rte. 19 and Fort Couch Rd., South Suburban, is a two-level all-enclosed mall with 120 stores and parking for 6,500

automobiles. In the mall are many lovely planters, an aviary and fountain. Ther
is a theater, a *Stouffer's Restaurant* and the *Harvest House Restaurant.* Thre
stores— *Horne's, Gimbel's* and *Sears*—have branches there. *Kaufmann's* i
nearby.

Pittsburgh Merchandise Mart in Monroeville features shops, exhibits, an
displays—public and private.

 WHAT TO DO WITH THE CHILDREN. In the *Pitt.
burgh Zoo* in Highland Park are 2,000 animals in
75-acre setting that includes a main zoo; children's zo
where youngsters may pet baby animals; a twilight zo
displaying nocturnal animals and featuring a 300-foot tunnel containing exhibit
of rare and diurnal animals; and an aqua zoo with piranhas, Alaskan king crabs
and a special exhibit showing the voltage produced by electric eels and othe
fish to stun enemies. And besides all the animals, there are picnic grounds, trai
rides and a merry-go-round.

Those who enjoy the zoo will also delight in the *Aviary-Conservatory* in Wes
Park at Ridge Ave. and Archer St., with its talking birds and free flight demon
strations. The *Nature Museum* on Schenley Dr. exhibits small birds, animal
and reptiles.

Buhl Planetarium and Institute of Popular Science at Allegheny Square fea
tures breathtaking "Sky Dramas" in its Theater of the Stars. The nation's oldes
planetarium is a place of many wonders, including three-dimensional exhibits
many of them do-it-yourself types; a Zeiss projector; a miniature railroad an
village; and a gigantic pendulum measuring the motion of the earth.

Dinosaur Hall at the *Carnegie Museum of Natural History* is guaranteed to
intrigue spectators of any age. The mechanical-minded will enjoy *Arden Trolle
Museum* in Washington, not far from the city; open on weekends May throug
October. For rides on real vehicles, don't miss the *Monongahela and Duquesn
Inclines;* and, by boat, the *Good Ship Lollipop* sailing from Memorial Day t
Labor Day.

For a shift from sightseeing rides to thrill rides, *Kennywood Park* at 480(
Kennywood Blvd. features four different roller coasters, and, for other recre
ation, a Kiddieland, gardens and picnic areas. *White Swan Park,* 3 mi. SE o
Greater Pittsburgh Airport, has amusement rides, miniature golf and picni
areas.

For children's theater, *Lovelace Theater* at 5888½ Ellsworth Ave. in Shady
side will delight audiences of any age.

 HOTELS AND MOTELS in Pittsburgh range from
glamorous establishments in the Golden Triangle to the
plain, but comfortable, motels surrounding the city on
its web of highways. In between is a host of accommoda
tions to suit every budget and taste. Double-occupancy lodgings in Pittsburgh
are categorized as follows: *Deluxe* $60 and higher; *Expensive* $50–60. *Moderate
$40–50 and *Inexpensive* under $40.

Conley's. *Deluxe.* 3550 William Penn Highway (US 22 Business). East of the
city, this motel offers kitchen units by the week, a rec room and putting green.
Restaurant, pool and sauna. Spa, health club, and facilities for the handicapped.

Harley of Pittsburgh. *Deluxe.* 699 Rodi Rd. The exercise-minded will espe
cially like this. Both outdoor and indoor pools plus whirlpool, wading pool,
sauna, lighted tennis courts. Rooms have private patios and balconies; suites
have refrigerators.

Holiday Inn-Airport. *Deluxe.* 1406 Beers School Rd. This link in the Holiday chain has a full line of luxuries: indoor pool, whirlpool, tennis privileges, rec room, color TV and coin laundry. Free airport bus.

Holiday Inn-Parkway East. *Deluxe.* 915 Brinton Rd. They have heated indoor pool, a rec room, banquet facilities for 350 people, a continental cuisine restaurant, European disco lounge, and happy hours every day from two 'til nine. Game room, disco club, swimming pool (indoors), and facilities for the handicapped.

Hyatt Pittsburgh at Chatham Center. *Deluxe.* In the Golden Triangle. More attractive facilities than the other deluxe hostelries: swimming pool, health club and theater. Checkout is at 3 P.M., they have a barber shop and newsstand too. Dining room and bar. Entertainment, facilities for the handicapped, foreign money exchange.

The Marriott. *Deluxe.* 101 Marriott Dr. 3 mi. W. off Mansfield Ave. 500 air-conditioned rooms, indoor and outdoor pool, whirlpool, sauna, pets allowed, barber and beauty shops, and free bus to the airport.

Pittsburgh Hilton. *Deluxe.* Gateway Center, Point State Park. There are barber and beauty shops here, room service from the bar and a drugstore. Comfortable rooms and suites available. Restaurant. Scenic location at tip of the Golden Triangle. Facilities for the handicapped.

Pittsburgh Marriott Hotel/Monroeville. *Deluxe.* 101 Mall Blvd., Monroeville. Indoor-outdoor pool plus whirlpool, lifeguard, even ice skating. Free bus service to shopping malls. For the romantic, honeymoon weekend plan available.

Ramada Inn. *Deluxe.* 1420 Beers School Rd. (State 60). Most of the rooms here have private patios or balconies, this being one individualizing feature of the chain operation. Heated pool and a free ride to the nearby airport. Facilities for the handicapped.

University Inn. *Deluxe.* Forbes Ave. at McKee Place. Newest luxury hotel in Pittsburgh. Gourmet restaurant. Live entertainment seven nights. Free valet parking. Located in Oakland, near Univ. of Pittsburgh and the medical school. Charming decor. Facilities for the handicapped.

William Penn. *Deluxe.* 530 William Penn Place, on Mellon Sq. Recently redecorated, this venerable hotel overlooks the green area of the downtown center. Restaurant. Checkout time is not until 1 P.M.

Hilton Airport Inn. *Expensive.* Cliff Mine Rd. 140 air-conditioned rooms in a four-story building. Rooms have color TV, some have in-room steam baths. Pool with lifeguard, dancing Tuesday through Saturday. A quick free bus ride to the airport provided.

Holiday Inn-Monroeville. *Expensive.* 2750 Mosside Blvd. Reliable choice for this area. Pool, wading pool, lifeguard, golf privileges, dancing and entertainment. Rooms with private patios and balconies.

Howard Johnson's-Airport. *Expensive.* 1500 Beers School Rd. in Coraopolis. Adjacent to the Greater Pittsburgh Airport. Indoor pool, cafe open 24 hrs., private patios, balconies, free bus service to the airport.

Howard Johnson's-Oakland. *Expensive.* Near the Medical Center. Eight stories with 119 air-conditioned rooms. Some have patios, balconies and/or steam baths. There are 24-hour coffee shop, room service, color TV and weekend entertainment and dancing.

Inn at Parkway Center. *Expensive.* 875 Greentree Rd. Located in Parkway Center, they have a barber and beauty shop, a Mellon Bank, the Pavillion Restaurant, The Giraffe Discotheque, game room, full health club facilities for all guests, an indoor pool, and gift and coffee shops.

Sheraton-North. *Expensive.* 4859 McKnight Road in northern section of city. Pool, Canterbury dining room. Golf and tennis nearby.

Holiday Inn-Allegheny Valley. *Moderate.* 180 Gamma Dr. (State 28). Heated pool with service, 2 units for handicapped complement the usual chain features at this northside location.

Parkway Center-Best Western. *Moderate.* 875 Greentree Rd. In south area, a hotel with all the trimmings: indoor pool, sauna, health club, disco, recreation room. When you're ready to leave, free bus to the airport.

Quality Inn-East. *Moderate.* 500 Lincoln Hwy. 80 rooms with weekly, monthly and group rates available. Pool, tennis privileges, Ping-Pong, lawn games and health club.

The Viking Motel-Best Western. *Moderate.* 1500 Banksville Rd. (US 19). Sauna and pool, where you can order from the bar or kitchen. There's dancing and entertainment; the dining room keeps long hours. Free bus to the airport.

Red Roof Inn *Inexpensive.* 6404 Steubenville Pike (15 mi. W. on Pa. 60). A modest inn of 122 rooms on two floors and comfortable for the price. Color TV, adjoining 24-hour coffee shop, and airport transportation available.

 DINING OUT in Pittsburgh offers a wide range of cuisines and all degrees of formality. If you have time, try at least one meal at a Mt. Washington restaurant. It will be at the upper end of the price spectrum, but the view is exceptional and you may choose to build an appetite by walking up. Unfortunately, a good many delicious nationality foods which are quite common on home menus here do not show up in restaurants—the *pierogi,* dough pockets stuffed with potato, cheese, cabbage or fruits; Polish *kielbasy,* or meat sausage; *golabki,* or stuffed cabbage. You will find them served at church suppers, open to the public, or at national day festivities held in local parks in the spring and summer. Easier to come by are the nut breads and nut cookies that you find in many of Pittsburgh's bakery shops. They are delicious.

Cost categories for medium-priced meals on each menu are: *Deluxe* $18 or higher, *Expensive $12–16 average, Moderate* $9–12 and *Inexpensive* $6.00 or under. These prices cover hors d'oeuvres or soup, entree and dessert. Not included are drinks, tax (6% on meals in Pennsylvania) and tips.

EDITORS' CHOICES

Rating restaurants is, at best, a subjective business, and obviously a matter of personal taste. It is, therefore, difficult to call a restaurant "the best," and hope to get unanimous agreement. The restaurants listed below are our choices of the best eating places in Pittsburgh, and the places we would choose if we were visiting the city.

New Meadow Grill. The neighborhood could hardly be characterized as a "high-rent district," but the roughness of the environs in no way detracts from the elegance of the fare. A cornucopia of Italian delights overflows with clams, mussels, and conch, plus fresh snails in a very special sauce. Veal and mushroom dishes are also a staple of the menu, and the sauces are a particular treat. Liquor is available but there is no bar. Not open for lunch. Average price for dinner (per person): $7. 420 Larimer Avenue (in the East Liberty area). *Italian Cuisine*

Anna Kao's. The owner is a teacher of Oriental cooking, and the menu is replete with offerings that represent such diverse Chinese provincial areas as Szechuan, Hunan, Peking, Canton, and even Fukien. All ingredients are fresh, and there is nary a trace of MSG. Excellent soups—especially one called "Bamboo Stick"—spicy fish and Moo Shu Pork with pancakes are specialties. Not open for lunch. Average price for dinner (per person): $7. 1034–38 Freeport Rd. (O'Hara Township). *Chinese Cuisine*

Alex Tambellini's Woods Restaurant. This small, crowded restaurant specializes in Italian seafood. Scrod, scampi, bay scallops, oysters, and Crabmeat Thermidor are the best bets. House dressing on salads is something special, as is the veal and filets. Average price for dinner (per person): $9. 213 Wood Street. *Italian Cuisine*

Sarah's. Pittsburgh's only example of the cooking of Mitteleuropa. Homemade moussaka, turkey stuffed with sauerkraut, salmon, and tasty crepes are the specialties. Particularly memorable strudel tops any meal. Reservations a must. Average price for dinner (per person): $7. 52 South 10th Street. *Eastern European Cuisine*

Park Schenley. An outstanding chef makes this more than just a posh, velvety eatery. Specialties include mousse of pike, almost all varieties of beef, and the hearts of veal with goose liver. Excellent wine list is a fitting complement to the exceptional food. Average price for dinner (per person): $13. 3955 Bigelow Blvd. (Oakland section). *Continental Cuisine*

OTHER RECOMMENDED RESTAURANTS

American-International

The Board Room. *Deluxe.* The Bank Center, 414 Wood St. An elegant former bank board room behind mullioned windows. The cuisine is similarly elegant: truffled sole, duck with plum sauce, beef Wellington and other delicacies. Dinner is fixed price ($25), lunch is a la carte. With just eight tables, the place is rather exclusive and reservations are advised.

Christopher's. *Deluxe.* 1411 Grandview Ave., Mt. Washington, atop LeGrande Apts. Experienced aficionados reserve their tables not only to taste the delicious cooking but to get the best view of the city below. Beef, veal and seafood are the favorites here. The service is excellent.

Grand Concourse. *Deluxe.* This is Pittsburgh's newest and largest restaurant, with a seating capacity of 500. Over two million dollars were spent to restore the magnificent Edwardian Grand Concourse to its original turn-of-the-century elegance. Raw oysters, clams, and shrimp are the fare in the Old Station Baggage Room. There are two more intimate dining areas, each lavish with the original ornamental decor.

Murphy's Backroom. *Deluxe.* Gateway Towers ground floor. Entrees include duck with raspberry or plum sauce, sole stuffed with salmon mousse in truffled cream sauce, cold veal salad with tuna. Fixed price $25.

Ben Gross Restaurant. *Expensive.* Route 30, 4½ miles west from Irwin exit of turnpike. Varied continental menu and a reputation for imaginative dining dating back to 1934. Some say this is also Pittsburgh's best wine cellar.

Bigelow Restaurant. *Expensive.* Bigelow Square, downtown. In summer, you may eat outside. Quiet atmosphere and good food.

The Butcher Block. *Expensive.* Parkway West at White Swan Park, in Hilton Airport Inn. The name certainly fits; you not only get to eat steak, but also to select it from a meat cabinet, then watch the butcher cut and trim it—and charge you by the ounce.

The Colony. *Expensive.* Greentree Rd. at Cochran (State 121). Jacket and tie required of men at this lovely restaurant, 20 minutes SW of the city. Limited specialty menu, pianist plays during dinner.

Hugo's Rotisserie. *Expensive.* Hyatt House in Chatham Center near the Civic Arena. Roasts of beef and ducklings turn on spits before your eyes. Other features include do-it-yourself desserts, hors d'oeuvres bar, Sunday brunch.

Hyeholde. *Expensive.* 190 Hyeholde Dr., off Parkway West, Coraopolis. Pittsburgh's answer to the New England country inn is in a gracious home with spacious grounds, and serves excellent food. Reservations required.

Landmark. *Expensive.* Fourth Ave. Downtown. Historical landmark building houses a three-level dining-entertainment facility with a downstairs rathskeller, first floor bar and dining area, and dining rooms on the second floor.

Rifle and Plow. *Expensive.* Pittsburgh Hilton Hotel, Gateway Center. Beef dishes are popular here and there's a special house dressing for spinach and bacon, other salads.

Sgro's. *Expensive.* Cambell's Run Road off Parkway West, in Robinson Township. The specialty is prime rib with the rib bone in and local gourmets say they have the best for counties 'round. The appetizer selection features great seafood. They're open for lunch and dinner.

Top of the Triangle. *Expensive.* 600 Grant St. A Stouffer's restaurant atop the US Steel building with, of course, magnificent views of the region. Jacket and tie for men, please.

Top Shelf. *Expensive.* 606 Liberty Ave. near Heinz Hall. Lunches are light—quiche and omelettes, but hearty dinners include mammoth 25 oz. T-bones, served to the tune of light jazz Thursday through Sunday evenings.

The Cheese Cellar. *Moderate.* No. 25 Freight House Shops, Station Square. Candlelit wine cellar ambience, with light menu of fondues, quiches, burgers, salads, omelettes. Convenient for lunch, dinner or late-night snack.

The Common Plea. *Moderate.* 308 Ross St. The food in this unpretentious restaurant is among the best in Pittsburgh. Menus are presented on a clipboard, written on a yellow legal pad. A delightful variety of dishes are offered. Only seats 50, but the food is worth the possible wait.

Cork 'n Bottle. *Moderate.* 527 Smithfield St. in the Oliver Bldg. Complimentary hors d'oeuvres in the lounge from 5–7 P.M. weekdays. American fare that includes a carafe of wine. Caesar Salad a specialty here.

Gateway Clipper Fleet. *Moderate.* All aboard for the "Captain's Dinner Dance Cruise." Not only do you get a hot buffet here, but also a three-hour three-rivers cruise and a combo for dancing. Weekends, plus occasional weeknight cruises. Board at 6 P.M., sail and eat until 10.

Georgetown Inn. *Moderate.* In Mt. Washington. Beautiful view of the city.

Horn of Plenty. *Moderate.* Butler, Pa. A two-level buffet with a huge selection from 70 items, both hot and cold. To add further adornment, local art is on display.

Houlihan's Old Place. *Moderate.* Freight House Shops, Station Square. Sunday brunch features fresh pastries, and any day the unusual and delightful atmosphere is enjoyable.

Johnny Garneau's Golden Spike. *Moderate.* 216 Sixth St. The ambience is rustic Western, and the fare is hearty—steaks, seafood, an eat-all-you-can roast beef buffet. Meals include salad and dessert buffets, too.

Lawrence's Restaurant. *Moderate.* On Penn Ave. across from Heinz Hall. Enjoy continental cuisine here before or after the concert. Veal is a specialty. Prices $12.95 to $18.25 for seven-course meal.

Old Allegheny. *Moderate.* 6th and Penn Ave. across from Heinz Hall. Traditional fare featuring lots of wine sauces. Prime ribs, and veal Veronica stuffed with crabmeat, grapes and almonds are especially popular choices here.

QQ's. *Moderate.* Hyatt House, Chatham Center near Civic Arena. Delicatessen-type fare here: light suppers, sandwiches, tasty desserts, all served in comfortable cafe atmosphere.

Red Bull Inns of America. *Moderate.* A chain of standardized restaurants spread through the suburbs. The menu is predictable but the atmosphere is

pleasant and the well-prepared food served generously. S of town: 3220 W.
Liberty Ave. (US 19 truck route), Dormont. SW of town: 13 W. Mall Plaza,
Carnegie. SE of town: 624 Lysle Blvd., McKeesport. Shadyside, 401 Shady
Ave., North of the city, 4550 McKnight Rd. These inns usually close early and
are closed between lunch and dinner.

The Rusty Scupper. *Moderate.* The Bank, 311 4th Ave. The Rusty Scupper
has recently opened in The Bank, a restoration development in the heart of
downtown. The decor is a magnificent mixture of multi-leveled spaces, bright
colors, live plants, California redwood, and antique bricks. Alaska king crab and
western prime rib of beef are the house specialties.

Settler's Coffee House. *Moderate.* Lobby level of Hilton Hotel at the Point.
Varied menu from hamburgers to sauteed calves liver, served in casual atmosphere. Breakfast, lunch, dinner all days.

Three Lions. *Moderate.* 429 Fourth Ave. in Law and Finance Bldg. An
English tavern aura with a bustling bar to cheer the heart of any Anglophile.
Lunch or dinner, the emphasis is on steaks and lobsters.

The Upper Crust. *Moderate.* Forbes Ave. and Cherry Way next to Kaufmann's. Soups, salads and sandwiches for lunch; gourmet fare for dinner; wide
selection of breads at any time—from Bavarian black to whole-wheat pita to
French toast for breakfast.

Encore. *Inexpensive.* 5505 Walnut St. (Shadyside) and 629 Liberty Ave.
(downtown). Cozy restaurant and lounge offer nightly entertainment, sometimes jazz.

Palmer's. *Inexpensive.* 437 Smithfield St. near Kaufmann's. In a quick service
down-to-earth coffee shop style, you'll eat with downtown office workers and
Pittsburgh natives who have frequented the place for years. Open for breakfast,
lunch and dinner, all but Sundays.

Chinese

Chinatown Inn. *Moderate.* 522 3rd Ave. The Cantonese cooking is well
thought of throughout the city. They're open 7 days a week.

Mandarin. *Moderate.* 322 Forbes Ave. Mandarin and Szechuan cuisine.
Menu includes Mongolian barbecues, exotic drinks, and, with advance notice,
gourmet dinners prepared for groups of eight or more.

French

De Foro's. *Expensive.* Lawyer's Bldg. on Forbes Ave. Formal French-Italian
cuisine—duck a l'orange, salmon in champagne sauce and more. Reservations
needed on weekends.

Le Mont. *Expensive.* 1114 Grandview Ave. Another fine restaurant on Mt.
Washington, this one serves authentic French dishes, including baked Belgian
endive rolled in ham and Côte d'Azur Poulet en casserole.

Le Normande. *Expensive.* 5030 Centre Ave. in Amberson Towers, Shadyside. Delightful quaint country-inn ambience is the proper setting for elegant French cuisine. Jackets requested.

German

Max and Erma's Allegheny Taverns. *Moderate.* Middle and Suismon Sts., Northside. Old-fashion pub specializing in German-style food. Very good.

Wiegand's Cafe. *Inexpensive.* 422 Forland St. This northside favorite serves seafood and German specialties.

Italian

Cafe Cappuccino. *Moderate.* In Bank Center. Indoor setting with atmosphere of outdoor café.

Piccolo Piccolo. *Moderate.* 212 Third Ave. An innovative trattoria. Menu spans pasta, strudel, fettuccini Alfredo, shellfish, roast chicken and peppers.

Nello's Golden Lion. *Inexpensive.* 400 Island Ave. In McKee's Rock, a northwest suburb, you'll find excellent seafood, steaks and an Italian selection.

Japanese

The Samurai. *Expensive.* 2100 Greentree Rd. Dinners served as in Japan, on low tables, prepared in front of you by the chef. Located in the suburbs, SW of town.

Jewish

Rhoda's. *Moderate.* 2201 Murray Ave., Squirrel Hill. Jewish food in deli-style. Near the university.

Lebanese

Samreny's. *Moderate.* 4808 Baum Blvd. In the university section, this establishment is popular for its Middle East cuisine. If you've never had baklava for dessert, there's a treat in store here.

Mexican

Tequila Junction. *Moderate.* Freight House Shops, Station Square. Mexican specialties served in south-of-the-border atmosphere. Fresh strawberry margaritas lift the spirits even more.

Natural Food

Gesundheit. *Moderate.* In Bank Center. Natural food and drink parlor.

Seafood

Klein's Restaurant and Seafood House. *Expensive.* 330 Fourth Avenue, downtown. Excellent seafood menu lists fresh fish in season, many shellfish dishes. Lobster Allegro an original creation by the chef.

Pilot House. *Expensive.* Wood St., Monongahela Wharf, downtown. Pittsburgh's only floating restaurant. The menu has great variety; the management suggests you reserve your table.

Poli's. *Expensive.* 2607 Murray Ave., Squirrel Hill. Specializes in excellent seafood, only ten minutes from downtown. Luncheon specialty is Omelette Francaise cooked and served at table. Featured dinners are broiled seafood platter, stuffed lemon sole with crabmeat, and lobster.

OTHER PENNSYLVANIA
HIGHLIGHTS

There is, obviously, an abundance of attractions in the Keystone State, as outlined in previous chapters. For visitors who want the most complete sampling of its scenic beauties and history, here are other highly recommended excursions.

Bushkill Falls

The Pocono Mountains has its own Niagara: a series of seven dramatic waterfalls, the largest with a 100-foot drop. Bushkill Falls originates as the pure mountain headwaters of Bushkill Creek, high in the uplands of the Poconos (2 miles N.W. off US 209). There, they begin their descent to the Delaware River far below. When Bushkill Falls first opened to the public in 1904, there were minimal facilities for viewing this splendor—just one path and a swinging bridge over the head of the main falls. Nature, of course, retained its beauty for the ensuing 77 years. But now there are more ways for tourists to enjoy the area: hiking on well-marked *nature trails, fishing* on Twin Lakes, riding in *paddleboats.* The area offers *picnicking* facilities, *miniature golf,* an *art gallery,* and a *wildlife exhibit,* the newest attraction. Housed in a new building and created by taxidermist Parker Riday, it features an exhibit of native Pennsylvania birds and animals mounted and displayed in 60 feet of natural woodland setting.

But the biggest attraction is still the outdoors, where the scenic splendor is best enjoyed on foot. Nature trails afford views of gorges, gigantic boulders, and the waterfalls themselves. The trails lead through forests lush with wildflowers and greenery. The explorer can choose one of three clearly marked and color-coded trails: the short route (green) averages ½ hour; the regular route (yellow) takes about ¾ hour; and for those with stamina and hiking shoes, the long route (red) lasts 1½ hours. The latter route covers 16 lookout spots and includes a one-mile hike along Bridal Veil Falls Trail, where one can see the pipeline that carries pure spring water to the village of Bushkill. At the top, there is a view of white foam tumbling down the mountains, a sight so misty and flowing it inspired the names for two of the three falls on this trail: Bridesmaid's Falls and Bridal Veil Falls.

Bushkill Falls is open daily 8 A.M. until dusk from April 1 to November 15. Adults $2.50, senior citizens $1. Those between 6 and 12 years, 75¢. Phone 717–588–6682 for information.

The Pennsylvania "Grand Canyon"

Pine Creek River Gorge can be compared to Niagara Falls and the Grand Canyon, too. Located in the town of Wellsboro in mountainous north-central Pennsylvania, it is known as the state's "Grand Canyon," fifty miles long and 1,000 feet deep at one point. Stop for a picnic in either Leonard Harrison State Park at the east rim of the gorge or Colton Point State Park at the west rim. Special *bus tours* for visitors allow close-ups of the panoramic views afforded by the gorge. For those who want to explore the rustic surrounding areas and their narrow gravel roads, the Wellsboro Chamber of Commerce can provide useful maps. This town of 4,100 is a year-round vacation center itself.

Hershey

This is the place for those who savor not only chocolate bars but a sweet American success story. Milton S. Hershey, son of a Mennonite farmer, completed the fourth grade, left school and took a four-year apprenticeship as a candymaker. He then set out to follow his sweet-tooth craving for success. He tried making ice-cream, salt-water taffy, cough drops, and milk-based caramels, and it was with the last that he finally struck big success. By the time he decided to devote himself solely to milk chocolate, he sold his caramel plant for $1 million. Today the Hershey Foods Corporation factory is the largest chocolate and cocoa plant in the world.

He founded Hershey, the town, in 1903, a place he planned and built for himself, his family, his chocolate-manufacturing plant and even the cows who produce the milk. He supervised—with meticulous attention —every detail, paid the mortgages for the churches, decorated his home in lavish style and founded a tuition-free school for needy students. During the depression, he started a number of construction projects—a sports arena, hotel, high school—so the townspeople would remain employed.

The city (population 7,400) naturally carries the flavor of its founder and his product; streets have names like Cocoa and Chocolate Avenue, street lamps are shaped like Hershey kisses; the numerals on the chocolate factory clock point not to digits but to the letters that spell HERSHEY COCOA—12 letters, conveniently.

Curiously, the one place you can't visit in Hershey is the Hershey factory itself. So many tourists were deluging it that the tours were discontinued in 1973. Now, **Hershey's Chocolate World** on Park Blvd. is the top attraction for those who want to absorb the full flavor of chocolate-making. Here, visitors step aboard an automated conveyance that takes them for a ride through a world of chocolate—from cacao bears in the tropics to Hershey Bar making in Hershey. The modern building, which also has chocolate shops and an indoor garden, is open daily. Admission is free.

The **Hershey Museum of American Life** nearby covers not chocolate but Americana, with an extensive collection of American Indian, Pennsylvania Dutch and Eskimo artifacts and decorative crafts of this Lebanon Valley region. Exhibits include: Colonial furniture, Conestoga wagons, Eskimo tools, German folk art, Steigel glass, Indian baskets. There is also an audio-visual program. Open daily except Monday in spring and fall, and every day from May 15 to Labor Day (closed in December). Adults $1.75, those under 18, 75¢. Free to children under 5.

The **Hershey Rose Gardens and Arboretum** on Hotel Road likewise have nothing to do with chocolate, but will satisfy any nature lover's hunger for lush and abundant flowers. The six themed gardens, spread over 23 acres, include 1200 varieties of roses, with 24,000 rose bushes in full bloom in June. Also blooming luxuriantly, depending on the month of year, are tulips, daffodils, azaleas, rhododendrons, forsythia, dogwoods, hydrangea, hollies, heath and heather. All of them are surrounded by vast numbers of trees and shrubs. Open from April 15 to October 31 daily, $1.50 for adults; children 5–18 years, 50¢.

At **Hersheypark** (just off SR 743 and US 422) it's back to chocolate amusements: a walking Hershey Bar, a Hershey Kiss 330 feet high and a myriad of other entertainments. 37 amusement rides; five theaters for live entertainment; a walk-through zoo of North America (or a ride-through if one chooses the mono-rail); demonstrations by blacksmiths, glassblowers, and other craftsmen and women; a display of old European villages; a Pennsylvania "Fest Haus," typical of the lifestyles of early regional settlers. There is also an arena for hockey, ice shows, concerts and public skating. Call 717–534–3911 for information on the arena; 717–534–3916 about the park itself. One-price all-inclusive admission to the park is $9.95 for adults; $8.95 for children ages 5 to 9; $4.95 for young-hearted adults over 62.

On a spacious campus area, the **Milton Hershey School** (on US 322) provides students from broken or one-parent homes with an innovative program in which they live in family groups. The **Founders Hall** has a striking rotunda, banquet hall and chapel. In the visitors' lounge, dioramas portray the school's program. A 30-minute film, shown in peak season (May 1 to Oct. 31), is devoted to the founding of Hershey itself. Founders Hall is open daily throughout the year. Admission free.

Erie

Pennsylvania's third largest city is also its only port on the Great Lakes. It is named for the Erie Indians who inhabited the region long before the arrival of the early French explorers and the later English conquerers. The American colonists created the permanent settlement in 1795.

Erie is a city of broad tree-lined streets, reminiscent of early Washington, D.C., for it was laid out on a modified plan of the nation's capital. It is also a center of widely diversified industry.

Presque Isle State Park boasts a seven-mile-long beach front that attracts some three million visitors annually. The park covers 3,200 acres of woods, lagoons and lily ponds, and contains wildflowers, deer, and 280 varieties of birds. There are seafood restaurants along the pier, picnic facilities, and skiing and ice-skating in winter (a season which also features fewer crowds).

Presque Isle holds an important place in American history, for it was in Presque Isle Bay that Oliver Hazard Perry, in 1813, constructed the ships that met the British in combat in the Battle of Lake Erie. A limestone monument to Perry stands at the northeast corner of the bay, while docked at the foot of State Street in Erie is the restored U.S.S. *Niagara,* the commodore's flagship.

At Second and French Streets, the **Perry Memorial House,** also known as Dicksons Tavern, served as Perry's quarters before the Battle of Lake Erie, and also was a "station" of the Underground Railway before the Civil War. The walls of the old tavern contain hiding places where slaves stayed until they could move on.

At 560 East Third Street is a **replica of the blockhouse** in which the Revolutionary hero "Mad" Anthony Wayne (whose "madness" was his unshakable courage) died in 1796. In **Lakeside Cemetery** is the grave of Captain C. V. Gridley, to whom Admiral Dewey said, "You may fire when ready, Gridley," at the Battle of Manila Bay. Also of interest to tourists is the **Land Lighthouse,** the first lighthouse on the Great Lakes, built in 1813 and reconstructed in 1866.

In contrast to Land Lighthouse, no longer in use, the **Presque Isle Lighthouse** on the peninsula has been in continuous use since 1871, flashing a red and white alternate beam visible for 16 miles out on the lake.

The **Public Museum and Planetarium,** at 6th and Chestnut Sts., is a 350-room mansion featuring local history and natural science. Among its more bizarre items is the kettle in which General Anthony Wayne's body was boiled after disinterment. The museum, with no admission charge, is open Tuesday through Sunday.

Bethlehem

A curious contrast pervades Bethlehem. A city rich in religious, musical and historic tradition ever since its founding by Moravians in 1740, it is also a booming industrial center famous for its iron and steel plants. Situated in the geographical center of the Greater Lehigh Val-

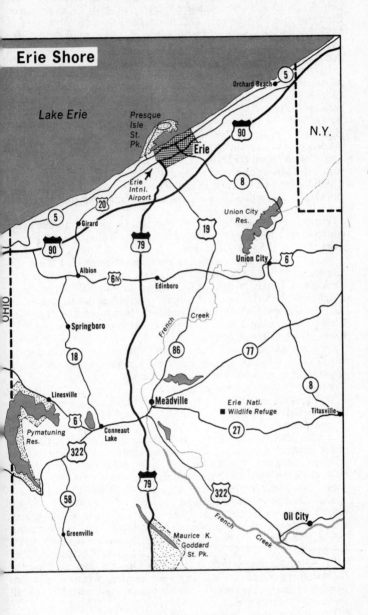

ley, its industrial development was stimulated with the opening of the
Lehigh Canal and the ensuing commerce in coal. Bethlehem Iron
Company, founded in 1861 and reorganized as Bethlehem Steel in
1899, became one of the largest iron works in the world. Today, the
industry-minded visitor can tour **Homer Research Laboratories,** a
major steel center, if advance notice is given.

But by far the most intriguing aspect for the visitor is the city's
Moravian heritage. The **Central Moravian Church,** at Main and West
Church Sts., is considered the foremost Moravian church in the nation,
and was the largest church in the state when it was completed in 1806.
At the time, the entire town could attend services at once—not a bad
idea for a city where, for 100 years, only Moravians were allowed
residence. (They are an ancient sect who look to the Bible as the sole
source of Christian doctrine. They have a tradition of beautiful music
with their services.) The church is now the site of the city's famed
Christmas service, when it is lavishly adorned with a huge Nativity
painting. A large choir and orchestra render chorales and traditional
hymns.

Yuletide is also the time when tiny candles glow in almost every
window and a 100-foot-high Star of Bethlehem in electric lights gleams
from the top of South Mountain.

Near the church is the **Moravian Museum** or *Gemeinhaus* (Common
House) at 66 West Church St., the oldest building still standing in
Bethlehem. It was in this log cabin that the original German-born
founders of the settlement held their first Christmas Eve service, led by
the just-arrived Count von Zinzendorf, Bishop of the Moravian
Church. They sang with fervor the German hymn, "Not Jerusalem-
lowly Bethelem 'twas that gave us Christ." This gave the town its name.
Today, the five-story structure displays silver, musical instruments,
needlework, seminary art and Moravian furniture. In the old chapel
adjoining the museum, built in 1751, Benjamin Franklin and many
Continental Congressmen worshipped.

Other buildings on Church St. serve as landmarks to early Moravian
life. The **Bell House,** built in 1746 and now part of Moravian College,
has a tower with the bell that called people to services and warned them
of danger. **Brethen's House** was first a residence for all unmarried
men in the community (unmarried women and widows had similar, separate
quarters) and later a hospital for the Continental Army. Near Main St.
is **Apothecary Museum,** with exhibits from the town's 18th-century
"apotheke," including the only complete set of Delft apothecary jars
in the U.S. The **Annie S. Kemerer Museum,** 427 N. New St., has on
exhibit many mementos of early Americana: Currier & Ives prints,
Chippendale chairs, Hepplewhite chests, locally made grandfather
clocks, and one of the best collections of Bohemian glass. At **God's
Acre** on West Market St., the founders of the town lie buried, together
with North American Indians and West Indians converted by the
Moravian missionaries. The "acre" has separate areas for men and
women, but all plots have uniform, flat gravestones, indicating that all
are equal in God's eyes.

Like their modern counterparts, the early settlers were industrialists
of a sort, and thanks to restoration, the visitor can now view a number

of the 32 industries they created. They're on display at the **18th Century Moravian Industrial Area** along Monacacy Creek. The Area includes a 1761 tannery, a waterworks (1762), springhouse (1764) and a grist mill (1869). Craftsmen demonstrate early trades, and guides in Moravian dress explain details. The exhibit is run by Historic Bethlehem Inc. Open Tuesday through Saturday. Adults $1.25, children 75¢. (Other tours can be arranged by the Bethlehem Convention and Visitors Bureau, 11 W. Market St., phone 215–868–1513.)

The biggest seasonal attraction, other than Christmas, is the springtime **Bach Festival,** stemming from the Moravian tradition of "service of song." Originally held in the Central Church, it is now given in Packer Memorial Chapel of Lehigh University. Music lovers flock every year to hear the massive 150-member chorus (its members are local residents) and renowned soloists. Music abounds in Bethlehem; besides the Bach Festival are many other musical performances, often free. Spring and summer concerts are held in the Rose Garden.

Fort Necessity

For history buffs, **Fort Necessity National Battlefield** is indeed a necessary excursion. It marks a crucial moment in the career of George Washington and in colonial American history. The site, 11 miles east of Uniontown (on US 40), was the actual battlefield where young Washington, then a lieutenant in the militia, waged his first campaign. On July 3, 1754, young Washington led a small company of Virginians against a strong force of French and Indians—and lost. The Battle of Great Meadows was not only his first campaign, but the start of the bitter French and Indian War.

On their original sites today are replicas of the fort built by Washington, entrenchments, and a log cabin. The **Visitor Center** offers a brief slide-and-tape presentation plus exhibits. It is open daily 8 A.M. to 5 P.M. and longer in summer. Admission free.

Near the fort is **Mount Washington Tavern,** a refurbished stagecoach inn. One mile west is the grave of General Major Edward Braddock, commander of British troops in the U.S. He met a disastrous defeat in 1775 near Fort Duquesne, where his army was ambushed and he was fatally wounded. The army, including his aide-de-camp Washington, buried Braddock in the road and drove wagons over the spot to prevent the Indians from discovering and desecrating the body. In 1804, the remains said to be Braddock's were moved to the present gravesite.

From Fort Necessity, it's not far to **Ohiopyle,** a resort that spans the Youghiogeny River and is in the heart of the Laurel Highlands, a vacationland spread out over two thousand square miles and including 3,213-foot-high Mount Davis, the highest point in Pennsylvania. This is good hunting, fishing, swimming, hiking and skiing country. For sightseers there's **Fort Ligonier** on US 30 in Ligonier, a restored 18th-century stockade with a good collection of French and Indian War mementos. Near Ohiopyle, at Bear Run, is **Fallingwater,** designed by Frank Lloyd Wright and one of the most famous modern houses in the world, with its superb location over the tumbling mountain stream.

On US 40 northwest of Uniontown is **Nemacolin (Bowman's) Castle,** a 1789 trading post overlooking the Monongahela River.

Laurel Caverns south off US 40 and east of Uniontown, has fascinating limestone formations, exquisitely lighted. **Mount Davis** is easily reached from Fallingwater. Head east on US 40 to Addison, a distance of seventeen miles, then turn north on State 53 and continue one mile to Listonburg. From there an unmarked road leads to Mount Davis, and down to a little village called Springs, where there is an interesting **museum of Amish farm life.** Continue along State 669 to Salisbury, which is about five miles away. From Salisbury, go north on US 219 to Meyersdale, where a **Maple Sugar Festival** is held early each spring. Continue on US 219 to Somerset, known as Pennsylvania's **mountain-top garden spot.** It lies more than 2,200 feet above sea level, and is graced with maple trees and lovely flowers.

Old Bedford Village

Old Bedford Village is a vignette of early American pioneer life created with modern American ingenuity. Many of the log cabins on this 72-acre site in the heart of the Alleghenies were transported from their original locales and rebuilt here. In all, the village comprises over 40 buildings that reflect life in colonial Pennsylvania during the late 18th and early 19th centuries. Inside, craftsmen dressed in colonial garb demonstrate the tools of the trade exactly as used by early settlers. The broommaker uses a 19th-century broom press; the potter uses a foot-powered wheel to shape bowls and plates. Others demonstrate gunmaking, tinsmithing, chair caning, quilting, shoemaking, spinning, weaving, needlepoint, leathermaking and woodworking.

Many of the buildings in this reconstructed village were original to the Bedford County settlers. The **Fungaroli House,** built in 1790, was, in the *old* Old Bedford Village, a furniture store and undertaking establishment. The **Semanek House** was luxurious among log cabins of the day, with fireplaces on each floor. Of special interest, too, are the **Eight-Square Schoolhouse** and Bedford County's only *slave house,* built in 1776. There is also a working colonial farm, complete with animals—a special delight for children. Inside the cabins, workshops and other buildings are "colonists" (although this time hardly the originals) who greet visitors and answer questions about colonial life and history.

Old Bedford Village, situated a mile north of Bedford Borough on a river bank among sycamores, was built for the Bicentennial. This was made possible through grants from state and federal commissions. Besides its ongoing exhibit, it features special seasonal events—a musket shoot, quilting bee, apple-butter boiling and a demonstration of colonial firearms. Before Christmas, there is a special three-day celebration. Open daily 9 A.M. to 5 P.M. from mid-April to the last Sunday in October. Call 814–623–1156 or 1157 for information, or write to Old Bedford Village, P.O. Box 1976, Bedford, Pa. 15522.

The area surrounding the village is rich in history. The town of Bedford was George Washington's headquarters during the Whiskey Rebellion. As long ago as 1795, **Bedford Springs** was popular for its medicinal waters, that included springs with traces of magnesia, limestone, iron and sulphur. In pre-Civil War days, this was a favorite vacation spot. Nearby **Bedford Springs Hotel** was President James Buchanan's summer White House. Even earlier, in 1758, the area began as Fort Taystown. It was later renamed in honor of the Duke of Bedford. **Fort Bedford Museum,** on North Juliana St., houses a reproduction of an early fort blockhouse and a scale model of the original fort.

Titusville

This small town (population 6,800), south of Erie (Rtes. 8 and 89), has a large claim to historic fame. The world's first productive oil well was first drilled here in 1858. It is a rather unusual success story. Edwin L. Drake, a clerk, train conductor and salesman, was hired by a syndicate that had leased land near Titusville in the hope of bringing up oil known to be present in this region. But no one knew exactly how it could be done, especially by this unlikely oilman, who had apparently been hired because he had a free train pass. Townspeople scoffed at "Drake's Folly," but he persisted. When water started to collapse the drilled hole, he drove a cast-iron pipe down to bedrock—32 feet. He also hired William Smith, a blacksmith who knew drilling techniques. On August 28, 1858, Smith visited the well, saw liquid near the surface, filled several barrels and ran through the town shouting, "Struck oil!"

While others dashed to dig oil and gain instant wealth, the unassuming Drake served as Justice of the Peace and oil buyer, but he drilled no more. Drake lived modestly, and only much later was he voted an annual pension of $1,500 by the legislature.

Drake Well Memorial Park, one mile southeast of town, is named in honor of the man who made Titusville famous. There is a full-size replica of Drake's oil well derrick and engine house. In the $2 million **Drake Well Museum** are parts of the apparatus from the first well, mementos of Drake's personal possessions, and exhibits of the development of the oil industry. They include dioramas, models and an electric map. A research library contains thousands of photographs of America's and Pennsylvania's early oil days. The museum is open daily except Monday. Admission $1; free to those over 64 or under 12.

PRACTICAL INFORMATION FOR OTHER
PENNSYLVANIA HIGHLIGHTS

 HOTELS AND MOTELS. In the listings below, price categories are, for double occupancy, *Super Deluxe* over $28–45, *Expensive* $22–27, *Moderate* $17–21, and *Inexpensive* under $17. A 6% sales tax will be added to your bill.

BEDFORD

Bedford Springs Hotel. *Deluxe.* US 220, 5 mi. S. of exit 11 from Pennsylvania Turnpike. This venerable resort, high in the Allegheny Mountains, is well over a century and a half old. Now a complete resort, operating on the American Plan, it's open May to October with elaborate sport and recreational facilities. There are indoor and outdoor pools, golf, tennis, trap shooting and water sports. Restaurant and lounge, dancing and entertainment, including movies.

Holiday Inn. *Expensive.* US 220, ¼ mi. N. of Pennsylvania Turnpike exit 11. Convenient stop for travelers in this difficult-to-drive section of the 'pike. There's a pool and sauna, dancing and entertainment.

Town House. *Moderate.* A quarter-mile from Turnpike exit 11, Penn and Richard Sts. Under 12 free, crib free, cot $2. Restaurant opposite.

Quality Inn. *Moderate.* Located at the Turnpike exit 11.

Lewis Inn. *Inexpensive.* Quarter-mile from Turnpike exit 11. Owner-managed, medium-sized facility of 32 units. Coffee shop, cocktails. Open all year.

Penn Manor. *Inexpensive.* A block N. of Turnpike exit 11. It has 41 rooms, heated pool, wading pool, playground, café a half block away. Crib, cot $2.

BETHLEHEM

Bethlehem. *Expensive.* 437 Main St. (State 191). Large downtown hotel, with 150 rooms. Under 12 free, crib or cot $4. Two dining rooms, cocktail lounge. Free parking, some kitchen units.

Howard Johnson's. *Expensive.* US 22 Airport exit. Spacious grounds, pool, café and bar, restaurant and cocktails. Free bus to the airport.

Holiday Inn. *Moderate.* US 22 at State 512. Has 195 rooms. Under 12 free, crib free. Heated pool, wading pool, playground. Dining room and coffee shop, cocktails and lounge, entertainment and dancing.

BUSHKILL

Fernwood. *Super Deluxe.* On US 209 1½ mi. SW of town. Golf, tennis, private lakes, swimming pool, horses, entertainment, ski area with school and rentals, snow-mobiling and gift shops. Restaurant and bar.

Wayne Newton's Tamiment. *Super Deluxe.* In Tamiment, between US 6–209 and State 402. Spacious grounds include a 90-acre lake, ten tennis courts, lighted for night-time play, winter snow sport areas and a skating rink. Excellent food and top-flight entertainment.

ERIE

El Patio Motor Lodge. *Expensive.* Located at the entrance of Presque Isle State Park. Olympic-size heated pool. Licensed heliport. Penthouse restaurant. Nightly entertainment.

Holiday Inn-Downtown. *Expensive.* 18 W. 18th St. Under 12 free. Heated pool, restaurant and coffee shop; cocktail lounge with entertainment and piano bar.

Downtowner. *Moderate.* 205 W. 10th St. (1 block W. of US 19). 75 rooms. Heated pool, free coffee in rooms, restaurant and cocktail lounge.

Holiday Inn-South. *Moderate.* I–90 at State 97. Has 116 rooms. Under 12 free. Heated pool, dining room and coffee shop, cocktail lounge, entertainment and organist every night but Sun.

Howard Johnson's. *Moderate.* I–90 at US 19. The familiar orange color marks this conveniently located motor lodge. Under 12 free, heated indoor pool, sauna, playground. Restaurant and bar.

Niagara. *Moderate.* 20 W. 2nd St. Many units in this downtown motor hotel have a view of Erie Harbor. Heated pool. Free coffee in room; restaurant and cocktail lounge.

Ramada Inn. *Moderate.* I–90 at State 8. Under 12 free. Heated pool, wading pool, playground. Restaurant and bar, dancing and entertainment on weekends.

HERSHEY

Hotel Hershey. *Deluxe.* Off US 322, 422, 1½ mi. N. of the city. A resort complex of 150 rooms in Spanish-design building surrounded by golf course and gardens. American sports, recreation room, pool. Restaurant and bar, entertainment. Private airstrip. Closed Dec. 18 to Jan. 5.

Hershey Motor Lodge. *Expensive.* Chocolate Ave. at University Dr. 200 rooms, health club, good recreational facilities. Under 17 free. Pool, playground. Restaurant and bar, entertainment.

UNIONTOWN

Mount Summit Inn. *Deluxe.* US 40, 5 mi. E. of town. Family rates prevail at this resort hotel. In a beautiful mountain setting, you'll find an Olympic-size heated pool, wading pool, cabanas, playground. Restaurant and bar, dancing and entertainment. Cookouts, Sun. evening buffet in season. Nine-hole golf course, putting green, tennis, recreation room. Closed Nov. to Apr.

Holiday Inn. *Moderate.* US 40, 3 mi. W. of town. 119 rooms. Under 12 free. Heated pool. Restaurant, cocktail lounge, dancing and entertainment Fri. and Sat., jukebox dancing Sun. to Thurs.

WELLSBORO

Penn-Wells. The two Penn-Wells operations are a few blocks apart. The older hotel (62 Main St., 724–2111) has *Inexpensive* family rates. Hotel guests can use motor inn's heated pool. There also is a playground. The hotel restaurant and bar is open to guests at motor inn (4 Main St.). Both are community owned. The hotel has 93 rooms, the *Moderately priced* motor inn 40.

DINING OUT. In the listings below, categories apply to mid-priced dinners on each menu. *Deluxe* $12–20, *Expensive* $9–12, *Moderate* $5–9, and *Inexpensive* under $5.00.

BEDFORD

Ed's Steak House. *Inexpensive.* US 220, ¼ mi. N. of exit 11 from Pennsylvania Turnpike. Wide variety of food served in pleasant dining room and coffee shop. Dinners à la carte and children's menu. Bar. Open 7 A.M. to 10:30 P.M. May 1–Oct. 1; remainder of year to 10 P.M.

BETHLEHEM

Aspen Inn. *Moderate.* Rtes. 512 and 22. Varied menu, pleasant surroundings.

BUSHKILL

Fernwood Gaslight Lounge Restaurant. *Moderate.* On US 209, 1½ mi. SW of town. Dinner, music, dancing, and entertainment nightly.

ERIE

The Station Restaurant. *Moderate.* 4940 Peach St. 2 mi. S. of I–90, exit 6 on US 19. Pleasant dining in replica of a railroad depot and restored dining car. Children's menu.

FARMINGTON

Nemacolin Inn. *Moderate.* Out of private hands and now open to the public. Airstrip beside the Inn. 29 rooms at $78 to $122 double occupancy. French cuisine. Golf course. (412) 432–2881.

HERSHEY

Hotel Hershey. *Expensive.* US 322 1½ mi. N. of town. This resort hotel opens to guests its Spanish-style dining room with giant windows looking out on fabulous flower gardens. Dancing.

TITUSVILLE

Harmon's Rams Head Steak House. *Expensive.* Petroleum Center Rd. Highly recommended for steak dishes.
Cross Creek Resort. *Moderate.* R.D. 3, Rte. 8 South. Popular family-type restaurant. Varied menu.
Rusty Nail. *Moderate.* Drake Mall. Continental cuisine, salad bar.

UNIONTOWN

Coal Baron. *Expensive.* Rte. 40, 2½ mi. west of Uniontown. Highly recommended for its interesting specialties.
Braddock Inn Restaurant. *Moderate.* U.S. Rte. 40, 9 mi. east of Uniontown. Continental cuisine.
The Moon Shadows. *Moderate.* 264 N. Dallatin Ave. Good American fare.

WELLSBORO

Penn-Wells Hotel. *Moderate.* 4 Main St. Fresh sole, veal Cordon Bleu are specialties.

INDEX

INDEX

The letters H and R indicate Hotel and Restaurant listings.